The West Breal

Book two of the "Guardian of Empire" series

By: William Kelso

Visit the author's YouTube site

William Kelso is also the author of:

The Shield of Rome

The Fortune of Carthage

Devotio: The House of Mus

The Veteran of Rome series (9)

Soldier of the Republic series (11)

Rome Divided

Published in 2024 by KelsoBooks Ltd. Copyright © William Kelso. First Edition

The author has asserted their moral right under the Copyright, Designs and Patents Act, 1988, to be identified as the author of this work.

All Rights reserved. No part of this publication may be reproduced, copied, stored in a retrieval system, or transmitted, in any form or by any means, without the prior written consent of the copyright holder, nor be otherwise circulated in any form of binding or cover other than that in which it is published and without a similar condition being imposed on the subsequent purchaser.

A CIP catalogue record for this title is available from the British Library.

Dear Reader,

I hope that you will enjoy this book. 'The West Breaks Away' is the second of the 'Guardian of Empire' series. A third book will be published later in 2024.

As an independently published author, I do not command huge marketing resources so, if you are so inclined, please do leave me a review or a rating.

For those visually inclined have a look at my short historical themed YouTube videos at

The Story So Far…

This book series is the story of one family of three brothers. Corbulo, Veda and Munatius. The brothers are the descendants of the characters from my Veteran of Rome book series. Their ancestral home is the estate on the isle of Vectis of the southern coast of Britain. It is 261 AD and the brothers have not seen or heard from each other in fifteen years. Since they were split up at an early age their lives and fates have developed separately. But the three of them share a secret that will always bind them together. A terrible secret that over time has come to effect each brother in different ways.

In the East, in Roman Syria Corbulo, eldest brother has become a high ranking Roman officer in the imperial army. A leader who fights for Rome and the honour of his illustrious ancestors. Book II of the Guardian of Empire picks up the story with Veda, the middle brother…

Chapter One – Veda

Autumn 260 AD. Noviomagus Reginorum, Chichester, Southern Britain

Sitting on the three legged stool at the table inside the tavern, Veda held up the leather cup and shook the dice. Sporting a little amused smile. His eyes glowing with a strange crazy light as he studied his solitary opponent. The six bones of chance rattling in the container. The hearth fire at the far end of the room was crackling and spitting sparks as a black dog lay curled up asleep beside it. A fresh pitcher of wine was resting on the table in front of Veda while in-front of him piled up in the centre of the table was a mass of silver coins. It was late at night and from the doorway the cold autumn air was seeping into the inn. The tavern, with its straw covered floor was tense and quiet like a mouse that knew it was being hunted. Standing behind the lonely and deserted bar the inn keeper's wife was nervously polishing a fine glass with a rag cloth as the few remaining clients at this late hour, half drunk or asleep, watched the gambling from their seats at the small wooden tables, nursing their drinks.

"You feeling lucky," the middle aged inn keeper said closely watching Veda from across the table. The older man's sweaty cheeks were unshaven and his breath stank of wine. His face was expectant. "It's all or nothing now, boy. You lose now, you lose it all. No crying afterwards."

"Always," Veda shot back, rattling his cup.

"You sure about that. I don't think the gods like a man such as yourself," the inn keeper said folding his arms across his chest and observing Veda with a sudden mocking smile. "What kind of a name is Veda anyway. Sounds like a pussy woman's name to me."

"It's a good name," Veda said. "Did you know that on the Rhine - in Germany, it means a man with huge balls."

"No it doesn't," the innkeeper retorted hooting. "You are so full of shit, boy. The gods are not going to favour you tonight. I served in the legions. Now that was a proper job. I was a soldier once. I did honest work," the older man continued. "A soldier has the respect of the gods. But what have you ever done but piss away your aunt's money? You boy are a disgrace to your family and the gods will not make you lucky tonight. It's because you have no guts."

Sighing Veda lowered his eyes, looking unperturbed.

"Is that really the best you can come up with old man," Veda retorted before rattling his cup again and turning to eye his opponent. "You think that because I have never served in the army that I do not have any guts. You don't think I have killed a man before?"

"Really, you have killed a man!" the inn keeper called out in an incredulous sounding voice, leaning forwards and jutting his chin towards Veda. "I don't believe a word of what you saying. Who did you kill, boy?"

For a moment Veda paused as he stared at the inn keeper from across the table. His hand raised, clutching the cup.

"My father," Veda replied at last in an even voice. "I stabbed him to death right here with this knife," he added lightly tapping his throat and indicating the short broad bladed pugio knife that was tucked into his belt. "I was twelve."

Looking startled the inn keeper hooted.

Then for a moment the tavern went still.

"You are so full of shit," the older man exclaimed at last looking away and shaking his head. "Your father! Right. More lies. I don't believe you. Throw the fucking dice!"

Ratting the cup a final time Veda poured the six die onto the table and as the result became clear the inn keeper hissed in delight.

"Ha!" the older man cried out raising a fist in triumph. "Told you the gods did not favour you! A one. Three twos, a five and six. You are going to lose boy. You are not as lucky as you think you are."

Staring at the throw lying on the table Veda sighed - looking solemn. Shorter than the average man - at twenty-eight he was a handsome man with a stylish goatee beard. The bone fibula pinned to his right shoulder holding his expensive white woollen cloak together. The small brooch depicting the face of the Batavian god Hercules Magusanus. For a moment Veda did not move or say anything as the inn keeper reached for the dice and started to gather them into the cup for his own deciding throw. Then looking up Veda glanced in the direction of the inn keeper's young wife who was watching the gambling with a fearful look and their eyes met. The silence between the two of them pregnant with growing tension as something unspoken passed between them.

"I fucked your wife earlier today," Veda said turning to the inn keeper. "Right here while you were out at the market."

"You did what?" the older man exclaimed taken aback, pausing to collect the dice.

"You heard me," Veda replied.

Staring at him from across the table the inn keeper hesitated, his face darkening.

"Ah just more lies boy," the inn keeper said at last dropping the six dice into the cup and preparing his throw.

"No, I really did," Veda continued. "In your own bed up there," he added pointing up at the ceiling and the second floor of the building. "Your wife - she has a birth mark on her ass. She squealed like a pig. She wants to leave you. She says you beat her and stop her from seeing her friends. You abuse her. She is sick of you. Go on. Why do you not ask her yourself?"

"What?" the inn keeper snarled pausing again and glaring across at Veda. "What is this? You mock me in my own home, boy."

But as Veda remained silent the man turned towards his young wife whose face had gone utterly pale. The woman's body trembling. Moments later the fine glass slipped from her fingers and smashed to pieces onto the floor and before anyone could react the woman had fled through the kitchen doorway.

"She liked it slow and deep," Veda said lifting his chin and staring straight at his opponent as the tavern went very still.

For a long moment the inn keeper remained silent as he stared in the direction in which his young wife had vanished. His mind working. Then slowly he turned his smouldering eyes back towards Veda. His face was dark as thunder. His mouth curling and twisting. His fingers tightening their grip on the edge of the table. The only noise in the room was the crackling fire and the man's laboured breathing while the black dog had lifted its head to see what was going on. Then with a furious bellowing roar the older man rose sharply to his feet and upended the table and all its contents across the floor. But Veda had anticipated the move and leaping backwards he avoided the tumbling table. The inn was suddenly alive with shouts and startled cries as the inn keeper lunged at him with a concealed knife. The blade slashing through empty air and just missing his throat. Emitting a crazy peel of laughter Veda's eyes widened. His cheeks flush with excitement from the thrill and the near miss. Stooping he seized his wooden stool by one leg and as the older man came at him again he smashed the chair straight into the inn keeper's face sending him stumbling backwards in a howl of pain.

"Beat her again and I will finish you!" Veda yelled as he glared at the stricken inn keeper. "That is a promise! This is your last warning, old man! I mean it. She is leaving you. The money on the table was meant for her you prick, not me! I was going to win it for her so she could leave you."

Then Veda turned and hurriedly reaching the door he opened it and fled into the night as the inn keeper bellowed in rage.

***

Pausing at the end of the alley Veda's eyes strained to see in the darkness. The small town around him however was silent and asleep. The night quiet. The streets deserted. The sky moonless and starless. Then once again he heard the approaching sound of crunching boots. Moments later a posse of flaming torches appeared as the group of vigilantes who were out searching for him rounded a corner and went hurrying down the street. The men, led by the middle aged inn keeper however did not notice him hiding in the darkness and as their footsteps receded Veda turned to cast a sombre glance in the direction of the inn. Wondering what had happened to the woman. But she had gone. She had probably already fled from the town. He had failed her.

For a moment longer he lingered before with a little resigned sigh he turned and started to retreat back down the alley until he found the building he was looking for - another inn. A proud sign hanging from a sturdy wooden beam above the doorway depicting a Roman merchant ship with a full set of sails upon the ocean.

Trying the tavern door he found it locked. Cursing softly he turned to look up at the shuttered window on the second floor. But he could not risk calling out. The inn keeper and his men were still about and may hear him and come to investigate. Turning to look around Veda spotted an old barrel used to catch rain water. Hurrying over to it he quickly tipped out the water before quietly rolling the barrel up to the side of the tavern wall and turning it upside down. Clambering up onto the barrel he softly cursed his lack of height as he found himself just a few hands length short of the shuttered window. Unperturbed he turned and lunged at the wooden beam from which hung the tavern's sign. Catching hold of it he strained and grimaced as he slowly hauled himself upwards, his legs dangling into space. His knees scraping against the wall. His breath coming in gasps. At last hanging suspended across the wooden beam above the tavern doorway he twisted around and catching hold of the window shutters he slowly prized them apart. Straining he pushed himself upwards until at last he managed to climb in through the window, tumbling into the dark room beyond.

As Veda came clambering in through the window the room was rent by a startled female shriek. As if the occupant had been asleep and his unexpected intrusion had abruptly woken her. Landing on the floor beside the window, in the darkness, Veda cried out as he was abruptly kicked in the head by a frantic, panic stricken female foot.

"Cata. It's me sister," Veda whispered hoarsely into the darkness. "Stop kicking me."

But from the darkness there was no reply just the sound of loud panicked breathing before the door was flung open and a young man appeared holding up an oil lamp in one hand and clutching a stick in the other. The newcomer looked no older than eighteen and he was clad in the simple woollen tunic of a slave. His alarmed eyes darting about, trying to locate the threat to his mistress. Advancing towards Veda the slave raised his stick to strike as a solitary woman rushed towards him and into the safety of the light of his lamp. Then abruptly the young man stopped as he recognised Veda.

"It's all right Caledonus," Veda said stiffly and painfully rising to his feet and holding up a hand. "It's me. Put that stupid stick away and close the door."

"What the fuck Veda!" Cata, Veda's sister hissed standing beside her slave and staring at him with large alarmed eyes. "This is how you come back! You scared me. I was asleep. What are you doing? It's the middle of the night. Where have you been?"

For a moment Veda said nothing as Caledonus, his sister's male slave and man servant, promptly lowered his stick and quickly closed the door behind him before silently placing his lamp on a nearby table. The glow bathing the room in a faint flickering light. Quickly closing the window blinds behind him Veda turned to Caledonus, ignoring his sister.

"I though I told you to make sure the inn door was open for when I returned," Veda said in an irritable voice. "But it was fucking locked. What kind of slave are you. You got ears haven't you."

Looking embarrassed Caledonus simple shrugged, his subservient eyes lowered and avoiding looking directly at Veda. Gazing back at the slave boy Veda slowly shook his head in disapproval. Caledonus - the teenage slave appeared to have been sleeping on the floor outside Cata's door as was his custom. His job to guard and accompany his mistress which he had been doing faithfully for years now. It had been aunt Helena who had first spotted Caledonus in the slave markets of Londinium years ago when he had been just a small boy. She had bought him specially for Cata and the slave had formed a surprisingly strong bond with his sister. His loyalty to her unquestionable. But apart from his loyalty no one knew much about Caledonus for he could not speak. Someone had cut out his tongue and he had never been taught how to write. No one knew his real name or even how old he really was. All that aunt Helena had gleaned from the slavers who had sold the boy to her was that he was from the north. So she had decided to call him Caledonus after the land of the Caledonians.

"We can't stay here, its not safe," Veda said at last turning to his sister. "So pack your things. We need to leave right now and get out of town."

"What? Why? What have you done?" Cata exclaimed taking a step towards her brother, looking annoyed.

"The inn keeper at the Legionary," Veda replied. "He is out there right now looking for me with his boys. I pissed him off tonight and he's out for blood. We're going to have to leave town for a while. He will be watching the city gates so we will slip out through the old lovers passage. You know the one."

Staring back at Veda, Cata looked incredulous. Then she groaned and placed both her hands across her cheeks in dismay. At twenty-one, clad in her loose white night clothes she had grown into a beautiful young woman with long blond hair tied back in a traditional Roman bun.

"You were screwing his wife weren't you," Cata exclaimed. "That is why her husband wants to cut off your head. What do you expect Veda? Why are you always getting yourself into trouble like this?"

"He was abusing her," Veda shot back, "I could not stay silent about that. He was beating her. I hate men like that. They remind me of my father. It had to stop. She wanted to leave him and I agreed to help her. I had to make it stop but I fucked it up and now she is gone…" Veda added looking away as his voice trailed off.

Groaning again Cata too looked away and for a moment the room remained silent.

"What about your job interview tomorrow?" Cata said at last turning back to her brother. "For the clerical position at the lawyers office. You can't miss that."

"Screw the interview," Veda replied shaking his head. "We need to get out of town for a while until things cool down and I cannot let you stay here. The inn keeper may try and hurt you in revenge for what I did. We need to go now before it gets light."

"Screw the interview!" Cata exclaimed her eyes flashing in alarm. "But that is why you came to Reginorum in the first place. Aunt Helena wants you to get this job and you promised her that you would give it a go. You can't Veda! You can't just give up on this. How many jobs have you now turned down? You are going to make Helena very angry."

"I am not going to that fucking interview tomorrow," Veda replied. "Screw it sister. I have no interest in becoming a lawyers clerk."

"What about a position in the army then, like Corbulo?" Cata said with growing desperation. "You could become an officer."

"Fuck the army. I am no soldier," Veda retorted. "I am not like Corbulo, sister."

Shaking her head Cata looked dismayed.

"Why do you always do this Veda?" she said at last sounding defeated. "You show no interest in getting a job or a profession. Julia left you because you can't stop sleeping around. She divorced you! You are aimless. You do nothing but drink, gamble and get into fights. You are nearly thirty. You are a mess Veda and it hurts me to see you like this. It hurts Helena too. You are my brother! I just wish you would change your ways and make something of yourself. It is not too late."

"Yeah well we can't all be like Corbulo," Veda replied bitterly, lowering his eyes. "Our brother the soldier. The war hero. The leader of men. The perfect son. Being a soldier and a war hero is not for me sister. I have no desire to die in some far off foreign field."

"Well I wouldn't know," Cata replied with a sigh, "for I was just a baby when he left but at least from his letters to aunt Helena, Corbulo seems to know what he wants to do with himself, unlike you."

"I will be fine."

"You are not fine Veda. You don't know what to do with yourself."

Shaking his head Veda remained silent.

"You can't keep getting into trouble like this Veda," Cata continued, reprimanding him with a concerned look. "I worry about you. We all do. One day I am going to find you dumped in an alley with your throat cut."

Advancing towards his sister Veda took her into a little fond embrace.

"My sister - always looking out for me," he said quietly addressing Cata as Caledonus looked on impassively. "and I appreciate it more than you know but don't worry about me. I will be fine. Now we have to leave right away. We have to go home. Back to Vectis."

"I can't," Cata said breaking free from his embrace. "You forget. I have to attend Hisauus's funeral tomorrow. Remember. Helena asked me to represent her at the funeral. To pay our respects on her behalf. I can't and won't miss that Veda. You know how many years of faithful service Hisauus gave us - looking after the cattle. We need to pay our respects to the dead. To Narina, his widow. That is right and proper."

Swearing softly Veda turned to look away with a frustrated look. "But we can't stay here sister," he replied. "I cannot show my face around town. Not for a while at least. They are looking for me." Pausing Veda sighed before lowering his eyes. "The funeral for Hisauus," he continued, "it is being held at his home by the lake, beyond the city walls?"

"Yes," Cata nodded, "at noon."

"All right, fine," Veda said quickly. "So I will compromise with you sister. Tomorrow you shall go to pay our respects to the old vet but right now we leave town and we go and stay with

Sulpicia. She will put us up. She is a good friend and we should be safe there. Agreed?"

Studying her brother Cata hesitated.

"Agreed," she replied at last slowly shaking her head. "But Helena is going to be so angry with you Veda, for missing that interview. You promised her that you would give it a go and now you have broken your word."

Chapter Two - "These Are Troubled Times"

It was just after dawn and a thick mist hung over the narrow Lavant river where it joined the wider Fishbourne Channel. The morning air was frosty and still. The land, silent. The ground along the river was covered in heaps of green, yellow and red leaves shed by the trees as the forest prepared for the coming of winter. While popping up in the river an otter was on the hunt. Lying drawn up along the bank were several sturdy sea going rowing boats. Their oars stowed inside while nearby a group of men, clad in their thick winter cloaks, were standing quietly chatting to each other and warming their hands over an open fire.

Standing alone in the doorway to Sulpicia's thatched cottage, Veda surveyed the country scene with a dissatisfied look. His quick, alert eyes roving about. Searching for signs of trouble. His nose taking in the smell of the wood smoke. His right hand resting on his leather belt from which hung his broad bladed pugio knife. His fingers fidgeting with the weapon.

Sulpicia, his mother's old friend, lived alone and from her home he should have been able to see the walls of Noviomagus Reginorum just a short distance to the north, but the open fields beyond were shrouded in mist. The narrow channel of the Lavant river, which the locals had diverted to supply the town with drinking water, fading away into the fog. While to the south in the direction of the sea all he could hear out on the marshes was the screech of a solitary sea gull.

"One of my men will row you across to Vectis," Sulpicia said as she came up behind Veda and placed a gentle, maternal hand on his shoulder. "Don't worry about the weather. My boys know what they are doing. They can handle almost any sea condition."

"I must pay you for your trouble and also the ferry fee for the three of us," Veda said hurriedly reaching into a pocket.

"Nonsense," Sulpicia replied quickly tightening her grip on his shoulder, "put away your money Veda. This is on me. You know that you and Cata are always welcome in my home. I will never stop being a friend to Tadia's children. It is the least that I can do."

"Thank you," Veda said with a grateful nod. "Thank you for everything you have done for us. It is appreciated."

Accepting the gratitude Sulpicia smiled and remaining silent she turned her attention to the river and her rowers. Sulpicia was in her fifties. A business woman and a spinster who had never married. She owned her own transport business. The only company operating a regular ferry service from the mainland to the isle of Vectis just off the south coast. Her boats transporting passengers and cargo to and from the island. Her face was drawn and wrinkled with age and beaten by a hard life lived largely outdoors, but the light in her eyes was strong and she'd kept herself in good health and shape.

"You know your mother Tadia and I," Sulpicia exclaimed at last in a wistful voice, "we actually met for the first time on one of these rowing boats that was going between Reginorum and Vectis. We shared the boat. She was a good friend to me, your mother. I still miss her - after all these years. Her death was such a tragedy. She was taken from us far too soon."

"She should never have married again. She should not have married Gamo," Veda said with sudden bitterness. "That was her big mistake."

"Oh I don't know," Sulpicia said looking away, her eyes suddenly distant. "Put yourself in her shoes Veda. Vennus your real father had been listed as missing in the east. The army told your mother that he was unlikely to return home and meanwhile you three boys were growing up and needed a father figure. It is not good for a boy to be brought up surrounded only by women. Your mother was thinking about your welfare and future prospects when she agreed to marry Gamo and move to be with him in Germany. She always had you three foremost in mind. You boys and Cata were her life."

"No it was a big mistake. She should not have married Gamo," Veda replied shaking his head, his expression set. "She should not have uprooted us and taken the three of us to live with him on the Rhine in Germany. We should have stayed here on Vectis with Helena and Cata - on the old farm. This is where we belong. Maybe mother would still be alive if she had stayed here. And my sister has never even met Corbulo and now will never meet Munatius! He's gone!"

"You can't say that Veda," Sulpicia said gently lowering her eyes. "The plague that killed Tadia struck here too. We here in Britannia are not immune. It carried off many in town. Gods I should know. It nearly broke my business. And as for Cata never meeting her brothers," Sulpicia added with another sigh. "She was just a toddler when you, Corbulo and Munatius left for Germany. Your mother decided that she was too young to travel, so she left her here in your aunt Helena's care. It was the right decision for Cata - for look at what a beautiful happy young woman she has become."

"Well we three got a tyrant," Veda snapped averting his eyes. "Gamo abused us. I was glad when he died."

"Helena tells me that Corbulo is doing well for himself," Sulpicia said quickly. "In his latest letter he says that he has been posted to Syria and that he is a centurion now in command of a hundred soldiers."

"Yeah sure. Corbulo is the golden boy," Veda retorted looking annoyed. "The eldest son who will inherit the old farm one day. He can do nothing wrong. The success and pride of the family. But if we had stayed here on Vectis maybe Munatius would still be alive. Maybe all of us would be together like we were supposed to be. I have not seen Corbulo since we were separated fifteen years ago. I barely know my brother any more."

"You do not know if Munatius is dead," Sulpicia replied withdrawing her hand from Veda's shoulder and folding her arms across her chest. "His body was never found after the attack on your party and I am told that the Franks are not as bloodthirsty as they are made out to be. Maybe instead of killing your brother they took him back with them as a slave. Maybe he is still alive," Sulpicia continued, "and living somewhere beyond the Rhine. It is possible Veda. You cannot be certain that he is dead."

"He is dead. Munatius is dead," Veda retorted. "I was there when those Frankish raiders attacked us. I saw what those barbarians did. They slaughtered everyone in our party."

"But you escaped," Sulpicia said. "So maybe Munatius did as well."

"So where is he then!" Veda said raising his arms in exasperation. "Why has he not returned to us? It's been fifteen years since he went missing. Fifteen years since the three of us were split up."

Taking a deep breath Sulpicia remained silent as she turned to gaze out across the mist shrouded country. Her expression sombre.

"You seek answers Veda but I do not have them," she said at last in a weary resigned voice. "But I do know this. Your mother would want the best for all of you and I shall be a friend to all of Tadia's children until the day I die. To honour the spirit of your mother - my dear departed friend."

Nodding Veda said nothing before after a pause he placed a hand on her shoulder and turned to stare out across the river.

"There is news from across the sea which you should know about," Sulpicia said at last glancing quickly at Veda. "Worrying news - which is likely to affect us here in Britannia and soon. In my business I pick up a lot of gossip. Travellers like to talk. Now I am hearing that there has been an army mutiny and rebellion against the rule of emperor Gallienus in Germany. That Colonia on the Rhine has been besieged and captured. They say that Postumus the imperial legate in lower Germany has seized power for himself. That he has declared himself emperor and that he has had Gallienus's young son put to death. There is already fighting between Gallienus and Postumus's troops."

"I have heard the same," Veda replied reaching up to rub his chin. "All of Gaul is said to have gone over to Postumus as have the German provinces along the Rhine frontier. I hope Hostes and his family are all right. They were in Colonia the last I heard. Maybe they got out in time before the siege began. The legions guarding the German frontier have all pledged allegiance to Postumus. They have started a civil war."

"Do you think it will spread. This war. Will it come here, to Britannia?" Sulpicia asked looking concerned.

"Probably," Veda said shrugging. "Britannia cannot remain neutral. We are going to have to pick a side at some point. My bet is that we shall side with Postumus. Gallienus is far away in Italy. The emperor can do little to help us here in the far west and most people will be anxious to avoid bloodshed. We already have enough to deal with - what with the Scoti and Picts agitating along the wall to the north and the Saxon pirates raiding our shores."

"I hope you are right," Sulpicia said quickly. "War is always bad for business. Taxes go up and trade decreases. I don't really care who rules us along as they bring prosperity and security."

"Gallienus is the legitimate emperor now that Valerian his father is no more," Veda said staring at the group of rowers warming themselves around the fire. "But he does not have the support of the people here in the west and he has other problems too. Postumus in contrast is a Batavian. He speaks German. He does have the local support in Gaul and the German provinces. They say that he is a competent general and administrator. That he will secure the frontiers and defeat the Frankish raids and bring prosperity. That he will be a good ruler."

For a moment Veda paused, suddenly looking troubled. "Ah I don't know," he continued. "It's all a huge mess if you ask me and its likely to get worse. These are troubled times Sulpicia. The empire is divided. In the east Valerian lounges as a prisoner of the Sasanians. Meanwhile I heard that his former chief treasurer, a man named Macrianus, has proclaimed his sons as co-emperors and now the west too breaks away. How many emperors can Rome have?"

"Yes it's worrying," Sulpicia said nodding. "You know about these things Veda. You have always had a head for politics and imperial affairs. What would you advise me to do. When the time comes - to whom should I pay my taxes? Who should we support?"

"For now you should wait and keep your thoughts to yourself," Veda said glancing at Sulpicia. "My advice - keep your mouth shut if someone asks for your opinion on the matter. Then back the winner when it becomes clear who has the advantage. That is what we on the farm are going to do when the time comes to choose sides. You are right. Who cares who rules us along as they bring prosperity and security. Those are the most pressing concerns after all."

"There you are," Cata called out cheerfully as she approached with a silent Caledonus in tow and came up to Veda. "Ah yuck, its misty," she added noticing the weather. "Right," she continued turning to Veda with a little resigned smile. "Are you ready to go home to explain yourself to aunt Helena?"

"I don't have to explain myself to anyone, sister," Veda shot back.

"Ah this is going to be fun," Cata said in a sarcastic voice. "I just can't wait until you tell her that you did not go for that job interview. It's going to make the conversation at dinner so very pleasant."

"Dearest Cata," Sulpicia said interrupting as the older woman reached out to fondly run her fingers across Cata's rosy cheek. "Please give my warmest regards to your aunt Helena. Tell her that I shall visit her before the Saturnalia festivities. Tell her that I still have some of that fine wine from Londinium and that I shall bring it along with me so that we can drink it together."

"It's so good to see you again Sulpicia," Cata replied grinning and turning to kiss the older woman quickly on her cheek. "I will indeed pass on your regards and thank you for putting us up at such a rude hour."

"You have become such a pretty young lady," Sulpicia continued looking pleased. "You look just like your mother did at that age. No doubt you shall have many young men seeking your hand in marriage. Please do not forget to invite me to the wedding when it is announced."

"Of course I will," Cata said with an embarrassed blush, "but you may have to wait for a while. I have not found anyone suitable yet."

"Look after each other," Sulpicia said turning to grasp hold of both Veda and Cata's arms at the same time, her eyes filled with sudden concern. "Your mother would want that. She would have wanted all four of her children to be together. You are right Veda. These are troubled times. I fear much change is coming. So look after yourselves."

Chapter Three - The Old Family Farm

The mist which had shrouded the three travellers for much of their journey across the straights to the Isle of Vectis had lifted and the skies were a dull, bleak autumn colour. Leading the way, clutching a stout walking stick, Veda had come to a halt upon the ridge. His boots caked in mud and his cloak soiled. It was afternoon and before him - to the south - the pleasant undulating country sloped down to the sea with an estuary separating a small island beyond. The patchwork of fields were empty except for a flock of grazing sheep. The copses of forest - all that remained of the mighty wilderness that had once covered the whole land. The geography hiding from view the fine expanse of sandy beach that he knew existed down along the southern shore. And sat in the middle of the clearings on a gentle slope overlooking the sea was a smart looking Roman villa. Its white washed stone walls and sloping tiled roof enclosed by a low boundary wall.

Surveying the old farm with a fond expression Veda sighed. This was home he thought and if he truly loved anything it was this place. His ancestral home - the villa had been in the family's continuous possession for over a hundred and seventy years. Ever since the plot of land and the original farm building had been given to the first Corbulo, his ancestor - by general Gnaeus Julius Agricola, the conqueror of Caledonia.

The southern range, the oldest and simplest part of the villa complex had been where his forefathers - Corbulo, his son Marcus and grandson Fergus - had once lived but that building was now used for storing grain, the animals and the farm equipment. While the family now lived in the north range, built just fifty years ago and which faced the original farmhouse across a grassy courtyard. A somewhat grander and larger building the current house had two floors, the upper level was where the slaves and farm workers lived and slept while the ground level was where he, Cata and Helena had their rooms.

Coming to a halt beside him Cata heaved a sigh of relief as she too caught sight of home while bringing up the rear Caledonus remained mute, carrying his mistress's belongings in a pack slung over his shoulder. For a moment the two of them said nothing as they surveyed the estate and the couple of small tenant farms that occupied the land not far from the main house.

"I am not going to cover for you this time," Cata exclaimed at last in a determined voice. "If Helena asks me the reason you did not get that job then I am going to tell her the truth. That you couldn't give a shit."

"I am not asking you too cover for me," Veda replied shooting his sister a moody look. "And just between me and you," he added. "Helena is getting old. She is letting matters slip. I have noticed. You know that Adron the farm manager has started sleeping with the slaves again? After Helena told him to stop doing that. It's not the slaves fault either. They are hardly in a position to resist him and I know they don't want to have sex with him. He is their boss but Helena is Adron's boss so he is disobeying her. And if you want my opinion sister I think that Adron is corrupt and he drinks too much. He steals from us. Helena should sack him but she refuses to do so. That is not right."

"You are always so full of opinions about others," Cata replied looking away. "But maybe you should be looking at yourself Veda. You are hardly a glowing example for people to follow."

"Go on - say it," Veda retorted. "Say what you mean."

"Julia, your wife," Cata said turning to face her brother, "you cheated on her. You neglected her. You were not a good husband and I do not blame her for running away and abandoning you."

"Yeah well at least I did not beat her or abuse her," Veda said turning to look away.

"Abuse comes in many forms," Cata retorted, her cheeks burning. "Not all of them are physical."

Remaining silent Veda took a deep breath as he stared at the farm down the gentle slope. Then he took another deep breath.

"Julia was a mistake," he said lowering his eyes. "Not my finest hour I admit but it is too late now to make amends. She is gone and she is not coming back. So I have to move on too."

Standing at his side Cata was staring at the farm. Then at last she reached out to lightly touch her brother's shoulder before - without saying a word -she set off down the slope towards the villa, swiftly followed by Caledonus.

***

As Veda, Cata and Caledonus entered the villa's grassy courtyard through a gate set in the low wall, two young slave girls, both of them no older than ten and who were busy feeding the chickens in their pens, turned to look around and recognising Cata they hurried on over to her. Their youthful faces lit up with sudden eager and expectant excitement. Spotting the children heading towards her Cata laughed. A happy laugh and as the youngsters came up to her Cata paused to dig around for something in the pockets of her cloak.

"Domina, welcome home," one of the little slave girls said in a respectful childish voice as the two slaves were swiftly joined by a third slave, an older girl who came running across the courtyard.

"Do you think that I forget my promise," Cata said looking pleased as the eager expectant girls clustered around her, the slaves completely ignoring Veda and Caledonus. "Of course not. Here," Cata announced as she pulled out a bag containing the boiled sweets she had purchased for them in Reginorum. "Share them fairly among yourselves. This is all that I have."

Receiving the sweets the girls fell silent as they quickly divided the spoils. Then one of the girls turned to Cata.

"Thank you domina," she said her cheeks blushing. "Mother says that you are most kind and wise. That we are lucky to have you as our domina."

"Hurry along now," Cata said looking pleased by the way she had been greeted.

Watching the three slaves return to their tasks Veda rolled his eyes. His sister was popular among the slaves and freedmen who did all the hard manual labour across the estate. Cata appeared to have a knack for getting people to like her. By treating them fairly and by simple bribery his sister had worked out how to get the best out of the workers. How to increase their loyalty, productivity and respect and because of this her authority on the estate was growing. Really - he thought - she should have been in charge of managing the farm and not Adron, the hired farm manager but Helena had wanted a man to do the job. Cata, his aunt had told him, was destined for other things, marriage and the raising of the next generation. Whether she agreed to that or not. That was his sister's duty.

Feeling something suddenly brush against his legs Veda looked down and spotted Bandit - one of the farm's black and white sheep dogs. The animal was muzzling his leg before sitting down and looking up at him with the loyal devoted look only a dog can give. Sighing Veda reached down to give the animal a stroke across its head. At least someone had come to welcome him home he thought. Someone who was not out to berate or beat the shit out of him.

Helena was sitting at her desk in her study sifting through a pile of accounts and ledgers, frowning and sporting a concerned look, while one of her freedmen was standing nearby waiting for instructions, when Veda and Cata appeared in the doorway. Spotting them Helena's expression abruptly changed and she quickly rose to her feet and came across to give them both a quick welcome hug.

"You are back. Good. All went well?" she inquired as she took a step back to scrutinise Cata. "So Hisauus's funeral - you paid our respects to Narina?"

"Yes aunty I did," Cata replied nodding dutifully. "It was a lovely service. Hisauus would be pleased so many came. I think he was popular. Even his bankers in Londinium sent one of their representatives to attend the funeral and pay their respects. Narina told me to tell you that she was grateful to you. She thanks you for your support."

Hanging back in the doorway Veda remained silent as he eyed his aunt, the family's matriarch and the legal owner of the estate, now that his father and mother were no longer around. At fifty-one Helena looked tired as if she was carrying the burdens of the whole world on her shoulders. A short plump woman with a round face, Helena's grey hair had been tightly bound back in a traditional and conservative Roman bun and she was clad in a long black stola whose robes and folds covered up every patch of skin. Her dress suggesting that she were in mourning, and she was Veda thought. She had been in mourning for years and years. A widow, whose own husband and children had all died young - their loss still appeared to haunt her, for Helena talked about them out loud in her sleep. Calling out their names. He and Cata had often heard her doing so at night.

"Good, " Helena said giving Cata a pleased look. "Well now that Hisauus is dead we are going to have to find a new veterinarian. Adron says that the cattle are in need of a vet but I am struggling to find someone suitable and qualified. Did you ask Narina if she could recommend anyone good, who would be willing to come and work here on the estate?"

"I did, and she said she would make inquiries," Cata replied. "Hisauus was the one who ran the business so she is still getting her head around how everything works. She said she needs a bit of time."

"Well I suppose that is something," Helena said wearily - looking away. "If we lived near town it would be easier to find someone but no one wants to come out this far and those that do are either too expensive or charlatans like the last one. I will not waste any more of the estate's money on them."

"And Sulpicia sends her regards too," Cata said quickly with a little smile. "She says she will visit before Saturnalia and bring some of that wine you like."

"Wine," Helena muttered to herself with a sudden absent minded look, "no, there is no escape that way."

Then Helena turned to gaze at Veda.

"How did your interview go with the lawyers office?" she asked.

"I didn't go," Veda replied folding his arms across his chest. "Changed my mind. The job was not for me."

"What!" Helena exclaimed her expression darkening. "You did not go. Is this true?" she added hurriedly turning towards Cata.

"It seems so aunty," Cata replied with a shrug.

Turning her gaze back to Veda, Helena gave him a long hard stare, her displeasure palpable and there was something else too, a sudden desperation in the old woman's eyes.

"You shame your father and mother!" Helena snapped jabbing a sudden angry finger at Veda. "You do nothing with your life. You are aimless. You do not contribute. You just live of the hard work of others. What am I to do with you? I needed you to get this job. We need the extra income and the contacts with the lawyers would be very useful to the business. But now you have let the chance slip just like you have let all the other opportunities go. You are wasting your life Veda. What excuse was it this time?"

"He was entertaining a young lady," Cata said quickly. "That and there was some trouble with her husband afterwards."

"Good gods," Helena sighed staring at Veda with growing despair. "Seriously. Your mother and I have spent years ensuring that you got a good education. That you could read and write. We hired the best tutors which we could afford. So that you had future prospects. A good start in life. And this is how you repay me? What am I to do with you Veda? You appear to be no good for anything or anybody."

"That is not true," Veda said taking a deep breath. "The lady in question was being abused by her husband. I could not let that continue. She needed my help."

Taking a quick step towards him, with a speed that caught Veda by surprise, Helena raised her hand and slapped him hard across his cheek, her eyes blazing. The blow making him wince.

"To hell with that woman," Helena cried out, "grow up! I need you Veda! The estate needs you, now more than ever. We're on the verge of bankruptcy. If I do not raise new capital within the next three months our creditors are going to call in our debts and we do not have enough to repay them. I will be forced to sell the farm and you know that I cannot do that. This place," Helena said gesturing at the room, "this has been our family's home for over one hundred and seventy years. And I am not going to be the one who loses it all."

As Helena stopped speaking a tense, startled silence descended across the study. Looking shocked Cata blushed while Veda gingerly reached up to rub his cheek where his aunt had struck him.

"Bankruptcy," Cata said at last. "But how is that possible aunty?"

"Easy," Helena said raising her hand in a little frustrated gesture, "taxes and costs are going up relentlessly as is inflation. The market for our grain is not what it used to be - but mainly its because of that fire. You remember the fire that gutted the farm years ago," she said lowering her eyes. "Well it was not only disastrous for our home but also for the estate's finances. Afterwards I had to take out loans to have the villa rebuilt and restored and the bankers well they have now raised the interest we must pay on these loans. The repayments are crippling us."

"Good gods," Cata whispered.

"So we are going bankrupt, we're going to lose our home," Veda said gazing at his aunt. "Why did you not tell us about this earlier? Why do we only learn about this now?"

"I was going to tell you both," Helena said looking away, the strain showing in her eyes. "I have tried everything I can think of to change our fortunes but every way I turn I find myself blocked." For a moment she paused. Then she turned to Veda looking him straight in the eye. "That is why I was hoping you would make something of yourself Veda," she said in a composed voice. "Now do you understand why I need you. Why the estate needs you. But you messed it up like you always do. What am I to do now?"

Staring back at his aunt Veda did not immediately respond, his expression unreadable. Then at last he sighed and turned to look away.

"Corbulo should be here," Veda said. "He is the eldest. He is the one who one day is going to inherit the villa and the estate. But he is not here. He is in Syria with his soldiers."

"No," Helena said and the sharpness and decisiveness in her voice cut through the room as she gazed across at Veda. "Corbulo may be the eldest but he will not inherit the farm. After I am gone, our home will pass to you Veda. In my will I have nominated you as my sole beneficiary. You are my heir. You are going to inherit everything. That is my decision."

Staring at his aunt, Veda opened his mouth in surprise. Then closed it again without speaking.

"You are the man in this house, the only man," Helena continued. "There is no one else. I have no one else to turn to. For they have all left me. But long ago before your mother took you and your brothers to go and live on the Rhine, she told me that no matter what, the family must continue and go on and that we must never lose our farm. Our home! She said that it was my sacred duty to retain possession come what may. For this place is where our family has lived for one hundred and seventy years. This is where we belong. Our ancestors are all buried here. Their spirits still reside here. They are watching us even now. They will never forgive us if we lose it all!"

"Is there nothing we can do?" Cata exclaimed looking alarmed. "Can we pay off these debts through another way perhaps."

"Would you want me to sell you two into slavery," Helena replied turning to her, "no I have suffered enough loss already. I will not lose you two as well. We have three months before the debt collectors arrive."

As the room fell silent the two women turned to look at Veda who was staring down at the floor. Then without saying a word Veda turned and stomped off down the hall and out of the house.

***

It was evening and darkness had fallen across the land. The air was chilly and the sky starless and moonless. Alone, accompanied by just a solitary burning oil lamp which he had placed on top of the low wall; sat upon the wooden stool he'd brought from the house, Veda raised the flask of wine to his lips and took a long drink before lowering the flask again; his eyes gazing at the array of headstones in the small enclosed cemetery that sat among a peaceful copse of trees. While across the empty field a few lamps in the villa complex glowed, pin pricks of light in the all consuming darkness. The headstones he knew, all belonging to his forefathers, had neat straight lettering carved into them recording their names and deeds, but in the darkness he could not read the writing. Moodily he stared at the markers. They were all here he thought. All of them. All except his own father who was still missing and the very first Corbulo to own the farm whose ashes had been scattered across the battlefield where long ago he had fought with the legions to destroy queen Boadicea and her army. Thus saving the province of Britannia from her wrath. Corbulo, his brother Veda thought had once boasted to him, that he could recall each ancestor by name going back hundreds of years, remembering them in a little song which their mother had taught him. But he Veda had been too young and mother had died from the plague before she could get round to teaching him the same song that Corbulo had been taught.

"Greetings Marcus. Greetings Fergus," Veda called out softly into the darkness raising his flask in salute. "Looks like we have fucked things up for the very last time."

From the graveyard there was no reply. The night remaining silent and undisturbed.

"Fuck," Veda swore softly to himself turning to look away. Then raising his flask of wine to his lips he took another sip. "Ah fuck it," he muttered again slowly shaking his head. "Fuck."

Across the fields coming towards him from the direction of the house he suddenly spotted two lamps. The glowing light steadily approaching. Then a voice was calling out to him and moments later two figures emerged from out of the darkness. Helena and Cata were both clad in their winter cloaks and Veda immediately noticed the look of concern on both their faces. But it was not concern. The two women looked positively alarmed.

"I am here. What is it?" Veda said sharply rising to his feet feeling a sudden sense of foreboding.

"Trouble," Helena said hoarsely, her hand, holding up her oil lamp, trembling in the flickering light while Cata's face was ashen. "Trouble Veda. A messenger just arrived at the house. Sulpicia sent him. She says that a party of soldiers have arrived at her place asking to be transported across to Vectis. One of the soldiers talked too much. He revealed that they are coming here. To our farm. They will be crossing over at first light tomorrow. Sulpicia thought she should warn us that they are coming. It doesn't look good."

"Soldiers!" Veda exclaimed, frowning.

"From the army camp at Isca," Cata blurted out. "That is what Sulpicia says. She did not like the look of them."

"Did they say why they are coming here, to our farm?"

"Sulpicia did not know," Helena replied hurriedly shaking her head. "She tried to find out but they refused to tell her. They only told her that they were here on official business. Now think. What would a party of soldiers be doing coming all this way to our farm? Whatever it is I don't think it is to do any good. That party is coming here because they want something from us."

"You are right," Veda said nodding. "This cannot be good. But we have done nothing to deserve such attention. We have no business dealings with the army and none of us has been to Isca in years. It does not make sense."

Looking worried Helena took a quick breath. "Maybe," she said turning to look eastwards, "this has something to do with Corbulo. Maybe these soldiers are coming because of something he has done which we do not know about."

"But Corbulo is far away in Syria fighting in the war there," Cata exclaimed looking confused. "What could he possibly have done to warrant the sending of a party of soldiers to our home. Who would be capable of organising such a thing? I don't understand."

Catching Veda's eye Helena's expression was suddenly cold as ice. "There is civil war in the east too," she said. "You know this Veda. I am sure that Corbulo has been caught up in that too. He will have had to choose a side. Maybe that is why these soldiers are coming."

"To punish us!" Cata exclaimed her eyes widening in horror.

"It's possible," Helena snapped. "If this is true it means that Corbulo has angered someone very powerful and influential. Powerful enough to order a detachment of men to settle scores half a world away."

"So we are in danger aunty!"

Nodding, Helena remained silent for a moment. Her face working on a response. Then gathering herself she raised her head in a defiant, composed manner. "Veda go and fetch our tenant farmers and get Adron to organise and arm the slaves," she said. "Then once that is done I will take our men down to the landing ground and meet these soldiers to see what can be done. They are not going to come to our farm. We will fight them if we have to."

"No," Veda said and the sudden firmness in his voice appeared to startle both women. "No," Veda repeated shaking his head. "I will take our freedmen and the tenants and go to meet these soldiers. You aunty will take care of our women, our silver and the family records. Hide them where they will not be found. We saved the family records from the fire and we must preserve them now again. They are priceless. It's a hundred and seventy years of written history. Get Caledonus to help you. Then you will hide yourself and Cata from these men. You know where to go. I will find you there."

"Veda!" Cata exclaimed. "No."

"Yes," Veda said sharply turning to his sister. "There is no other way. I am not going to let these soldiers take our farm. This is our home and I will fight to defend it like Marcus did all those years ago. We are of his blood and no one is going to take this sacred land from us. No fucking way!" Then to Helena, "the family must go on. That is what you said," he snapped. "So do it. Hide and survive! That is what I need you to do right now."

Chapter Four - I am Expendable

Emerging from the forest, his boots crunching onto the stony beach, Veda turned to gaze northwards across the narrow straights that separated the isle of Vectis from the mainland. His expression was set. Clad in his thick woollen winter cloak, underneath which he was wearing a coat of leather body armour, he was carrying a spear and an old battered shield and he was bareheaded. The gentle sea breeze playing with his black hair. It was early in the morning and across the straights the sea and overcast sky seemed to merge into one. Following on behind him in single file was a ragtag band of armed men and boys. A dozen strong. The silent tenant farmers and a few of the freedmen armed with a motley assortment of spears, scythes, swords, hammers, shields and hunting bows. None of them sporting any proper metal body armour or helmets. None of them looking as if they wanted to be out here on this cold morning.

Gazing out across the sea Veda's expression tightened as one of the estate's freedmen suddenly cried out pointing at something.

"There," the man shouted.

Spotting the two rowing boats heading straight towards him and the landing ground, their oars rhythmically working the sea like the legs of some insect, Veda came to a halt not far from the edge of the water and thrust the butt of his spear into the soft ground. The boats appeared crowded with men. At least two full squads of soldiers, sixteen heavily armed men and crouching at the front of one of the boats, gazing straight back at him across the water, was a centurion, identifiable by the red cloak and fine plumed helmet that he was wearing.

The boats were coming straight towards him, steadily drawing closer to the beach intent on making their landing. Watching them for a while at last Veda turned to Adron, the estate manager who was standing beside him. Adron was a big slightly overweight man in his forties with a slumping pot belly and choppy cheeks that had always reminded Veda of those of a feeding rabbit. Glancing at the estate manager now Veda saw that Adron too looked like he really did not want to be here. Duty compelling him, but only just. The big man looked on edge. Out of his comfort zone. Swallowing nervously as he eyed the approaching soldiers. Quickly shifting his gaze to the others Veda saw that it was the same for them. His band of farm workers would not stand their ground for long.

"All right. Form a line," Veda cried out to his farm workers. "We will let them land but none of these soldiers are going to leave the beach. Those with bows move to the flanks. You shoot when I tell you. And you shoot to kill. You have my permission to do so. The rest of you will stand your ground. No one is to move until I tell you to move."

"This is fucking suicide," Adron hissed biting his lip beside Veda, his breath still stinking of wine. "These are professional soldiers Veda. What chance do we stand against them. None of us are trained for this kind of thing."

"They are fucking bullies, that's what they are," Veda retorted, his mouth curling in contempt. "And no one is going to bully me. That ended when I was twelve."

Out on the sea the first of the rowing boats slid up onto the beach and leaping over the side and into the surf the Roman centurion and his men began to wade ashore. The group of silent soldiers heading straight towards the spot where Veda stood waiting for them. The legionaries were clad in their metal body armour, helmets and were carrying their large oval shields and spears. Their long spatha swords were hanging from their military belts. Leading his men up onto the beach the centurion, an older and experienced looking man in his forties at last came to a halt a few paces from Veda and with a wary frown he turned to scrutinise the line of armed farm workers that blocked his path.

"Who the fuck are you? What are you doing blocking my way?" the officer called out turning to Veda as his men assembled behind him. The soldiers professional gear, appearance and weapons creating a stark contrast with the farm workers. The soldiers grim faced. The two sides squaring up to each other as the waves surged up and retreated back down the beach. The crisp morning air was cold and damp. The tension was growing.

"No, no, you will wait! You are staying right here," Veda suddenly shouted, ignoring the officer and instead raising his hand towards the party of Sulpicia's rowers who had transported the soldiers across the straights and who were preparing to set off back to the mainland now that they had accomplished their job. "You are to stay here! You will be taking these soldiers right back to where they came from. They won't be a moment. So you will you wait for them!" Then turning to the centurion Veda's eyes gleamed with a sudden crazy light. "Hello Centurion my name is Veda and I am from the farm where you are going," he announced. "Now we are hospitable people on this island so I thought I would come and greet you here myself. To have a chat with you. So now that we are acquainted - why have you come here to the island? What do you want from us?"

Staring back at Veda the centurion remained silent for a moment. Then he sighed as he quickly turned to survey the line of armed farm workers standing spread out behind Veda.

"You are from the Brading estate?" the officer asked in a stern voice. "I was told it was owned and run by a woman. A domina by the name of Helena. She is aunt to an imperial officer named Corbulo - prefect of a German battle group operating out east."

"Prefect!" Veda said, arching his eyebrows. For a moment he paused. "Well that would be my brother and aunt you are talking about," Veda said at last with a little amused smile. "But the last time I heard from my brother he was just a centurion like yourself. He must have got a promotion. Good for him. Now answer the fucking question. What are you and your men doing here?"

"I have orders to arrest your aunt, your sister Cata and you too," the centurion said raising his eyebrows as he stared back at Veda. "Then I am to burn down the estate and confiscate everything of value. Punishment. For your brother's disobedience and disloyalty."

"I see," Veda said nodding calmly. "On whose orders and why? We have done nothing to deserve such harsh treatment."

"On the orders of the praetorian prefect Balista," the centurion replied, his expression darkening. "Seems your brother crossed him. Your family appear not to be in Balista's good books for some reason. But that is not my concern. I am just here to arrest you, your sister and your aunt. Now I am a reasonable man. So we can either do this the hard way or the easy way. Tell your men to stand down and disperse and I promise you my soldiers will not harm you or your family. My orders are just to take you back to Londinium with us."

"And then what?" Veda shot back. "What will happen to us in Londinium?"

"Fuck knows," the older man replied with a shrug. "That's for my superiors to decide. That is none of my concern. I have my orders."

For a moment Veda remained silent as he stared at the Roman officer. "Balista," he said at last mulling over the name, "the emperor's praetorian prefect - I see. Must be one gigantic prick. Well done, Corbulo for pissing him off."

Then Veda turned to his farm workers and finally he shifted his gaze in the direction of the family estate.

"No I don't think so," Veda said at last turning back to the centurion. "You and your men are not going to leave this beach. There will be no arrests and no burning. You are just going to have to get back in those boats over there and return to Londinium without us."

Sighing as if he had expected such a reaction the centurion turned to scrutinise the farm workers blocking his way. His weathered face looking displeased.

"Your men," the officer said at last, "won't stand a chance if it comes to a fight. We'll go through them like a knife through butter. You can't stop us. Are you not afraid to lose your life?"

"Lose my life," Veda exclaimed - a crazy light glowing in his eyes. "You got the wrong brother. You think I care what happens to me! I am already going to hell for what I have done so I really don't care whether I live or die. You see I am expendable. I am a nobody. You see I am fucking crazy," he added tapping his head with his finger. "I really have nothing to lose. I got nothing. No woman. No home. No job. No children. Your threats mean shit to me - but here is the thing - I really don't like bullies so I promise you this. You and your men will not be arresting anyone today. Nor will you be burning anything on this island."

"You can't stop us and this is your last warning. Stand aside!" the centurion cried out raising his voice and taking a menacing step forwards. "I have my orders."

"Oh yes I fucking can," Veda retorted taking his own step towards the officer. Their noses nearly touching. "You say your orders came from the praetorian prefect Balista. Well I have news for you. His writ and authority no longer apply to this province. In case you have not heard we have a new emperor now here in west. His name is Postumus and he is a good friend of my family. We live under his protection."

"Postumus, the imperial legate!" the centurion exclaimed hesitating with a surprised look.

"Yes, you didn't expect that did you," Veda said with a laugh. "Yes that fucking Postumus. The man who has just proclaimed himself emperor and who has a whole army behind him."

"Postumus does not rule here. He is across the sea. On the German frontier."

"Oh but he is going to rule here in Britannia too and soon," Veda retorted in a gleeful voice, "and I speak fluent German. My uncle Hostes is a senior officer with the XXX legion on the Rhine and he knows Postumus personally. So imagine what the new emperor is going to do to you when he hears that you have had his friends arrested and that you have burned down their farm. That you have harmed a family who were under his protection. The world is changing centurion," Veda snapped, "and you are in danger of being left behind. Your orders are out of date or soon will be. You need to start thinking about your own prospects, your own career."

"You! You know Postumus?" the centurion replied and there was a sudden unease in his voice. "I don't believe a word of it."

"But you can't be sure," Veda laughed again, a crazy laugh. "Maybe I am lying, but maybe I am not. So please go ahead and try and carry out your orders and see what happens. Or," Veda said raising his chin, "you can play it safe. Return to Londinium and file a false report. You could tell your superiors for instance that you could not find us and I will pay you five silver coins for your trouble and one each to your men. But in return you get on those boats right now and promise never to come back to this island again."

Watching the two boats out on the sea, crowded with Roman soldiers, departing towards the main land Veda said nothing. His hand gripping the shaft of spear which was still embedded into the beach. His expression inscrutable. The farm workers gathered around him looking visibly relaxed and relieved now that a fight had been avoided. Standing at Veda's side Adron too was staring at the departing party. Then the big man slowly blew the air from his chubby cheeks in relief and his shoulder slumped, releasing pent up tension.

"You really know general Postumus?" Adron said at last quietly turning to glance at Veda.

"Do I fuck," Veda said drawing a deep relieved breath, "Postumus in all likelihood has no idea who we are."

Chapter Five - Changes

Running his fingers down the long row of leather bound files that occupied the shelf along one of the walls in Helena's study inside the main house, Veda looked thoughtful as he stood studying the books containing the precious parchments upon which generation after generation of his ancestors had recorded their lives. It was afternoon and the room was quiet except for the crackle of a small wood fire burning in the hearth. Seated in their chairs in opposite corners Helena and Cata were watching him in silence while Caledonus had folded his arms across his chest and was standing in the doorway. The slave looking impassive. Helena looking exhausted. Cata fidgeting nervously with her fingers.

"Do you think the soldiers will return?" Cata asked at last, breaking the silence.

"It's possible but unlikely," Veda replied keeping his eyes on the books. "Sulpicia says that she will warn us if they return and I have sent messages to the other estates on the island. To alert them. Our neighbours have promised to warn us if they see anyone who should not be here and I have also posted a guard. I think we should be safe for now."

"Thank the gods," Helena muttered, lowering her eyes. "Thank you Veda."

"The centurion," Veda said turning to gaze at his aunt from across the room, "he told me that it was Corbulo who has caused all this trouble. It seems that Corbulo has made an enemy out of Balista the praetorian prefect. Not a very smart thing to do if you ask me - to anger a senior imperial officer like that - but lucky for us Balista is far away in the east. Lucky for us too that Postumus has taken charge in Gaul and the German provinces."

"Corbulo is not to blame," Helena said looking away. "He is a good man. He was raised by decent people."

"Ah yes Corbulo can never do anything wrong. The perfect son. The pride of the family," Veda snapped gazing at Helena. "But we nearly ended up as collateral damage because of things he did half a world away. So no more," Veda added sounding suddenly decisive. "You Helena have nominated me as your heir and I am going to take care of this estate. I am going to save our home but there are going to be changes around here. Changes in how we run the place."

"Changes?" both women said at the same time, gazing back at Veda.

"For a start I am getting rid of Adron," Veda said. "I am sacking him and you Cata will take his place as the new farm manager. You have the respect of our people and the slaves and you are more than capable of running the estate. You know what is required."

"What?" Helena exclaimed looking alarmed. "You can't get rid of Adron! He has been with us for years. He's not all that bad."

"He's going today," Veda said sharply folding his arms across his chest. "He disobeyed you aunt. He has started sleeping with the slaves again after you told him to stop doing that. That is disrespect to you and disrespect breeds contempt. I don't want him here any longer. He's out."

"But. But…Cata," Helena blurted out in confusion turning to stare Cata. "What about finding a husband, marriage and children? Cata is a lady, not a farm worker. She was always destined to marry into society."

"Cata is more than capable of doing Adron's old job," Veda said before Cata had a chance to speak. "Our home has seen women successfully managing the estate before. A whole line of them. I have read the accounts. Dylis, sister to Marcus did much for our home as did Briana, Fergus's eldest daughter. Cata is of their blood, their descendant. And I need you to take care of this," Veda added turning to his sister with a serious look.

"Cata!" Helena exclaimed turning to her.

Sitting on her chair Cata took a deep breath before leaning forwards. "I can do Adron's job, aunty," she said. "I had been thinking about asking you for more responsibility in the running of the estate. We can all see how the burden of running this place is exhausting you aunty. I want to help. If Veda needs me to do this then I will."

"Good gods," Helena muttered looking away.

"Secondly," Veda continued. "Caledonus!" he said turning towards the slave standing in the doorway, surprising the young man with the sudden attention. "How long has he served this family? Sister - he follows you around like a faithful dog but he is no longer a boy. He is a man. So I think it is time that he was freed and allowed to choose his own path. We should set him free. As a reward for all his years of faithful service. That is the right thing to do. So you aunt," Veda said turning to Helena, "you are his legal owner, I am asking you to free him."

Looking shocked Helena did not immediately reply, her eyes turned towards Caledonus who had gone very still.

"But what would he do?" Helena said at last in a slow measured voice. "He has no skill, no education. He can't even speak. Who would want him? Cata?"

Sitting in her chair Cata too had gone very still. Her eyes fixed upon Caledonus as she carefully bit her lip. Her mind working. Then at last she took a deep breath. "I knew this day would come," she replied quietly. "Caledonus has been a very good and loyal friend to me but Veda is right. He is no longer a boy. He should be allowed to choose his own path in life. I will miss him terribly but we should free him aunty. That would be the decent thing to do."

"My, my," Helena murmured lowering her eyes.

For a moment she remained silent thinking it over. Then Helena raised her head and slowly got to her feet and came over to where Caledonus was standing. The mute teenage slave staring at her with large astonished eyes, blushing furiously with sudden emotion.

"All right," Helena said in a grave voice. "All right then. You remember the day you and I first met," she said gazing at Caledonus with a sudden fond expression, like a mother addressing a son. "That day in the slave market in Londinium all those years ago. You were so small and skinny then. Sitting their alone in your cage. And no one knew your name or even how old you were and I named you Caledonus. Because that is where I was told you were from. Well, all right then," Helena continued taking a deep breath. "So our association finally ends here. I will free you Caledonus. I will write the official manumission and see that it is properly recorded. You will be free to go where you please and do what you want. And thank you," Helena said reaching out to touch the young man's shoulder, "for looking after my Cata. We are grateful and we are going to miss you."

Staring back at Helena a little tear welded up in Caledonus's eye and he opened his mouth but the sound that came out was unintelligible. Then with a heaving chest Caledonus abruptly turned and fled down the corridor, his boots thudding rapidly across the fine mosaic floor.

In her chair Cata groaned and hurriedly wiped away a little tear of her own. Then forcing herself to remain composed she turned to look at Veda and for a moment the room remained silent.

"Next. Our debts," Veda said taking a deep breath, "they need to be settled and we are running out of time."

"How?" Helena threw up her hand in frustration as she retrieved her place in her chair. "I have tried to think of a way. I have tried everything."

"No one is blaming you," Veda said, his eyes gleaming. "But we need to try something new. Now we could cut back on our expenditure," he continued. "We could raise the tax our tenants pay us. We could sell some of our slaves or cattle. But I don't think it will be enough. I have had a look at our accounts. They are very bad."

"The main problem we face is the interest that we have to pay on those loans I took out to recover from the house fire," Helena said wearily. "If those bankers at First Imperial in Londinium would have kept the rate at what it used to be - we could have managed. But they put it up by fifty percent and there is nothing legally we can do about it. I tried to renegotiate the repayment of our loans but those bankers would not budge. They continue to insist on their new terms. They are deliberately trying to ruin us. Probably so that they can then pick up our estate at a fire sale price. It's disgusting."

"No aunty," Veda said quietly raising a finger in a thoughtful manner. "I think there is something we can do. I have a plan."

"You! You have a plan?" Cata exclaimed giving her brother a dubious look.

"Yes," Veda continued. "It's fairly simple. If our bankers at First Imperial will not offer us new and better terms then screw them. We will find ourselves new bankers who are more reasonable."

"New bankers!" Cata exclaimed. "But we have been with First Imperial for decades."

"How? Who do we do know?" Helena said quickly, her eyes narrowing. "These money merchants are all the same. Thieves and arm twisters, the lot of them."

"You," Veda said turning to his sister, "you mentioned the other day that at Hisauus's funeral his bankers sent a representative - to pay their respects to their client. That sounds like a decent thing to do. Maybe they are a firm of reputable, decent people who are willing to do business with us. So I suggest we ask Narina who her bankers are and arrange a meeting with them."

Looking startled Helena blinked while Cata looked down at the floor.

"I told you that changes are needed to be made in how we run this place," Veda said as the room went quiet. "We cannot keep doing things the same way as we have always done them. We do not have the time. If we do not turn things around and quickly we will lose everything."

"So what do you want me to do?" Helena said at last looking despondent. "I presume you are not sacking me too."

"We will work together, you and I," Veda said nodding. "This is still your farm Helena and I am your heir. You can show me what is what and I can learn from what you know. You wanted me to get a job, to do something with myself. Well I think I have found what I want to do. I am going to save our home and make it prosper. So how about that. Does that meet with your approval?"

In her chair Cata squealed with sudden delight and clapped her hands together, her face beaming.

***

Climbing the stairs to the second floor of the house where the estate's slaves lived and slept Veda appeared brooding. His fingers tapping impatiently against his thigh. His short broad bladed pugio knife stuffed into his belt. It was late in the evening and outside darkness had come. The autumn cold trying to get in through the walls of the house. The rain pattering against the roof tiles over his head. Entering the slaves quarters Veda said nothing as he stomped passed the rows of beds. A burning fire in a hearth providing some light and warmth. The slaves were preparing to go to sleep but as they saw him they stopped what they were doing surprised by the unexpected sight of their master paying them a visit. Some of them hurriedly glancing at each other. No one saying a word. But Veda had not come to speak to them. Heading down the length of the long communal space, with its sloping roof, Veda's boots clattered across the wooden floor beams. His dark eyes fixed upon the door leading into the farm manager's bedroom at the far end. And as he reached the door he heard the sound of soft groaning coming from beyond.

Opening the door Veda paused as he was confronted by the sight of one of the young slave girls on her knees servicing a semi-naked Adron. The farm manager's penis stuffed into her mouth, his undergarments lying down at his ankles, his hand resting on the girl's head. But as he saw Veda Adron yelped in surprise and stumbled backwards against the wall.

"Get out," Veda said quietly turning to the slave girl.

Blushing the girl quickly scrambled to her feet and fled through the doorway. Sighing Veda stepped into Adron's room and closed the door behind him so that the two of them were alone.

"I am sorry you had to see that," Adron exclaimed as he hurriedly reached down to pull up his under garments.

"So am I," Veda said coolly gazing back at the big farm manager as he casually dropped a small bag of coins onto the man's bed. "Here are the wages that we still owe you. I am here to tell you that your services are no longer required. So pack your things and get out of my house. I mean right now."

"What?" Adron stammered staring at Veda in shock. "You are sacking me! But I have worked here on the estate for your aunt for years. This must be a mistake. Helena would never let me go."

"This is not her decision, it is mine," Veda replied. "Now pack your belongings and get the fuck of my property," Veda continued taking a step towards Adron, a crazy light appearing in his eyes. "I said your services are no longer required. You are done here. I don't want to ever see you on this estate again."

Staring back at Veda, one hand trying to hold up his undergarments, Adron remained silent for a moment, shock slowly giving way to resentment. Then suddenly his lips curled with bitterness.

"Fine!" Adron hissed. "But know this Veda. I know things about you and this farm. I know a great deal of things. Secrets. I could make things very difficult for you and your family."

"Listen," Veda said a little dangerous smile playing across his lips. "If you utter one bad word to anyone about us I will find you and cut you into little pieces, starting with your prick. You think I am not capable of killing you. I stabbed my fucking father to death when I was just twelve. Killing a piece of shit like you will be easy. So you will keep your mouth shut."

Glaring back at Veda, Adron's eyes widened. "You are fucking crazy you know," the big man snarled at last. "You are mad! Something is very wrong with you."

"Pack your things and be gone," Veda replied.

"Its fucking raining and its night," Adron growled looking displeased.

"Then get wet," Veda shrugged.

Veda had just returned to the house after escorting Adron off the property when in the hall way he was accosted by Cata. His sister was looking determined, her arms folded across her chest as she came up to him.

"Brother," she said in a serious tone. "It's about Caledonus. He has told me something. It's important."

"What?"

"He does not want to leave our home," Cata said taking a deep breath. "He has nowhere else to go to. He has nothing. He says that he wants to stay here with us as a freedman and work for his living like the others do. He will do anything. He says he wants to learn to read and write. But he has no money to pay for a tutor. I think," Cata added with a sigh, "I think we should pay for him to learn to read and write. We owe him that too."

"Why does he want to learn to read and write?" Veda asked, frowning. "It's expensive. A good tutor costs a lot."

"I don't know," Cata said with a shrug. "He just does."

For a moment Veda remained silent as he considered what Cata had just said. "No I am sorry. No fucking way," he muttered at last pushing passed her, "we don't have the funds to spend on that and besides if we did, every one of our other freedmen would want the same treatment. I am not going to become a charity. It's not going to happen sister."

Chapter Six - Entering a New World

"They are coming. They are here!" Cata called out in an urgent voice as she came hurrying back into the house, her cloak draped over her head. It was nearly noon and outside the snow was falling in a grey and deeply overcast winter sky. Standing at Veda's side in the middle of the living room in Sulpicia's cottage, that occupied a patch of high ground close to the Lavant river, Helena straightened up and took a deep breath, composing herself. The older woman looked tense in her respectable black stola - the dress denoting her social rank. She had clearly prepared for the meeting and the contrast with Veda, who was clad in a casual tunic and cloak, could not be more stark. But where Helena looked nervous, a bemused smile was playing across Veda's lips as if it were all a joke and he was just here to enjoy himself. A leather waterproof satchel was slung across his shoulder.

"I shall go and greet them and show them into my home. Then I shall leave you alone to discuss your business," Sulpicia said gracefully, giving Helena a little encouraging smile. "I hope it works out for you. There is some wine and food over there if they are hungry. Call me if you need anything. I will be in the barn working on the nets."

Then she was gone disappearing out of the doorway of her home and into the falling snow. Leaving Helena's side Veda quickly stepped up to one of the shutters that covered a window and peered out through a crack. Outside across the white winter landscape, trundling down the track towards the solitary cottage, was a horse drawn carriage escorted by six mounted men. The side of the high box like carriage engraved with a logo and a name written in large silver coloured letters - B&M Brothers. The guards woollen cloaks were drawn tightly around their bodies against the cold and the driving snow and the men were clutching spears, their shields slung across their backs, their horses splattered in mud. The procession appearing strangely out of place among the deserted fields while the walls of the city of Reginorum were just visible in the distance.

"How can you be so calm," Cata whispered giving her brother a frown as she fidgeted with her fingers.

"They would not have agreed to come if they were not interested," Veda murmured as he watched the carriage draw to a halt outside the cottage and Sulpicia move up to greet the newcomers. "These bankers - they must smell a bargain. They are going to be tricky bastards."

"Senovara seems all right," Cata said sniffing and looking away. "He did not strike me as a tricky bastard. He was rather young I thought, to hold such an important job, but I think he is clever. He was good with numbers."

"He's a tricky bastard," Veda muttered as he stared at the scene outside.

"Don't say anything to upset them," Helena said giving Cata a quick disapproving look. "Let me and Veda do the talking - dear."

Retreating to the far wall Cata did not reply as she quickly folded her arms across her chest.

Leaving the window Veda returned to his place beside Helena. The two of them standing in the middle of the room as they waited in silence. Their eyes turned towards the doorway. A moment later from outside there was a little commotion, followed by a few voices, the stamping of feet and the whinny of a horse. Then Senovara, the banker's agent appeared in the doorway. His sharp alert eyes quickly surveying the space.

His smart winter cloak emblazoned with the logo of the B&M Brothers banking house.

The young blond agent was in his early twenties with a large birthmark blotting one cheek that spoiled an otherwise handsome face. Recognising Veda and Helena he nodded a quick silent greeting before coming up to them and shaking their hands in a curt, professional manner. Then clearing his throat he turned to introduce an older man who had followed him into the building.

"This is my boss Buccaddus," the agent said deftly extending his arm towards the older man. "He is the B in B&M Brothers. He and his brother Mato run the banking house. Buccaddus runs credit, Mato looks after deposits. I act as their agent along the south coast. Sir, this is Helena who owns the estate at Brading and her nephew and heir Veda."

Gazing across at the old elegant looking banker Veda remained silent as Helena advanced to shake the older man's hand. Buccaddus was in his fifties. A tall man with a bald head, he too was clad in a smart dark cloak bearing the logo of his banking house in silver letters. The man's sharp eyes radiating a calm confidence. For a moment he said nothing as he gave both Helena and Veda a polite nod as they shook hands. Then as the preliminaries ended an awkward silence settled across the room.

"In my work I do not often get to do business with a woman," Buccaddus said at last breaking the silence and addressing himself to Helena. "Most of my clients are men. It is nice now and then to see that a woman has the talent to make it to the top. Why may I ask, did you approach us for your banking requirements? I am curious that's all."

"It's because of him," Cata said raising her arm and pointing at Senovara before anyone could answer. "He came to attend old Hisauus's funeral. I saw him there and we thought that was the act of a decent man. Of a company that was not just interested in profit but who showed some respect for their clients. That is why we approached him."

"I see," Buccaddus said turning to stare at Cata. "And who are you, young lady?"

"She is my sister," Veda replied interrupting. "And she is right. We chose your firm because you appeared to be decent people. I hope that we shall not be disappointed. We can do good business together."

Studying Cata for a moment longer Buccaddus frowned. Then at last he turned his attention back to Veda.

"So you are Veda," Buccaddus said sizing him up with a careful practised look. "Yes we are good people," the banker continued with a nod, "but whether we can do business together remains to be seen. I hope that I have not wasted my time by coming all this way to see you."

For a moment the banker paused eyeing Veda.

"Any way that is why I am here," he said turning to Helena. "To see if we can do business together. My job is to assess the risk and the reward. In my long experience in the lending business it is our clients who tend to need us more than we need them. I am not saying that this is your situation but these are challenging times and I must be careful to who I lend the bank's money. Too many bad loans and we go under."

"Yes of course, I understand," Veda said a little bemused smile playing across his lips as he studied the banker in turn. "And we too have not yet decided whether we want to use your services. Our last bankers proved to be a bunch of arseholes and I am still making up my mind whether you are like them or not. For us too there is a risk and a reward."

"Previous bankers?" Buccaddus snapped raising his eyebrows and showing no sign that Veda's words had insulted him.

"First Imperial of Londinium, Sir," Senovara said hastily stepping up to stand by his boss's shoulder. "It was in my due diligence report on the estate. They were with them for decades but then their bank put up the interest rate that they had to pay on their debts. First Imperial refused to renegotiate so now the family are seeking a new bank Sir."

"They put up their rates by fifty percent," Veda said giving Senovara a tight displeased look. "Its obscene."

"Ah First Imperial," Buccaddus said with a little laugh. "Then I must agree with you Veda. They are a bunch of crooks. I know them well. When they were being run by the father they were not bad but now that the son has taken over he has changed all their practices and turned the operation into a shit show. I do not blame you for wanting to shift your business away from them."

"So we are in agreement then?" Helena said raising her eyebrows with a hopeful look.

"Not quite," Buccaddus said smoothly, smiling. "Senovara, remind me please of who I am being asked to lend money to?"

"Well Sir," Senovara said smoothly, speaking clearly as he stood at his boss's shoulder. His youthful, competent looking face set. "I went to see the estate after the family initially approached me. To do the due diligence. The young lady is correct. The initial contact with them came through one of our other clients in the area, a vet named Hisauus who is now deceased. So I went to inspect the Brading estate on Vectis to see what was what and to check up on their financial situation. To see wherever it was accurate and to get a better understanding of who our clients are. In my conclusion Sir," Senovara said his eyes slipping towards Cata who was gazing back at him, her arms still folded across her chest, "I found that the farm is profitable. They own a sizeable area of good fertile land and they have a long established position in the grain market. I counted a sizeable cattle herd, a flock of thirty sheep, twelve slaves, two tenant farmer families and six horses and oxen. The estate appears to be well managed but they are weighed down by debts caused by having to rebuild after a house fire some years ago. The interest they have to pay on these debts is crippling them. But," Senovara continued pausing to take a breath. "Everything being what it is - it is my considered opinion Sir that if the interest rate burden were to be removed, the estate would be able to survive and return a healthy profit. They have a sound business."

"You forgot to mention the sheep dog," Veda said giving Senovara an annoyed look.

"And the dog," Senovara said hurriedly turning to his boss, the changed expression on his young face making Cata giggle.

Then for a moment no one spoke.

"I see," Buccaddus said at last turning to Veda, the banker's eyes gleaming like a hunter who had just spotted its prey. "So you need help. You need a bank who will lend you the money to cover your debts at an interest rate that you can afford or else you will go under. You will lose your farm. Essentially I have got you and your estate by the throat. You are not in a very strong bargaining position are you and I will let you know - I detest weakness."

"Yeah you can be an arsehole if you want to be," Veda replied smiling, appearing unruffled by the verbal assault, "and you are right. We are not in a strong position, but I have a proposal for you."

"A proposal?" Buccaddus said raising his eyebrows as he sized Veda up again. "Go on."

Sensing Helena's confusion as she stood at his side Veda nodded. "Yes. These are our terms," he said. "We will agree to shift all our financial business to B&M Brothers. All of it. You will take over all our debt with First Imperial and you will charge us no interest on this loan, for perpetuity."

"You want an interest free loan - for all time!" Buccaddus exclaimed looking surprised. Then he laughed. "That's insane," the banker added. "I have to make a profit. I don't hand out money for free."

"It would not be for free," Veda replied coolly. "In exchange for this interest free loan I will agree to work for your banking house. I will join your business as an employee. I will work for you for free."

"What?" Helena and Cata called out at the same time turning to stare at Veda in shock.

"You want to come and work for me," Buccaddus said grinning as he stared back at Veda. "Well I sure did not see that coming."

"It's a good offer," Veda said smiling. "I can be very useful to your organisation."

"You surprise me," Buccaddus replied still grinning, "and not many manage to do that young man. But what would you do for me? What can you do? What qualifies you to be my employee? Are you versed in the money lending trade?"

"Your man here," Veda said gesturing towards Senovara, "he is smart. He has a head for numbers and he has a good business sense. He will be you one day. But he is also soft and way too nice. What you need, what every business needs," Veda said taking a step towards Buccaddus with a sudden gleam in his eye, "is someone who will handle the dirty work. The work that no one else wants to do because its dangerous and unpleasant. Well I will do that for you. I will do the bank's dirty work. I don't mind doing that. I will do anything."

"Dirty work?" Buccaddus said arching his eyebrows, his smile abruptly vanishing.

"Yeah, you know, the jobs for which you struggle to find someone," Veda said with a shrug. "The dangerous shit. For at the end of the day I am expendable. If you guarantee to take on our debts and ask us for no interest, I will do anything for you and I will do so for free."

For a moment the room remained silent as Buccaddus appeared to think it over. Lost in thought.

"Veda," Cata said quietly shaking her head as she stared at him.

Then Senovara spoke up.

"Sir," Senovara said turning to his boss. "It may not be such a bad idea. He speaks fluent German and when I was at their farm I learned that he spent time on the Rhine in his youth and that he has contacts among the Batavian community. He knows the ways of these German barbarians."

"Does he!" Buccaddus exclaimed.

"He could work on the German account Sir," Senovara said hurriedly.

"And if you are worried that I am a thief," Veda said smiling back at Buccaddus, "I assure you that I can be trusted and that I shall keep my mouth shut about your affairs."

"He's divorced," Senovara replied turning to his boss. "I learned that his wife ran off some time ago."

"What would you know about that?" Veda hissed angrily rounding on the young agent.

"And he has a temper," Senovara retorted unperturbed. "He is not the most popular man in town right now. He has a tendency to sleep with other men's wives. But that should be manageable."

"Shut the fuck up," Veda growled staring at Senovara. "Before I change my mind about you."

Wrenching his eyes away from his boss Senovara hesitated as he gazed back at Veda with a strange calculating look. Then his expression softened as he glanced across at Cata who was watching him closely and attentively. A blush spreading across her cheeks.

"We could put him to work on the German account Sir," the agent repeated. "You know we have been struggling to find a replacement for Jonas. He would make a good fit for that role."

"What happened to Jonas?" Cata called out in an anxious voice before anyone could speak.

"He went missing," Senovara replied lowering his eyes.

Once again the room went silent. Buccaddus looking thoughtful. Cata fidgeting nervously. Veda calm and expectant. Helena subdued. Senovara suddenly blushing, his eyes gazing down at the floor.

"In your inquiries into the family, Senovara," Buccaddus said at last speaking in a measured voice. "Did you discover any other issues that may disqualify him from working for us. Are there any other risks? Is he being sued or pursued by anyone which I should be aware of. Does he have political connections that may prove problematic or damaging to the reputation of the bank?"

Opening his mouth Senovara hesitated as he locked eyes with Veda and as he did something unspoken appeared to pass between them. "No Sir," the agent said at last shaking his head. "He does not appear to have dabbled in politics. I did not come across any outstanding issues. He's clean. I think he would make a good addition to the firm."

"Right," Buccaddus murmured.

For a moment the banker paused, frowning. Then he took a deep breath, contemplating what had just been said.

"Seven years," Buccaddus growled at last turning to Veda. "You will give me seven years of service without pay in exchange for a life time free interest loan to cover your farm's debts."

"Five years," Veda retorted raising his chin. "I get released on my thirty-third birthday and when I am done the debt that my family have with you will be completely written off. All of it. On my thirty-third birthday my family will be debt free."

"Six years," Buccaddus growled, his eyes glowing. "You will be released on your thirty-fourth birthday and if you die in my service your family will still pay what is owed on their debt minus the time that you have worked for me. That is my final offer. Take it or leave it."

"So don't die," Senovara said fixing Veda with a helpful look.

"Done," Veda snapped.

"Good," Buccaddus replied as Helena looked aghast. "Then it is settled. Your employment with me starts the moment we take over your family's debts from First Imperial. Forfeit this agreement for any reason and I will call in your loans and take over your farm. Senovara," the older man growled turning to his young agent, "you will act as go between on this. You will ensure that Veda knows what is required from him and when the time comes I will summon him to Londinium. Welcome to B&M Brothers!" the old banker then called out with a little smile as he stepped up and slapped Veda across the shoulder. "Welcome to the old firm."

Chapter Seven - The Deal

Winter 260 AD

Standing by the gate to the Brading estate Veda gazed at the approaching horseman. It was morning on a clear and beautiful winter's day. The deep blue sky uncluttered by clouds. The empty rolling fields that surrounded the Roman villa covered in pristine white snow. Moving excitedly around Veda's legs, Bandit the farm's sheep dog, barked again as he too stared at the lone rider. The animal's tail wagging furiously.

Approaching the farm Senovara slowed his pace, the collar of his smart expensive cloak decorated with the familiar silver logo and initials of his company - B&M Brothers. Raising his hand in greeting Veda left his position by the gate and headed towards the young agent who had dismounted and was holding his horse's reins in his hand. A leather satchel slung across his shoulder. A whip was coiled and tied to his belt.

"Veda," Senovara said giving him a curt, stiff nod in greeting. "Good to see you again."

"Likewise," Veda said with a bemused smile, extending his hand. "Sulpicia warned me that you were coming. Any trouble on the roads?"

"None that could catch me," the agent responded with a shrug as he grasped hold of the proffered hand. "Any bandit would have a hard time outrunning my horse and if they were to get close I would mark them with my whip. It's a ferocious weapon if you know how to use it. No the weather was the worst part. The bridge was down across the Trisantonis river - which delayed me."

Nodding Veda studied the young man. "I take it then that you have news," he said.

"Yes I do," Senovara said stiffly. "I have come straight from head office in Londinium. I can confirm that B&M Brothers has now taken over your family's debts. As of now you are employed by the firm. Your work with us has started. I have been instructed to bring you up to Londinium to be briefed. I have brought all the official documents with me for you to look at and sign. The deal is as discussed, no more, no less. B&M Brothers keeps its word."

"So are you to be my boss?" Veda asked folding his arms across his chest.

"No," Senovara said turning to cast his eyes across the white fields. "Not exactly. We are to work together you and I. I am to show you how things work around the bank. If you have questions I am to answer them. Buccaddus however will issue the instructions. He is the managing partner."

"I see."

For a moment Veda remained silent. Then he turned to gaze at the villa.

"So our deal still stands?" Senovara asked lowering his voice.

"Yes - you kept you word," Veda replied turning to the agent. "Our deal still stands."

"Good glad to hear it for I took a big risk in supporting you at our last meeting with Buccaddus," Senovara said looking away. "It was my advice, my good word on your behalf that got you this job. I covered for you Veda. I broke the bank's rules. I have never done that before, nor do I ever want to do that again. Buccaddus knows nothing about the incident with the soldiers that the praetorian prefect sent to arrest you but I do. Remember that. Remember that like it or not, we are now bound together, you and I."

"There is a first time for everything," Veda replied with a little chuckle. "But don't worry. You will find that I keep my word. I shall honour my end of our deal. I may have a temper and sleep with other men's wives like you said, but I do still possess some integrity. Some. You will see."

"Good," Senovara muttered.

"All right then, great," Veda continued rubbing his hands together. "So I am in. Then we should get started. We shall leave for Londinium tomorrow. Tonight you shall remain here at the house and be our guest. You must be tired from your journey. So come. I will have one of the pigs slaughtered and we shall have a feast. A farewell banquet."

"Business before pleasure," Senovara said sharply. "I insist."

Gazing back at the young agent Veda's sighed. Then he nodded. "Come, lets meet the others and then you and I will take a walk on our beach," he said beckoning for Senovara to follow him through the gate and into the villa's courtyard. "It is a most splendid beach."

***

The sound of the waves crashing and breaking onto the deserted stretch of beach and Bandit's excited barking rang out as Veda and Senovara walked across the sand followed by the sheep dog. The icy breeze tugging at their cloaks. A trail of footsteps visible behind them.

"There is news from across the sea," Senovara said looking serious as he turned to stare at the foaming, unsettled waves.

"Postumus is coming to Britain. Not with an army - but to talk. From what I have heard he is coming to Londinium to try and convince the governor and the army commanders to pledge their loyalty to him. To recognise him as their new emperor. He wants to take the whole province without a fight."

"Postumus is coming to Britain," Veda said raising his eyebrows. "What took him so long. Do you think he will succeed in his mission?"

"The smart money says yes," Senovara said nodding. "I believe Postumus will succeed and that is the bank's position as well. This is still classified," the agent added glancing at Veda, "so you are not to tell anyone, but B&M Brothers is one of the new emperor's backers and supporters in this province. Postumus is going to be good for business. Good for us. He is a capable general and he also understands that it is money which forms the basis of everything."

"So the bank is supporting Postumus," Veda replied, a little bemused smile playing across his lips. "But is that not sedition and illegal? What about Gallienus? He is still the legitimate emperor is he not?"

"Gallienus," Senovara snorted, his contempt clear. "Listen Veda," the agent said rounding on him, "I hope we are not going to have any problems on this issue. That would not be a very good start. The bank's position is that we support Postumus. That is the official line and all employees of the bank are expected to support that position."

"So legitimacy counts for nothing?"

"Screw legitimacy and screw Gallienus," Senovara snapped exasperated.

For a moment Veda remained silent. Then he turned to Senovara.

"I am just joking," Veda said lightly, his eyes twinkling. "I have no problem with Postumus or a change of government. I was more interested in seeing what kind of a man you are. You need to lighten up or else working together with you is going to be such a bore. I like to joke."

"I don't joke," Senovara said stiffly.

"Ah that won't go down well with my sister," Veda replied quickly shaking his head in disapproval. "If you want to impress her my friend you need to appreciate a good joke."

Giving Veda a caustic look Senovara hesitated.

"Postumus will succeed here in Britain because there is no appetite among our soldiers and officers for civil war," the agent continued, "and Postumus has a powerful army at his back. The Rhine legions are still a formidable force. Postumus also controls both the German and the British fleets. He has command of the seas and can strangle us if he wanted to. And as for Gallienus, no one cares about him. He is in Italy. He cannot solve our problems. Everyone recognises that. The people have more pressing concerns than dealing with abstract issues such as legitimacy," Senovara snapped. "We have an economic crisis. We are under threat from every direction. From the Scoti and Picts up north along the wall. From the Saxon sea pirates and the Franks who are raiding across the Rhine."

"Abstract issues," Veda said his eyebrows knotting together. "An interesting way of putting it."

Taking a deep breath Senovara paused again, his expression pained. "It is like Ceasar once said," he growled at last, "obey the law at all times and if you must break it, then only break it to seize power. Postumus has the authority and the strength. He will be our new emperor and B&M Brothers plans to prosper from his rise to power. That's it. That is all there is to it."

"And the German account?" Veda inquired. "The one that I am to work on. What is all that about?"

"I can't tell you yet," Senovara sniffed. "All I can say is that it will be dangerous. So tonight, at the feast," the young agent said coming to a halt and turning to Veda with a serious look. "You should say goodbye to your family. You may be gone for a long time and you may never come back. You should prepare them for that. There is a risk."

"You are going to spoil the mood, my friend."

"You said you would do anything for the bank," Senovara said as he resumed walking. "That you would do the shit that no one wanted to do. Well this is it. The German account is one of the most difficult and dangerous accounts that we own. You are going to need all your wits."

For a while the two of them walked on across the beach in silence.

"Your sister, Cata," Senovara said at last. "If she agrees I would like to take her with us to Londinium when we leave tomorrow. I have a house in the city and I would like to get to know her better, with your permission."

Looking thoughtful Veda did not immediately reply as he turned to gaze out across the disturbed, boiling sea. When Senovara had first arrived at his estate - to do his due diligence and make his recommendation to his bosses, he had quickly noticed the young agent's interest in Cata. His sister forming the basis of the subsequent deal he had struck with him. Senovara would support his plan to get a job in the bank in exchange for Veda not disapproving or standing in the way of his courtship with Cata.

"Listen," Veda said patiently. "My sister is a free woman. Our agreement was only that I would not block you from seeing her. That I would not forbid the match. If Cata wishes to go with you to Londinium then she is free to do so. I shall raise no objections. But I cannot guarantee that she will want to go. That is the risk you are going to have to take."

"You said you would encourage our courtship," Senovara said quickly. "That you would promote me to her. That was part of our deal."

"Yeah," Veda said with a sigh. "I remember what I said. But you need to understand something about Cata. My sister can be very headstrong. She knows her own mind and she is no fool. She has had other suitors before and she has turned them all down because they did not recognise who she is. She will never be some trophy wife. She can be successful in her own right. Now having said that," Veda continued. "I think she does actually like you. She says you are smart and good with numbers. But to me," Veda said turning to the agent with a little bemused smile, "you are still a tricky bastard. Break my sister's heart and our deal is off."

"Hurt Cata," Senovara said taking a deep breath. "I would never do such a thing. She is the most beautiful woman I have ever laid eyes upon. My intentions are honourable, I assure you."

"Good, glad to hear it," Veda said smiling as Bandit came bounding up to him. "For if you were to hurt her I would stick a knife in your throat."

***

Inside the long rectangular dining room that occupied half of the lower floor of the villa the wood fire roared in its hearth. The flames shooting upwards, crackling and sizzling as a slave knelt beside the hearth tending to the roasting pig that was suspended over the fire on a pair of beautifully engraved iron fire dogs. The heat blasting into the room. The shutters were closed against the cold and dark winter night outside. The atmosphere was cosy and relaxed as Helena, Cata, Veda, Caledonus and Senovara sat around the oak dining table. Plates, cutlery and cups of wine, mead, beer and water arranged before them.

Surveying the feast from her position at the head of the table, Helena at last cleared her throat and stood up and as she did the table fell silent and all turned to look at her.

"To the spirits of the departed," Helena said solemnly raising her cup of wine as her eyes turned to the empty plate on the table that had been left undisturbed. "To Veda to whom we say goodbye tonight. To us. May the gods bless us and provide us with good fortune."

Repeating the toast the room once again fell silent as Helena remained standing, her eyes fixed upon Veda and as he eyed his aunt in return Veda could see that she was worried. Her face was drawn and pale with foreboding. Her black stola dress doing nothing to lighten the sudden sombre mood that threatened to spoil the banquet.

"Senovara," Cata said quickly breaking the awkward silence as she turned to the young agent who was seated opposite her. "You have asked me much about myself but we have not heard anything about you. Please - tell us your story and how you became a banker?"

"Well," Senovara said smiling and lowering his eyes, "I am not sure that is such an interesting story. My father was a banker you see. He worked in the forum in the very heart of Londinium. I was brought up to follow in his footsteps from a very early age. From when I was still small I was meant to follow him into the family trade and so here I am."

"You never wanted to do something else?" Cata said smiling sweetly back at Senovara.

"No, not really. I enjoy banking," Senovara said, his expression set. "It is not all boring accounting and risk assessment. We can make a real difference to people. I have seen how our loans have helped create work and prosperity where none existed before. How we have made people improve themselves and their lives. Money lending can be a force to do good."

"I told you sister that he is a tricky bastard," Veda said glancing across at Cata. "The only thing these people are really interested in is profit."

"Shut up," Cata replied frowning at Veda. "I for one am excited to be going to visit Londinium. The big city, our capital. You know. I have not been there for years. And I would like to hear more about the banking business and so should you brother. This is the world that you are now part of after all."

"To survive everyone must make a profit," Senovara said shrugging. "It is just the way of things. Now I am just a junior member of B&M Brothers but one day I want to reach the top and when I do I will be able to make a difference to many people. I will be able to do great things. Money lies at the base of every ambition and nothing can be achieved without it."

"I like that," Cata said beaming. "So you are ambitious."

"I am," Senovara replied smiling back at her.

"Yeah he has a heart of gold," Veda said, his eyes twinkling, "a fine young man from an upstanding family. I am sure that many women are seeking his wallet and hand in marriage."

"What?" Cata exclaimed turning to shoot Veda a confused look.

"Never mind," Veda said with a sigh as he raised his cup of wine to his lips. "Aunt," he added after taking a sip, "you look worried. Please. Tonight should be a celebration, not a wake. What is it that you fear so much?"

Once again the room went silent as all turned to look at Helena. Sat in her chair Helena took a deep breath.

"I fear that you will not be coming back," she said at last in a quiet, dignified voice as she gazed back at Veda from across the table. "They all left me," she sniffed, her tone suddenly hard. "My husband, my children. They are all gone and now I have the feeling that I will not be seeing you again either Veda. That tonight will be the final time."

"Aunty, Veda will return," Cata said quickly. "We're just going to Londinium."

"I am forced to live alone," came Helena's bitter voice, cutting across the room. "They said that before, that I would be left with at least one of my loved ones but they were wrong. They all died. The gods took them all from me. All of them. They did not show me any mercy and they will show no mercy now either. Cruel evil spirits curse me."

Silence followed her outburst before, to everyone's surprise, Caledonus rose from his seat, where he had been his usual quiet and subdued self. Turning to Helena the eighteen year old's face was flush with sudden youthful emotion and before anyone could react Caledonus placed both his fists on his heart before turning to point a finger at Veda. The noise coming out of his mouth like a series of grunts. Staring back at the freedman, Helena's eye became moist and she bowed her head as she seemed to understand what Caledonus meant.

"What is going on?" Veda called out with a frown. "What is he saying?"

For a moment no one spoke.

"I was going to tell you after dinner, brother," Cata said as she too rose to her feet and placed a hand upon the freedman's shoulder. "This concerns Caledonus's future," she continued turning towards Veda, raising her chin with a little defiant gesture. "Now that you refuse to pay for him to be educated he says that he wants to earn his education by working for you. Caledonus says that he wants to go with you to wherever it is that they are sending you. He will do anything and he will serve you loyally like he served me. He doesn't care what he does as long as you promise him that he will earn his education. He wants to learn how to read and write. You need to do this Veda, you need to agree to this."

"I don't need that boy's protection," Veda hissed, frowning. "I don't need him to accompany me. It's a ridiculous suggestion."

But as Veda fell silent Caledonus stared at him and there was something pleading, something desperate about the freedman. Then silently the youth got up from his seat and came round to kneel before Veda. The teenager's head bowed to the ground in a touching sign of homage.

"No Veda - you are going to have to take him with you and you will agree to my terms," Cata said folding her arms across her chest with sudden determination. "For if you refuse I will not be your friend any more. You will do this. If not for Caledonus then you will do it for me."

Once again the room fell silent. The roar of the fire in the hearth the only noise. The wild flames leaping to be free. Staring across the table at his sister, Veda looked thoroughly annoyed. He had not seen the ambush coming. Then swearing softly he shifted his attention back to Caledonus, who was kneeling before him, his head still bowed.

"It seems you are not the only one who knows how to strike a deal," Senovara said turning to Veda with an amused smile. "Just to be clear. The bank has no problem with your freedman accompanying you although we shall not pay him a wage or expenses. What arrangement you have with him is entirely your own private business. So I agree with Cata and I too recommend that you accept your freedman's offer, my friend. Where you are going Veda - you are going to need all the help you can get."

Chapter Eight - The German Account

Sitting at the table in the busy city tavern Veda gazed across the room at the stage where a semi-naked girl was performing an erotic dance. The pretty young woman slowly gyrating around a wooden post. Her dance accompanied by the seductive tones of a solitary flute player. It had just gone noon and the London public house was packed. The punters drinking and watching the performance. Some of them calling out to the dancer while others were whistling. Laughter erupting here and there among the crowded tables. The smell of stale beer and wine mingling with the scent of urine and unwashed bodies. The wooden bar with its open barrels of wine and beer adorned with several small hand held stone statues of the image of emperor Gallienus which were up for sale. While at the door three burly looking bouncers were keeping a wary watchful eye on the clientèle.

At the table, sitting directly opposite Veda, Buccaddus however appeared completely uninterested in the dancer. Instead the old banker was frowning as he concentrated on reading a parchment which he had retrieved from his satchel and had placed on the small table. For a moment Veda observed his boss in silence. Then he shifted his attention towards the doorway where Caledonus was standing among the crowd who could not find a seat. The teenage freedman staring at the exotic dancer with a healthy blush. And as he gazed at his companion, Veda muttered something to himself before lowering his eyes.

Fighting his way through the crowd, returning to the table from where he had been getting the drinks at the bar, Senovara placed three mugs of beer on the table before hurriedly taking his seat beside Veda.

"So is this where you conduct all your business?" Veda asked turning to Buccaddus as he took his cup. "An interesting choice for a briefing."

"No, most of it is done at our offices in the forum," Buccaddus replied without looking up from his parchment. "Why? You don't like the girls?"

"Nothing wrong with the dancers," Veda replied as on the stage the girl's act finished and her place was taken by a new dancer. "It's just that I thought we would be meeting in a more private location that's all. Are you not worried that we may be overheard?"

Reading his parchment Buccaddus did not immediately reply. Then at last he sighed and rolling up the letter he replaced it in his satchel before turning to eye Veda with a solemn look.

"Oh I am not worried about that at all," the old banker said reaching for his beer and taking a quick sip. "There is nothing particularly secret about what I have to discuss with you. So what is someone appears to overhear us. You are to be briefed on the job we want you to do. That's all. And besides - these young girls," Buccaddus exclaimed gesturing at the erotic dancer, "they may be slaves but by watching them they tell me how the slave market is doing. This place is where I gage the state of the market. If the girls are of poor quality that tells me that the best ones have already been snapped up by private buyers. If the girls are poor performers then the slave market is doing well and thriving. For it means that people are buying and a good slave market is good news for everyone. It means business is booming and people have money to spend. You only have to start worrying if the best of them end up in a cheap establishment like this. That means the market is down and no one has any money to spend on buying slaves."

"So, are we up or down right now Sir," Senovara said eyeing his boss with a little forced, humorous look.

"What the fuck do you think?" Buccaddus replied giving Senovara a reproachful look. "Does that girl look attractive to you?"

"Nothing secret," Veda interrupted regarding his boss sceptically, "then why has no one been able to tell me about the German account. About the job that you want me to do and where I am going?"

"We are not keeping secrets from you," Senovara said quickly turning to him. "It is just a matter of timing. It was better for all if we waited until you were here in Londinium and were ready to be briefed which you are."

"You mean after you had managed to lure Cata to your house."

"That is ridiculous," Senovara said with an unhappy look. "What has she got to do with anything? The bank and I have not been keeping secrets from you Veda. We are here now to brief you are we not?"

"No," Veda said rounding on the agent, "you are afraid that I will change my mind once I learn what you want me to do. You don't trust me. But it was my idea to come and work for you."

"I trust you."

"No I don't think you do," Veda replied.

"Listen Veda," Buccaddus said shaking his head before fixing his eyes upon Veda. "There are no secrets between us. I believed you when you told me that you would do the shit no one else wanted to do. I can spot a liar from a mile away and you were speaking the truth then. You are a desperate man, Veda, but we are all desperate men and now you are one of us. You are a member of this firm and I treat all my employees in the same way. Do your best for the company and the company will do its best for you. We are not as heartless as you think we are. We take care of our employees."

"Banking is based on trust," Senovara replied as he caught the look in Veda's eye, "and you can trust me and you can trust Buccaddus. And we trust you too or else you would never have been offered a contract."

For a moment Veda remained silent. Then he nodded and his expression abruptly changed. "All right then. Good. Just checking. But you are still a bunch of tricky bastards."

Gazing across the table Buccaddus hesitated. Then he leaned back in his seat. His expression grave.

"If you want to know a real secret," the old banker said," here's one. Banking is a dying business. Our industry is finished. Sure we can hobble on for a while longer but the future of long distance trade is getting bleaker and that is where traditionally the greatest profits could be made. When I first started out in this business nearly forty years ago," Buccaddus continued, "the good merchants of Britain were doing business with every province in the Roman world. From the Rhine frontier to Egypt and the Greek east. Hell we even sent traders to the far north. Our merchants were exporting and importing every kind of good you can think of and we were providing them with insurance, foreign exchange, advice and credit. But now! Now long distance trade has become nearly impossible. It is a shadow of what it used to be. What with this political instability. Civil war. Rising taxes. One emperor following another before they even have time to mint their own coins - and the increase in barbarian raids and attacks. No one dares to trade over long distances any more. The risk is simply too high and don't get me started on inflation and the continued debasement of our silver coins. When I started out there were numerous argentarii based in the forum but many have now packed up and left. No one wants to be a banker any more. Profits are dwindling. Our industry I am afraid is heading for crisis if nothing changes."

Staring back at Buccaddus as the older man finished speaking Veda did not reply. Then he turned to Senovara who was sitting beside him.

"Well there go your hopes of reaching the top one day," Veda said as a little amused smile appeared across his lips. "Looks like you have chosen the wrong career my friend. Cata will be ever so disappointed."

"It's not all so bad," Senovara replied with a light embarrassed blush. "Buccaddus is right though. These are challenging times."

"Which brings me to the German account," Buccaddus said eyeing Veda with a sudden serious look. "I want you to take over the account but first a word of warning. This is a dangerous and challenging job as your predecessor discovered to his cost. Jonas is still listed as missing but I presume he is in fact - dead. Now having said that your mastery of German and your knowledge of the ways of those people will come in handy. So I have every confidence that you can carry out your task, which is why I agreed to employ you in the first place."

"You are sending me across the Rhine and into free Germany," Veda said gazing back at his boss.

"Yes," Buccaddus nodded. "To give you the background. One of the ways the bank has tried to mitigate our declining profits from long distance trade is by working more with the government and the imperial court. To that end some years ago we managed to win a contract which became the German account. Now I do not need to tell you about the Frankish raids across the Rhine frontier," Buccaddus added, "as you and your brother were once attacked by them. But the Frankish threat is growing and getting more dangerous. Every year these German war parties cross our frontiers to raid, destroy and loot. The government and the army do what they can to stop it but our troops are stretched thin and are often away on other duties. And of course the Valerian disaster and now this civil war have made things worse. Far worse. So some time ago a few bright sparks on general Postumus's staff came up with an idea. If the Franks attacked us we would get other German tribes, enemies of the Franks, to attack them in turn. And within free Germany the greatest rivals and enemies of the Franks are the Thuringii!"

"I have heard about them," Veda muttered, nodding. "The Thuringii - I believe they live around the middle stretch of the Albis river. I remember that some of their traders would come to Colonia to trade when I was still a boy. They speak in a very peculiar accent. We made fun of them when we were boys."

"Their homeland is just north of the Giant Mountains from which the Albis rises," Senovara said quickly. "To the east of the Franks."

"The Thuringians and the Franks are sworn enemies of each other," Buccaddus continued. "They hate each other. Their mutual enmity however works to our advantage and has given us an opportunity. Recognising this - some years ago when he was still governor of lower Germany, Postumus therefore made an alliance with the Thuringii. In exchange for payment the Thuringians agreed that they would attack the Franks from the east if the Franks dared to cross the Rhine to attack us.

The idea being that the threat from the Thuringians to their east would deter the Frankish warriors from leaving their homes. For who would want to go raiding knowing that they would be leaving their own women and children defenceless in the face of their neighbours aggression."

"So we are paying one German tribe to attack another on our behalf," Veda said with an amused smile.

"Correct and it works," Buccaddus replied, "well at least so far it has prevented a major Frankish invasion. But as I mentioned there is a cost too us," the banker continued. "The agreement we have with the Thuringii stipulates that each year by the full moon of the fifth month we are obliged to deliver to them a chest full of gold coins. Our payment. Now the renewal of our alliance with the Thuringii is once again approaching and this is where you and the bank come in Veda. The bank provides Postumus with the gold that he needs to pay this subsidy. Our contract with him states that one chest of gold coins to the weight of sixty-six pounds must be delivered to the public purse each year. The gold is then transported across free Germany and handed over to the Thuringians. Our alliance with the barbarians is renewed and everyone is happy. Now the delivery is normally done by one of our legate's and his staff but every year the bank has insisted on sending along one of our men too. The task of this man, his only task, is to keep an eye on that chest of gold. To make sure that it is not stolen and that it is correctly delivered to the right place. It is our money after all. That is the job. That is the German account. That is what I need you to go and do."

As Buccaddus fell silent Veda stared at him, his expression giving nothing way to what he was thinking. Then at last he stirred.

"I can do that," Veda said smiling. "So all you want me to do is escort and safeguard a chest full of gold through the midst of free Germany."

"That's it. Welcome to the German account," Buccaddus replied.

"Veda," Senovara said and there was a sudden note of caution in his voice as the agent turned to look at him. "Banking is often about assessing risk. We do it all the time. Weighing risk against reward. And this account, it is one of the riskiest accounts which we have. The subsidy that we pay to the Thuringians is large. It is a lot of money and the danger may not always come from the barbarians or the weather. The Roman soldiers who will be accompanying you on this task - transporting the gold across country. Some of them may be inclined to take the money for themselves. I am not saying they will but there is always a risk. We still don't know what exactly happened to Jonas your predecessor but we suspect some form of foul play. To mitigate the risk therefore the bank feels that it is imperative to have one of our own safeguarding the gold. A man who answers to us and us alone. A man we can trust."

"No I get it," Veda replied smiling. "I can see why people would want to steal that money and why you want your own man there to prevent that. Not that I would be able to do much if those soldiers decided to take it for themselves in the middle of nowhere."

"That is why we need a man with his wits about him," Buccaddus said leaning forwards, looking serious. "A man who is no fool and who can spot danger before it strikes."

"You will be provided with the only key to unlock the chest," Senovara said giving Veda a sympathetic look. "On no account are you allowed to give this key to anyone else. And if the gold is in imminent danger of being lost you are authorised to hide it as best as you can."

"Your instructions," Buccaddus continued, "are to see the gold successfully delivered and to get a receipt from the Germans."

"A receipt?" Veda answered knotting his eyebrows.

"That's right. The bank needs a receipt to prove that we have kept our side of the contract," Buccaddus replied. "It's a necessary formality. Welcome to banking."

"Right and what exactly does the bank stand to gain from this arrangement?" Veda asked turning to his boss. "You talked about weighing up risk and reward. Well if this is so risky then what is the reward?

For a moment Buccaddus hesitated as he and Senovara quickly exchanged glances.

"In return for supplying Postumus with the gold each year," Buccaddus said at last lowering his voice, "the bank buys itself political favour. Postumus and his council give us preferential treatment in the provinces which he controls when it comes to a host of government and public contracts. The worth of this preferential status easily outweighs the value of sixty-six pounds of gold coins. So you see this account may be our riskiest but it is also one of our most lucrative. We do not want another bank getting their hands on the German account," Buccaddus said fixing Veda with a serious look.

"I see," Veda shot back, "but if this is Postumus's idea then why does the general not use his own gold, from his own province. Surely he could use the money raised from general taxation for this. Why does he need us?"

Again Buccaddus and Senovara exchanged glances. Then Buccaddus took a deep breath.

"It's a sensitive matter. There are, lets say," Buccaddus said in a delicate voice, choosing his words carefully, "political reasons which are still playing themselves out today. Paying the Thuringians to attack the Franks was Postumus's idea when he was still just a provincial governor but not everyone in the imperial court at Mediolanum agreed with this strategy. Some of the advisers around emperor Gallienus were resolutely against the idea of subsidising the German tribes even though we have been doing it for hundreds of years. They wanted a new approach. They claimed it was a waste of precious and valuable resources saying that the Thuringii would attack the Franks anyway with or without our subsidies. So they blocked the idea and emperor Gallienus forbade Postumus from proceeding. So in response," Buccaddus added before pausing. "Well Postumus, he approached us because we were discreet and we were willing to take a risk."

"You mean," Veda said smiling, lowering his voice and leaning towards Buccaddus in a conspiratorial manner, his eyes gleaming, "that Postumus implemented his subsidy policy without the approval of emperor Gallienus and the imperial court at Mediolanum? Postumus was disobeying an imperial decree and that is why he could not use official government funds. Sounds like we are backing another tricky bastard if you ask me. Sounds like the fortunes of the bank are now firmly tied to the fortunes of Postumus himself."

"Postumus's Frankish policy works," Senovara said shrugging, "and is that not all that really matters? A policy that provides security on the frontier. Is that not what people want? Last summer Postumus destroyed a large band of Frankish raiders at Empel in the territory of the Batavians. Military action combined with our alliance with the Thuringii now has a chance of ending the Frankish threat for good and re-establishing peace."

"One has to take risks to get ahead in life," Buccaddus said eyeing Veda with a shrewd look.

"If you say so," Veda murmured. "But I don't think anything will stop those Franks from crossing the Rhine and doing what they do. They killed my brother. And another thing. Now that Postumus has declared himself emperor in the West he no longer needs us. He can do what the fuck he likes without restriction. That's the great thing about being emperor isn't it? He does not need to be discreet any more, nor does the bank for that matter."

"Nonsense," Senovara retorted - fired up. "We have and are providing Postumus with a useful banking service. We have been doing so for a number of years now. He still needs us. Postumus will remember who his friends are. He is not the kind of a man who forgets. I am sure that he will continue to reward us."

But as Senovara finished speaking Buccadus held up his hand in warning.

"No. Veda is right," the old banker murmured, "now that Postumus has promoted himself to emperor the situation has changed. We must hope that this change does not negatively affect us for it is true that Postumus does not need us any more. But right now he has given no indication that he wants to cancel our contract and I will be damned if I lose the German account. The bank must always benefit so we shall continue to kiss Postumus's arse to prevent him from handing the account to one of our rivals. But that is my job gentlemen, not yours."

"So you are the chief arse-kisser," Veda said wistfully leaning backwards and turning his eyes towards the erotic dancer on the stage, "and I get to see the unchanged beauty of free Germany while Senovara gets to hang out with my sister. So the dice roll. So they roll, my friends."

"You are to leave for the naval base at Portus Ritupis at the start of spring," Buccaddus said. "The bank will place the chest of gold into your care before you leave and Senovara and some of our men will accompany you to the port to make sure that everything is as it should be. At Ritupis you will join the legate Laelian's party. The legate is the government's official envoy to the Thuringians. He will be leader of the expedition. Our chief diplomat and negotiator. You will obey his instructions but you do not fall under his command. You work for us, for me, you understand," Buccaddus added fixing Veda with his eyes. "Your principal concern is the gold. You are to protect the interests of the bank first and foremost. If you feel that the interests of the bank are being threatened you are at liberty to take what action you think is necessary. Now the legate is an experienced man. One of Postumus's top allies. He has helped deliver previous consignments of gold to the Thuringians. He knows these people. Nevertheless my advice to you is not to trust anyone. Gold has a way of changing people and from my experience people are greedy. Clear?"

"Wait, did you say the port of Ritupis," Veda said hastily. "I don't understand. Why am I not meeting this legate on the Rhine frontier?"

"Because you won't be crossing the Rhine," Senovara said lowering his voice. "The Franks control most of the right bank. You would have to cross two hundred miles of enemy territory to just get to our allies. It would be far too dangerous. So we have come up with an alternative route. From Ritupis you will head north across the German sea working your way along the Frisian coast until you reach the entrance to the Albis river. From there you and your party will sail upstream and into the heart of free Germany. There are no roads beyond the Rhine and the country is teeming with war-bands looking for trouble. The rivers act as major highways - the safest routes into the heart of that country. You will use them. You will be using the same route as Drusus Germanicus first took during his invasion of Germany two hundred and seventy years ago."

"So I am going by boat," Veda muttered.

"For most of the way," Buccaddus nodded. "Now do you have any questions?"

"Yes, why gold coins and not silver?" Veda asked.

"The Thuringii will not accept our silver coins," Buccaddus said with a sigh. "The debasement of those coins has got so bad that they only want gold ones. Our gold coins are fortunately still in demand."

Veda was about to ask something else when he suddenly noticed a man approaching the table where he was sitting. The stranger looked fierce-some with his hair tied back in a ponytail and he was sporting a full face tattoo in green ink depicting a howling wolf. Clad in a long brown cloak he appeared to be in his early thirties with a pair of shifty, mean looking eyes.

"Buccaddus, Senovara," the man exclaimed with a cold grin, "what a surprise seeing you both here. Couldn't get your pricks to stand up so you had to come and see one of the girls in this fine establishment did you?"

"Shut up Dubnus," Buccaddus growled looking displeased. "We are here to discuss business."

"Oh I see," Dubnus said turning from Buccaddus to Senovara. Then his eyes settled upon Veda and he smirked. "You must be the new boy," Dubnus continued. "Don't tell me they are giving you the German account. That job is a death sentence. No one comes back alive. But I bet they didn't tell you that. I bet they didn't tell you what happened to poor Jonas?"

"No they didn't," Veda replied looking up at the tattooed man. "So what did happen to Jonas?"

"He was fucking eaten alive man," Dubnus grinned, "devoured by a pack of starving wolves."

"That's such bullshit," Senovara snapped rising from his seat, anger flaring across his face. "You are always so full of bullshit Dubnus that I am surprised that it does ooze out of your ears and nose."

"Yeah fuck off Dubnus," Buccaddus said. "We are busy."

"You made a mistake by joining this lot," Dubnus said sounding unperturbed as he turned his attention back to Veda. "Get out while you still can. There are a lot better firms to work for than these cheats."

"Veda, meet Dubnus," Senovara said unhappily. "Dubnus is the chief debt collector for First Imperial bank. He specialises in roughing up his clients and is never impartial to a bit of private looting afterwards."

"You work for First Imperial?" Veda said looking up at Dubnus with a little smile. "Never heard of them. Are they any good?"

"Better than B&M fucking Brothers," Dubnus replied. Then the man shifted his attention back to Senovara who was glaring back at him. "Sit down boy," the debt collector growled. "I am not going to hurt you. Not here anyway. Saw you the other day strolling around the forum with a pretty blond on your arm. Now how does a man with such a small cock like yourself get to go out with a tart like that or was she one of the prostitutes you like to keep company?"

Slowly Veda rose to his feet so that he was suddenly standing nose to nose with Dubnus. A crazy little smile playing across his lips.

"That is my sister that you are talking about," Veda said in a dangerously calm voice. "You insult my sister again and it will be the last thing you do."

"Your sister!" Dubnus chuckled standing his ground as he stared straight back at Veda, the two men's noses just inches apart. "Well that is quite something and for a new boy you got some nerve talking to me like that. But I am a reasonable man so suit yourself. I won't call her a tart then. But I bet she opens her legs for anyone who shows her the right amount of money."

For a moment longer Veda stared at the tattooed man. Then with a speed that caught everyone off-guard he head-butted Dubnus. The sickening crunch of bone slamming against bone drawing sharp startled cries of alarm from the punters. Dubnus crying out in shock. A woman screaming. Then before anyone could intervene Veda had grasped hold of Dubnus by his collar and was pushing him before him - driving a destructive path straight through the packed tavern. Sending people and furniture crashing and tumbling to the ground until with a mighty shove he sent the debt collector stumbling backwards onto a table that collapsed under his weight as he landed upon it, spilling its occupants and their beer onto the ground.

"You want to fight!" Veda roared as around him the tavern descended into chaos. Voices raised. People scrambling to get out of his way. The erotic dancer up on the stage folding her arms across her naked chest as she looked on in growing dismay at the disturbance to her act. "You want to fight me, come on then," Veda roared raising his hands as he glared back at Dubnus who was scrambling back onto his feet with a furious, murderous look.

Then Dubnus was coming at him. His fists were clenched. His face looking enraged. But as he swung his fist Veda ducked and kicked his opponent in the groin. The vicious well aimed blow sending Dubnus stumbling backwards. His face exploding with silent pain. Leaping onto his opponent Veda did not waste any more time and catching hold of the man's pony tail he yanked it backwards before smashing Dubnus's face straight into the stone wall. The blow breaking his nose and knocking him unconscious and staining the bricks with blood. But as Veda straightened up and staggered backwards, his eyes blazing as he stared at his handiwork, his chest heaving, he was suddenly aware of movement behind him. But he was too late. With a yelp he tried to turn towards the new threat to defend himself as a man loomed up behind him and in the light he caught the flash of a blade.

But just as the man was about to strike he was hit over the head by someone wielding one of the small stone statue of emperor Gallienus. The blow shattering the statue into pieces and sending the knife man crashing unconscious into another table whose occupants fled yelling in panic and dismay. Cups and pitchers shattering onto the floor while up on her stage the dancer had finally given up and had vanished behind a curtain. His eyes widening in shock Veda turned towards the man who had saved him and saw that it was Caledonus. The youth was still clutching the base of the statue which he seemed to have taken from the bar. His large eyes staring at the man he had just knocked out. His chest heaving with exertion. Then the freedman turned to Veda and jabbed a silent warning finger at the knife lying beside the man.

But there was no time to thank Caledonus for Veda suddenly noticed the three bouncers were already advancing towards him. The burly men, wielding stout wooden truncheons, meaning to end his rampage through their tavern in the fastest way possible. However as they closed in on him Buccaddus suddenly intervened, stepping in between Veda and the security men. The tall and old banker showing not the slightest fear. His eyes fixed upon the doormen.

"You know who I am," Buccaddus called out in a stern, authoritative voice. "This man is with me. He is not to be harmed. We are going to leave now and I will send a man round later to pay you for the damage we have caused and that shall settle the matter."

Staring back at Buccaddus the lead door man came to an uncertain halt, his truncheon raised in the air but it was clear from his expression that he recognised the old banker.

"Right, lets go, Follow me," Buccaddus said sharply turning to Veda and beckoning for him to follow. "We are leaving."

Giving the unconscious Dubnus a final despising look Veda quickly wiped his forehead with his hand before, with Senovara and Caledonus following quickly behind him, he pushed on passed the stationary, silent doormen before following his boss out of the tavern and into the street outside.

"I am sorry that you had to see that," Veda said as the four of them swiftly started to make their way down the narrow street towards the Roman forum and the heart of the city of Londinium.

"Nonsense," Buccaddus said leading the way. "Dubnus had it coming. I for one am glad that someone finally beat the shit out of him. And don't worry about the damage you caused. I will cover it. Like I said you are now one of us Veda and the bank looks after its own."

"Well done Veda!" Senovara said looking suddenly pleased as he softly pressed his fist into Veda's shoulder. "That was most satisfying. It was about time someone paid Dubnus back for all the evil he has done."

Saying nothing Veda walked on following his boss through the maze of narrow streets and alleys. But as they drew closer to the forum the streets appeared to be getting busier with people hurrying on past. The public mood growing more and more excited as if something had happened. Until, with the forum in sight, Veda noticed a crowd of eager people flocking into the main market square where the government, city council and the banking community had their offices. The eager crowd thronging the streets as if they were trying to get a glimpse of something or somebody.

"What is going on?" Buccaddus called out turning to a passer-by with a frown.

"It's Postumus," the man called out over his shoulder. "The new emperor. He is here. He is greeting people in our forum."

"Postumus!" Buccaddus exclaimed raising his eyebrows.

Then the old banker was hastening onwards with his companions following. Joining the back of the large crowd that had gathered in the Roman forum Veda sighed as his boss began to push his way through the throng. And as they reached the front he spotted a gaggle of Roman officers and dignitaries, clad in their splendid military uniforms and togas standing together on the steps of the city council building. And among them smiling and raising his hand to the crowd in greeting was a dapper looking soldier with curly hair and a fully grown beard that went right around his cheeks and chin.

"There he is," Senovara called out in an excited voice. "That's Postumus! He must have come to an agreement with our soldiers. Look. They are all standing together as if to show that they are united. This is a good sign. I told you that Britain would go over to Postumus and now it looks like it has happened. Oh this is a great and joyous day!"

Gazing at the group of senior officers standing on the steps to the council building in the Roman forum Veda said nothing as the crowd suddenly began to chant Postumus's name. The triumphant chant swiftly taken up by thousands of voices. Excitement sweeping through the crowd like an infectious disease. Then at last he turned and seizing hold of Caledonus's shoulder he began to steer his freedman back the way they had come until at last finding a quieter spot he came to a halt. For a moment Veda remained silent, his eyes turned towards the ground, thinking through what he was about to say, as Caledonus studied him with a silent, inquiring stare.

"All right," Veda said at last, turning to look at Caledonus, his eyes gleaming with a strange light. "So if you must accompany me. If you insist on working for me, then we are going to have some rules. First rule is you don't tell Cata or Helena anything about what I get up too. You work for me now, not my sister. What I do stays between us boys, understood. Second rule, you don't question me. You don't judge my methods, understood. And thirdly," Veda said grasping hold of the youth's shoulder and starting to march him down the street away from the forum, "anyone who works for me cannot be a virgin. So I am going to pay for you to get laid at a whore house that I know here in town. And that is my way of saying thank you for saving my arse back there in that tavern."

Chapter Nine - A Chest full of Gold

With his hands clasped behind his back Veda frowned as he slowly circled the chest that sat upon the table in the middle of the underground bank vault. His eyes taking in the beautiful handles, crafted to look like imperial eagles, that had been attached to either end of the box. The rows of small metallic buttons that decorated the outside of the chest and the silver logo of the B&M Brothers banking house that had been expertly engraved into the metal.

The vault around him was illuminated by a few oil lamps that were placed along the walls on metal place holders. It was just after dawn and outside the B&M Brothers head office the Roman forum was coming alive. The shouts and marketing cries of the traders, lawyers, bankers and merchants drifting down the narrow flight of steps that led to the underground room. Standing by the door one of the bank's employees was holding a bunch of large iron keys which were used to lock the sturdy, reinforced door.

"So this is our chest of gold," Senovara said quietly as he came up to the table and reached out to gently and proudly run his fingers over the box as if he were touching a lover. "Purpose made for the bank by the finest blacksmiths. The chest is waterproof and made entirely of iron to give it added protection. On its own it weighs thirty pounds and it measures exactly two feet long, two wide and two deep. It is the most secure strong box that we can make. This," Senovara continued turning to Veda and holding up a solitary iron key, "is the only key that can unlock the box, so do not lose it."

Then quickly he inserted and twisted the key in the lock and opened the lid of the chest with a little metallic click, to reveal a mass of small gold coins lying within. The gold gleaming a dull yellowish colour in the light.

"There you go," Senovara said taking a deep breath as he gazed down at the coins. "The German subsidy. Sixty-six pounds of gold. Three thousand three hundred and one aureus coins to be exact. I counted them myself."

"Fuck that is a lot of gold," Veda murmured as he stared at the pile of coins lying in their box.

"The coins are twenty four carat gold. Over ninety-nine percent pure. Each aureus weighs exactly one fiftieth of a pound. It is our best money. Impressive isn't it. Very few people get to see so much gold," Senovara said smiling as he noticed the look on Veda's face.

For a moment the two of them remained silent, staring down at the gold. Then at last Senovara stirred, solemnly handing Veda the key. "This is yours now. Don't lose it," the agent said, "and I am going to need you to sign a receipt that you have taken possession of the chest. One of our formalities I'm afraid. The chest is not part of the deal and remains the property of the bank."

"Don't tell me you want me to bring it back from Germany?" Veda said turning to Senovara with a pained expression.

"Well actually we do," Senovara sniffed. "Once you have successfully delivered the gold and got a receipt from the Thuringians you are to return with the empty chest. Those are your instructions."

Gazing down at the chest, as Senovara closed the lid and he locked the strong box, Veda said nothing. Then reaching for something within a pocket of his tunic he produced a small wooden writing tablet.

"What's this?" Senovara exclaimed frowning as he accepted the tablet.

"I thought I would compose a will and last testament," Veda answered with a shrug. "Seeing that I am heading into the unknown and may not be coming back. So here it is. My will. I am going to give it to you for safe keeping."

"Right," Senovara said staring at the closed and sealed wooden tablet.

"Listen," Veda said in a changed voice, looking away, "for I am going to say this only once. Cata appears smitten with you. So if I do not return then promise me that you will look after her. Don't break her heart. Will you do that for me?"

Staring down at the tablet Senovara did not immediately answer. His body suddenly rigid before at last he looked up at Veda and nodded.

Then with the silence in the vault lengthening Veda took a step forwards and quickly and lightly embraced Senovara. The two men breaking away with sudden awkward and embarrassed looks.

Chapter Ten - A Good Start

Spring 261 AD, Portus Ritupis, Richborough, Britain

Veda was still clad in his mud spattered boots and winter cloak as he followed Senovara down the corridor of the Roman naval HQ. The banker leading the way while two armed bank employees were carrying the chest of gold between them. A silent Caledonus bringing up the rear. The men's hobnailed boots rasping across the polished stone floor. It was his first time inside naval HQ and appearing slightly amused Veda glanced at the stone busts of long deceased Roman naval officers who had once commanded the Classis Britannica, the British provincial fleet, that lined the corridor ahead. The stern, stony faces glaring back at him as if to say - who the fuck are you.

Entering the operations room at the end of the corridor which was decorated by numerous wall paintings of ships at sea, Senovara gestured to his companions to place the chest on a table. Then the banker turned to the three men who were already in the room. One of the strangers appeared to be a naval officer. The other two however were civilians. The older of the civilians appeared to be in his thirties, a tall man with a deep sun tan and the arrogant and confident look of a man born to great wealth and power. While his companion was in his late twenties. A slight, small man with a pale sickly face and a pair of shifty eyes. Taking an instant dislike to both Veda paused beside the table upon which the chest had been placed as Caledonus took up position by his right shoulder. The young freedman staring at the wall paintings in wonder.

"Gentlemen," Senovara said curtly as he stepped forward to shake the strangers hands and from their expressions and greetings Veda could see that everyone already appeared to know each other.

"You brought the gold. It's all there?" the older of the pair of civilians exclaimed as he came round to the table, completely ignoring Veda as if he were not there. His eyes fixed upon the chest.

"It is," Senovara said nodding solemnly, "but before I show it to you. May I introduce my colleague Veda and his freedman Caledonus. Veda is Jonas's replacement. He is our man. The bank has assigned him to this mission and tasked him with looking after the chest and the gold. Veda," Senovara said smartly, turning to him with a professional flourish as he introduced the elder of the pair of civilians, "this is Ulpius Cornelius Laelianus. Laelian. The imperial legate who I told you about earlier. Laelian is being sent to renew our treaty with the Thuringii. And this is his private secretary, Hannibal. Laelian is our official envoy to the Thuringians. He will be in overall charge of the mission."

"Right, so you are the new Jonas. The bank's man," Laelian said straightening up and turning to inspect Veda and for a moment Veda was conscious that he was being examined, like a horse that was for sale in the market.

"My name is Veda," Veda said forcing a little cold smile onto his lips.

"Laelian has just returned from Spain," Senovara said hurriedly, shooting Veda a warning look. "He is a close and trusted ally of our new emperor Postumus. He is a career diplomat. One of our best. A legate from an old and noble Spanish family. He has extensive experience dealing with the barbarian world. He has been involved before in renewing our alliance with the Thuringii. This will be his third consecutive visit to the Thuringians."

"Senovara is right," Lealian said raising his chin with a hint of pride as he gazed at Veda. "I know the Thuringians well. They are valuable allies of Rome. And I am not one of our best - I am THE best," Laelian said turning to Senovara with a pleased smile. "I have just returned from Spain where I helped secure the province for Postumus. A triumph! Thanks to me Postumus now controls all the western provinces without any blood being shed and any loss to the public purse. His star is rising. Postumus is going to make a great emperor."

"As is yours I see," Senovara responded, his expression inscrutable.

"Impressive. I did not know that Spain had abandoned emperor Gallienus and gone over to Postumus," Veda said with a faint whiff of sarcasm in his voice as he studied the imperial legate. "You must possess a very cunning tongue to have talked the Spaniards round into supporting our new emperor."

Turning his attention back to Veda Laelian hesitated, his eyes narrowing. As if he sensed Veda's challenge. "Yes. Some may think so," the diplomat sniffed at last. "And I am good at my job because I come from a very accomplished family. I can count emperor Trajan among my ancestors. The Ulpii have a famous name and I have been trained by the best. You will do well to remember that. Now tell me," Laelian barked in the voice of a man used to being obeyed. "All my staff are familiar with the language and culture of free Germany. My bodyguards are all accomplished soldiers and experts with considerable experience. So what exactly qualifies you in particular for this job? I like to get to know the character and quality of the men who will accompany me. Have you ever been to free Germany?"

"No," Veda responded with a shrug, "can't say I have, other than that time when I had to swim across the Rhine to escape from an enraged storekeeper who accused me of theft. But talking about qualifications," he added switching to German, "let me turn the question around and ask you Laelian, what qualifies you for this particular task?"

"What?" Laelian growled in Latin, his face darkening in embarrassment.

"The legate does not speak the language of the Germans," Hannibal, Laelian's secretary interrupted glaring at Veda and speaking in crisp and fluent German as he came to his boss's aid. "It is my job to translate for him during the diplomatic discussions and record the renewal of the treaty of alliance. And you will refer to the legate as Sir from now on. He is your superior on this mission."

"Oh fuck that," Veda retorted in German. "No one is my superior. This is not the army. I am a civilian. I am a free man."

"You should know your place," Hannibal whined in German.

"And you should shut the fuck up."

"See. Veda speaks fluent German and he knows the ways of these barbarians," Senovara said hurriedly in Latin, turning to Laelian with a quick smile. "Veda grew up in Colonia on the Rhine. The son of an officer who was stationed there. The bank feels that he is well suited for this mission."

"Well we shall see about that," Laelian growled glaring at Veda before turning to the banker with an annoyed look. "But if you ask me your standards are slipping Senovara. Jonas was an experienced man. Unlike this novice here, he knew how to handle himself."

"About Jonas," Veda said switching back to Latin as he addressed Laelian, "no one appears able to tell me what happened to him? It's curious. Maybe you know? What can you tell me?"

Coolly Laelian turned his attention back to Veda, examining him for a moment in silence as a strange tension seemed to filter into the room. "Yes I was there when he died," the legate said at last. "It was a tragedy. I have been to visit the Thuringians three times in the last three years. The journey is long and dangerous, crossing the territory of multiple tribes. Much can go wrong and does. The tribes can be fickle and a chest of gold like that can excite men's imagination. Like I said Jonas was an experienced man. A good man. He knew the risks but on our last trip he disobeyed orders."

"Disobeyed orders?"

"We were on the river moving through the territory of the Semnones. Heading back after successfully completing our mission," Laelian sniffed. "In country where you do not want to linger for too long. Jonas disobeyed my orders and left the ship and a party of Semnones found and killed him. Those Semnones really don't like us Romans! We are lucky that they live far away on the eastern banks of the Albis. And that is all there is to Jonas's death. Like I said it was a tragedy. But every one of my men, who were with me that day, will testify that that is the truth. There was an inquiry afterwards and B&M Brothers agreed with the final judgement."

"So the Germans killed him," Veda said arching his eyebrows. "That was not what you told me," he said turning to Senovara. "You said Jonas was simply listed as missing."

Taking a deep breath Senovara looked frustrated.

"Look. Officially the inquiry concluded that Jonas is listed as missing because no one ever found his body," the young banker replied. "He is most likely dead but we cannot confirm that without a witness who saw the body and we have no witnesses and no body. You don't hang around when there is a hostile war-band on the move close by with blood on their minds. From what little we know the Semnones must have thrown Jonas into the river or disposed of his body another way. We simply do not know. And if we cannot confirm his death we are not obliged to pay compensation to Jonas's family for their loss. I don't make the rules, the bank does, so there it is."

"Convenient for the bank then," Veda said fixing Senovara with a cold smile. Then the smile vanished as he turned towards Laelian. "No witnesses," Veda snapped, "it seems you had a whole boat full of witnesses. I find it hard to believe Jonas can disappear like that without someone knowing something. Like I said it is curious. Why did he want to leave the ship? Where were you? How do you know the Semnones killed him?"

"The legate is not under interrogation here," Hannibal interrupted, his pale face flush with anger. "You are not in a court of law. You will desist from asking these questions."

"I would just like to know what happened to my predecessor," Veda said ignoring the secretary, his eyes resting on Laelian. "It's a fair request. As I am to do Jonas's job. I just want to make sure that there is no foul play at work here. Like you said, a chest full of gold can incite men's imagination."

"Foul play?" Laelian exclaimed as Senovara groaned and reached up to run his hand across his face in frustration. "No there was no foul play," the legate continued shaking his head. Looking shocked by the thought. "I am a professional. I run a tight ship. I would never allow something like that to happen. My men are all carefully hand picked and I have known them for years. I trust all of them and they trust me. Jonas did all three journeys to Germany with me but on the last one he disobeyed me and left the ship and he was killed by the Semnones. There is really nothing more that I can tell you."

Studying the diplomat Veda remained silent. Then at last he smiled.

"Well this is a good start. Shall I show you the gold now," Senovara said quickly and breezily trying to move the conversation on.

"That would be a good idea," Laelian agreed.

But as the two men turned towards the chest that sat upon the table Veda reached out to lay a hand on the lid of the strong box.

"No. You have to ask me," Veda said still smiling. "If you want to see the gold you have to ask me. I have been entrusted with looking after this chest and so I will. But no one gets to see the gold without my permission."

Appearing caught off-guard Laelian hesitated, his expression once again darkening.

Catching Senovara's warning look from the corner of his eye Veda however stood his ground. "He has to ask," Veda said sharply. "My job is to protect the gold and that is what I am going to do."

"He is the legate!" Hannibal, Laelian's secretary hissed glaring at Veda with an outraged look, "he does not need to ask you for anything. He is in charge here, not you. Stand aside!"

"Hannibal is it," Veda retorted turning to the secretary, "you bear a famous name but I am yet to decide whether you deserve it. The gold is in my charge and I alone determine who gets to see it. And just so that we are clear. If anyone tries to touch the gold without my permission I will happily cut their throat and social rank be damned. Everyone bleeds the same way in the end."

"You threaten us now!" Hannibal gasped taking a step towards Veda. "You threaten us here in the very heart of fleet headquarters!"

"You don't want to test me," Veda said, his voice suddenly hard and cold. The smile vanishing from his lips. "I stabbed my father to death when I was twelve. Doing the same to anyone of you will be a lot easier than that. He has to ask me, if he wants to see the gold!"

Silence followed the outburst. The men suddenly unsure of themselves. Staring at Veda, Laelian's mind appeared to be working fast. Then to Veda's surprise the legate threw back his head and boomed with laughter. The sound reversing the growing tension.

"Naturally," Laelian called out as he finally quietened down, "your job is to guard the gold - as it is my job to do business with these barbarians. Good. You have passed your test. Well done for doing your job. I can see I was mistaken about you Veda. My apologies. I was too hasty in my judgement. Now I shall ask you, politely, may I see the gold with my own eyes?"

Keeping his hand on the lid of the strong box Veda hesitated, his eyes fixed upon the legate and suddenly he felt troubled. There was something disturbing in how easy and fast Laelian had switched between arrogance, aggression and making his apologies. Like an actor performing on stage. As if there was something about the man that was utterly fake. As if he were dealing with multiple personalities. Never quite sure who the real man was. Laelian was another tricky bastard Veda thought with growing consternation.

"Veda, please," Senovara said in a quiet voice and as he noticed his friend's silent pleading look Veda abruptly raised his hand and bowed his head in a little display of magnanimity and approval. Producing the key he inserted it in the lock and opened the box and as the men crowded around to stare at the gold the room once again fell silent.

"Good. Good," Laelian murmured at last. "Sixty-six pounds of pure gold?"

"Sixty-six pounds of pure gold," Senovara confirmed. "Three thousand three hundred and one gold coins. It's all there as agreed."

But as Hannibal inched closer to the strong box to get a better look Veda slammed the lid shut and inserting the key he once again locked the chest.

"Right so now that the bank has completed our part of the contract and delivered the gold to you," Senovara said sounding relieved and turning to Laelian, "I am going to need you to sign a receipt that you have accepted the funds. Then I suggest that you introduce Veda to your close protection detail. The men who will be accompanying you on your journey. They are here I take it?"

"Yes they are," Laelian said sounding satisfied. "Five of my best. They are the same men who came along last year. Ex-special forces. Experienced professionals to a man."

"And when do you plan to leave?" Senovara asked.

"Tomorrow if the winds are favourable," Laelian replied looking bullish and puffing himself up. "The weather on the German sea at this time of year is unpredictable but it cannot be helped. We shall just have to risk it. The Thuringian Thing, their tribal assembly takes place on the full moon of the fifth month at Thor's Oak and I do not intend to arrive late. These Germans have a reputation for not being a very punctual race. It is a sign I suppose of their belief in individual liberty that they do not try very hard to arrive on time on the assigned day, even when they are summoned to do so. But they treat us Romans differently. We cannot be like them. If I were to arrive late for the Thing that would be treated as an act of bad faith and trust between us and them is always limited. But don't worry I will get the treaty of alliance renewed for another year."

"A naval warship is waiting for us down in the harbour," Laelian continued. "We will take the usual route there and back avoiding the Franks and their allies. First across the narrow seas to Portus Itius where we pick up our transport that will take us north along the Frisian coast to the estuary of the Albis. Then inland up the river through the territory of the Saxons. First to Drusus's old outpost at Treva, before continuing onwards through the land of the Semnones and Langobardi before we finally reach friendly territory at the confluence of the Marsh river with the Albis. Once we reach the Marsh river we should be safe among friends. The journey to the Thuringian Thing at Thor's Oak will be easier after that."

"You have a good local guide?" Senovara asked.

"Yes a good one," Laelian replied. "His name is Walaric. He was there with me last year as well. He is Thuringian and will help smooth matters with his people once we reach their territory."

Nodding Senovara paused, his expression suddenly solemn.

"If the gold is lost or not delivered to the Thuringii, for whatever reason," Senovara said at last, "the usual caveats apply. I know you are aware of them but the bank obliges me to state them again to you in person. B&M Brothers will not be liable for the loss of the gold until we have received the report on the matter from our man, which is Veda here. The bank will not consider replacing the lost gold unless it has received this report. So it is in the government's interest to keep my colleague Veda alive. You understand."

"Like always," Laelian said with a weak smile. "I intend to bring all my men back alive. Losing Jonas was most unfortunate."

"Good," Senovara said before glancing at Veda, "then I have done all that I can from our end. I wish you all a safe and successful journey."

"We have made a sacrifice to the Gods," Hannibal said turning to Senovara. "You would do well to make a similar offering for our safe journey, for it is in all our interests that we succeed."

But in reply Senovara looked away.

"No I don't think so," the young banker replied in a quiet voice. "The bank does not believe in omens or sacrifice to the gods. Those are the old ways. Nothing more than superstition. No," Senovara said turning to eye Veda, "we believe and trust in the cold, hard power of money."

Chapter Eleven - A Son of the Northern Light

Veda was standing at the bow of the "Frisian Glory" as the narrow, flat bottomed barge pushed on across the gentle sea swell. His foot was resting upon the iron chest that had been placed upon the deck while he was holding onto one of the taught mooring ropes that secured the solitary mast behind him. It was after noon and the ship was heading north and sticking close to the coast. With the deck gently tilting and creaking and the breeze playing with his black hair, Veda looked thoughtful as he studied the wide deserted beach and the line of sand dunes some several hundred yards off to his right. Behind him the Frisian Glory's square and reddish coloured sail bulged in the fresh salty sea breeze. A gaggle of screeching sea gulls hovering overhead.

Nearby Caledonus, his heavy leather back-pack resting at his feet, was half hanging over the side of the ship's hull, emptying the contents of his stomach into the water, his violent sea sickness drawing mocking smiles and a smattering of laughter from the rest of the crew.

Ignoring his freedman Veda turned his attention away from the coast and back to the barge. Aware that he was being watched. At twenty five yards long and three wide the Frisian Glory was just like any other light freighter that plied the shallow inland waters of the Rhine delta. The ship narrowing elegantly towards stern and bow with its flat bottom, cargo hold, cooking area and small cabin. Sturdy oak planking making up the deck - an orange pennant flying proudly from the top of the mast.

Sitting together cross-legged in a circle upon the deck near to the cabin in the centre of the barge, the five burly Romano-German soldiers; Felix, Atticus, Catuvolcos, Thiemo and their leader a Goth named Hulmu; were playing a game of dice.

The soldiers now and then pausing to cast a curious glance in Veda's direction as they chatted quietly with one another. While Hulmu was wearing a little sealed leather pouch on a cord around his neck. There was however no sign of Laelian, his secretary Hannibal or the Thuringian guide Walaric who made up the remainder of the party. The three men had to be in the cargo hold or inside the cabin Veda thought. Ignoring the five bodyguards sitting out on deck Veda's eyes finally settled upon Abbe and as he gazed at the ship's captain Veda frowned.

The owner and civilian captain of the Frisian Glory was standing at the stern holding onto the tiller that was connected to the rudder. Guiding the ship across the water. His eyes fixed upon the sea ahead with a calm, competent expression as if he had done this a thousand times before. A tall, straight backed and quiet man with an honest face and yellow blond hair Abbe was in his early forties. The oldest man aboard the ship. While sitting on the deck close by, Abbe's sixteen year old daughter Jorina was busy with thread and needle repairing a pair of leather shoes. The girl's braided hair as yellow blond as her father's as it flapped around in the wind. Her round cheeks rosy and freckled.

For a while Veda continued to observe the father and the daughter. Then as Caledonus swayed over to him carrying his heavy back-pack, the freedman appearing miserable and pale, Veda turned to him.

"Guard the chest for a moment," he murmured reaching out to squeeze the youth's shoulder and giving him a little sympathetic look. "And cheer up. The sea sickness will not last. It will get better once we reach calmer waters."

Nodding that he had understood Caledonus quickly reached up to wipe his mouth with his hand. Then silently without turning around, using his thumb, he pointed behind him at the five bodyguards while at the same time he shook his head with a disapproving facial expression.

"Yeah I don't like them either," Veda said quietly as he turned to study the five soldiers. "Fucking mercenaries think they are so cool."

Raising a finger to his eye in warning Caledonus fixed Veda with a wary look and seeing his freedman's expression Veda nodded. "I know. I am keeping an eye on them too," he murmured.

Then leaving Caledonus in charge of the chest of gold, Veda broke away and carefully made his way along the moving deck towards the stern where Abbe was standing holding the tiller. And as he approached, the tall skipper gave him a silent indifferent look.

"They say that you only travel to free Germany if it is your homeland," Veda said in German with a broad amused smile as he came up to the captain. "That it is really a rather bleak place. That there really is not much there other than treacherous bogs, forests and terrible food. That when the German women sing it can put a man off music for the rest of his life."

Keeping his eyes on the horizon and his hand on the tiller Abbe remained silent. A stoic, rugged character. Then at last, looking unimpressed, he turned eye Veda, pausing before speaking.

"They say that all roads lead to Rome," the captain and master of the 'Frisian Glory' said speaking German with a thick regional accent that made Veda struggle to keep up. "But when you get there everyone wants to return to the country as quick as possible."

"You have been to Rome?" Veda exclaimed looking impressed.

In response Abbe simply nodded. "It's a shit hole. Full of slums and people who do not want to work for a living," he murmured.

"I have never been," Veda said looking away as if talking to himself. "Strange. I really ought to go one day." For a moment Veda paused as he came to stand beside Abbe and turned to survey the 'Frisian Glory'.

"Well you have a fine ship, captain," Veda said breezily. "You must be proud to posses such a boat. She must be worth a lot of money."

"Yes. She has served me faithfully," Abbe said after a pause, keeping his eyes upon the horizon. "I have had the 'Glory' for four years now. Her flat bottom is ideal for the shallow waters of these lowlands where I do most of my work but it gets tricky out here on the open sea. The German sea is the roughest and most dangerous sea there is. She does not do so well in heavy weather which is why we shall hug the coast as close as we can."

"Your accent," Veda said, "it is from the north?"

"Yes," Abbe nodded looking serious. "I am of Frisian descent. A son of the northern light. And your German is atrocious. So speak slowly so that I can understand you properly."

"No one has ever told me that."

"I am not trying to be rude," Abbe continued, refusing to take his eyes off the horizon. "I am told by foreigners that my people are often direct, which can be mistaken for being rude.

But we Frisians are a free people who will speak our mind freely. It is just the way we are."

"I am not offended."

"You speak with a Batavian accent," Abbe added before stealing a quick glance at Veda, "but you are not a proper Batavian. You are not even a proper Roman. You are a half cast like so many these days. Perhaps you are from the northern districts of Gaul."

"You can tell?" Veda said with a little amused smile.

"Yes," Abbe nodded again. "Jorina and I - we are true sons and daughters of the northern light. We know who we are and where we come from unlike the half casts who are born in the Roman camps along the limes. Those people are neither Roman or German. You speak with a Batavian accent because, if I had to wager a guess, you learned to speak like that at one the Roman settlements along the Rhine. Felix, Atticus and Catuvolcos over there," Abbe said gesturing contemptuously at the three bodyguards, "they are the same like you. Only Thiemo is a proper Batavian and as for Hulmu he speaks the coarse eastern dialect of the Goths. He has the cruel eyes of that tribe."

"And what about Hannibal?" Veda said raising his eyebrows. "The legate's secretary and our official translator."

"The man is an idiot," Abbe replied coolly. "Every time he speaks he reminds me of a thief protesting his innocence and as for our fat guide Walaric he carries the heavy burden of being born a Thuringian. I feel only pity for him. It is not his fault that he is a Thuringian."

Looking amused Veda gazed out across the sea.

"You are right," he said at last as Jorina stopped what she was doing to look up at him. "In my youth I spent time in Colonia - on the Rhine. That is where I got my accent but you are wrong about us half casts. I do know who I am and where I come from. I have always known. My ancestral home is on the isle of Vectis in Britannia and my family have a long and distinguished record of service to Rome. One of my ancestors was even a Roman senator. His son was the legionary legate of the Twentieth. My brother Corbulo fights for the imperial eagle in the east. Service to Rome runs in our blood. Rome is the light in this dark, cold world. It binds us all and gives my family purpose."

"But you are not a soldier?" Abbe said keeping his eyes on the sea.

"No, I am not. I work for the bank that provided me with that chest over there."

"Ah the gold," Abbe responded, his eyes gleaming as he turned to stare at the spot where Caledonus was standing guarding the iron chest. "Was it really wise of you to show the whole crew the gold coins which you carry in that box? You protect a fortune but who protects you?"

"Yes I think so," Veda said turning to look away with a philosophical look. "Everyone on-board is risking their lives to get this gold to its destination. I thought it only fair that everyone saw the gold for themselves so that they know it is real. This crew I have been told can be trusted."

Staring out across the sea as he held the tiller Abbe said nothing and nearby Jorina returned to her repair work.

"Listen," Veda said seizing his chance and turning to Abbe, "what can you tell me about my predecessor? His name was Jonas. He was one of your companions. I am told that he travelled with you three times into free Germany as part of this diplomatic mission."

"I can't help you," Abbe said stoically. "Sorry. I did not know the man. He was not my companion. Like you this is the first time that we are doing this trip. I had never met the legate until he hired me for this job a few weeks ago. Jorina has never even been beyond the outer islands before."

"What! This is your first trip to the Thuringians?" Veda exclaimed looking surprised. "But everyone else on-board has been there multiple times. You are all veterans of this expedition. You all know each other!"

"No. I only met the legate a few weeks ago when he hired me. I didn't know any of you until you came aboard the 'Glory'," Abbe replied.

"So what happened to the previous boat crew? Why are they not doing this journey again?"

"Who knows. I don't have an answer for you," Abbe said with a shrug. "You should ask the legate that question."

"Right," Veda murmured.

"As for me and Jorina," Abbe said changing the subject. "We only have each other now. And we have this ship. The 'Glory' is our home. We live and work on this barge. I served Rome before as foederati," Abbe said glancing across at Veda. "I was a soldier once just like those five over there."

"So what happened?"

"I retired and bought the 'Glory'," Abbe replied. "Now I work as a repairman. I have a set of tools in my cabin over there," the captain said gesturing with his head. My daughter and I - we move up and down the rivers of the delta, repairing the forts and installations along the Limes. But work is increasingly hard to find so when they came asking for a crew and a ship to undertake this voyage I said I would do it. The legate pays me good money. And the money. It's all for her," he said gesturing at his daughter.

Looking thoughtful Veda remained silent.

"There is a rumour," Abbe said in a sudden changed voice, giving Veda a careful searching look, "that you murdered your father. That you admitted it yourself. I heard the others discussing it. Is it true?"

For a moment Veda did not reply as he stared out across the sea. Then his eyes came to rest upon Jorina who had again paused what she was doing and was gazing up at him in stoic silence.

"Yes, its true," Veda said with a sudden weary look. "Stabbed the bastard to death when I was just twelve with this very knife," he added patting the pugio that hung from his belt. "My father was abusing me and my brothers and we'd had enough. I thought that one act would free me but instead it has fucked up my whole life. I am twenty-eight and I have done nothing that deserves respect. I have done nothing of any importance. This voyage," Veda continued with a sudden wistful look, "it's like a journey of redemption for me. For the first time in my life I am actually doing something that has meaning."

Holding onto the tiller Abbe said nothing, his stoic eyes fixed upon the horizon. Then at last he stirred.

"Then I hope it works out for you," the captain said.

Chapter Twelve - The Warning

"There! See!" Atticus yelled pointing again with his finger.

It was morning and crashing through the sea swell the 'Glory' groaned, pitched and rolled, the barge's timbers creaking. The driving rain lashing the deck. The shoreline to the south was a smudge of low lying land and small treeless islands. Lining the side of the ship, clad in their bad weather poncho's, with their hoods lowered over their heads, Veda and the others were peering intently at the unsettled waves. Then Veda spotted the huge dark shape lying in the water and moments later, to a roar of excitement from the men, the huge gray whale sent up a spout of water before slowly sinking beneath the waves.

"Did you see that!" Felix bellowed looking awestruck. "A monster from the deep boys!"

"A good omen or a bad one?" Thiemo called out.

"A good one," Laelian cried looking pleased. "The gods have sent one of their own to escort us lads. This is a sign that they want us to succeed."

"Let's hope so," Hulmu growled reaching up to touch the small pouch that hung around his neck on a leather cord as if to ward off some evil. "The damned thing is large enough to sink us."

"If you are lost at sea," Felix cried out again, "your spirit will never find a final resting place. You will be homeless for eternity!"

Staring at the spot of water where the whale had vanished Veda remained silent, sharing the others excitement. Then he turned his head as Jorina came scampering past. The silent girl too was clad in her bad weather gear. Water glistening and streaming from her poncho. Ignoring both men and beast she hurriedly started to lower the square main sail. Working the rigging like a woman who knew what she was doing. For a moment Veda observed her as she worked before quickly shifting his gaze to Abbe who was standing at the stern holding the tiller. Guiding the barge through the choppy sea. And whereas the attention of the rest of the crew was fixed upon the whale sighting, the captain had his eyes firmly fixed upon the horizon and instead of excited he looked worried.

"Trouble?" Veda called out as he staggered up to the skipper on the swaying deck.

In response Abbe nodded.

"Legate! Storm coming," the captain shouted turning to address himself to Laelian and pointing towards the horizon where dark clouds were massing. "The weather is turning so I am heading for land. We have no choice. The 'Glory' cannot handle rough seas."

Hearing Abbe calling out to him, Laelian hurriedly made his way over to him accompanied by Hannibal and Walaric the Thuringian guide. A fat German in his thirties with a large hooked nose.

"All right. If you say so. You are the captain. You know these waters best," Laelian conceded turning to study the distant storm clouds with a sudden wary look. "But where around here can we find shelter?"

"There are no harbours along this coast," Abbe responded as the 'Glory' began to turn towards land. "There is nothing but low lying islands and marshes stretching for hundreds of miles. This is Frisian land Sir. Flat as a pancake and soggy as porridge. Now I need your men to man the oars and propel us for the final stretch. The wind is picking up in strength and will rip our sail to pieces if we are not careful. I will beach her on those mud flats," he said gesturing at the low lying coast. "In between those two islands. We will wait out the storm over there. Hopefully it will pass quickly and we will be on our way again."

"I don't see any mudflats!" Hannibal exclaimed peering suspiciously in the direction Abbe was pointing. "I just see more sea."

"Those are islands?" Laelian murmured raising his eyebrows in disbelief as he stared at the low lying coast. "Good gods man - the land barely rises out of the water. A large wave could swamp the place."

"The coast line around here shifts," Abbe growled unhappy that he had to explain himself. "It does not stay in the same place. It's intertidal. Right now it looks like the sea extends past those islands but that is because the tide is in - which means a barge like the 'Glory' can gain access. But once the tide goes out we will be left stuck on a mudflat. On dry land. The sea over there is very shallow and the water vanishes completely twice a day."

"On dry land! Stuck!" Hannibal exclaimed, frowning as he picked up on his boss's unease. "Is that wise?"

"We will be stuck only for a few hours until the tide comes back in and sets us free," Abbe snapped.

"But why not seek shelter on one of those islands instead?" Hannibal gasped pointing.

"No," Abbe said sharply - refusing to look at the secretary, "not on the islands. There are people there. It will be better to beach her on the mud flats. Hopefully the storm will pass quickly. Let's pray it does. With our flat bottom we will not get stuck. We will just have to wait until the tide comes back in to free us. The 'Glory' was designed for such shallow waters."

"What a treacherous place," Laelian exclaimed looking concerned as he turned to study the grey coast. "There is not even a clear boundary between the land and the ocean. Damn it. We have never had to set foot here before on the previous missions. This is a stroke of bad luck."

"Maybe the whale sighting was a bad omen after all," Walaric said turning to Laelian with the faintest whiff of discord.

Studying Abbe, Veda opened his mouth to speak, then hesitated before deciding to remain silent and he did Abbe shot him a quick, displeased look. The captain conveying some unspoken message. Abbe appeared concerned but it was not to do with the approaching storm Veda thought suddenly. Something else seemed to have unsettled the stoic Frisian. Something he was not willing to share with the rest of his crew.

***

Sitting on top of the iron chest on the deck of the 'Glory' Veda silently accepted the bowl of steaming hot soup that Caledonus had brought him. The young freedman settling down beside him to consume his own bowl using a wooden spoon. His backpack nestling securely between his knees. It was morning and the storm had passed. The ferociously cold northern wind had died away and the blue sky was clear of clouds and rain. Around the solitary, stranded barge the mudflats extended to the horizon. A bleak desert like landscape of mud, pools of trapped water and sand banks. The sea was gone. Retreating to the north and a line of small dune covered islands was the only reminder of where the coast began. The eerie mudflats were deserted except for huge flocks of screeching sea birds and a colony of seals basking in the warm sunlight.

Eating his soup Veda idly gazed at Jorina who was tending to a large metal pot that was suspended over a small fire. Wisps of smoke were curling up into the blue sky as outside the ship, on the mudflats, Felix and Thiemo were laughing at Atticus who had got stuck in the knee deep mud. The soldier struggling to free himself with growing desperate fury. While Laelian and Hannibal were sitting together eating their breakfast inside the cabin as the crew waited for the tide to come back in and the sea to set them free.

Nudging him with his elbow Caledonus suddenly caught Veda's attention. The freedman making an unintelligible throaty noise and gesturing with his head in Abbe's direction. Spotting the captain standing at the stern of the barge Veda frowned as he saw what Caledonus had noticed. Abbe appeared uneasy. The older man peering out across the mudflats this way and then that way as if he were searching for something. The enforced wait on the mudflats doing nothing to lighten the captain's mood.

Veda was finishing off the last of his soup when Walaric, the Thuringian guide approached and sat down on the deck beside him. For a moment the fat German with his large hooked nose, peered at the antics of the three bodyguards, who were out exploring the mud, with a little perplexed expression. Then Walaric turned and pointed at the iron chest that Veda was sitting on.

"I have noticed that you drag that box out of the ship's hold every morning," the German said speaking in his thick tribal accent. "Why do you do that? Would it not be safer to leave it stowed in the hold? You have the only key. No one is going to steal the gold or throw it overboard."

"My job is to guard the gold," Veda replied. "And it is only safe when I or my freedman have eyes on it. We take shifts. So if I left the chest in the hold I would not get to see what was going on out on deck. It's more pleasant up here than down below."

Staring at Veda, Walaric hesitated. Then he smiled and turned to look towards the stern of the marooned barge.

"The others," Walaric said, "they think you sit about on this chest because it gives you an excuse not to help man the oars. They grumble that you and your freedman do none of the hard work."

"I don't care what they think," Veda said breezily giving his spoon a final lick before stowing it away inside his tunic. "We all have our tasks. I could say the same about you. Abbe is the one who knows the way. He is our guide right now. What use are you to this mission?"

"Yes," Walaric said nodding. "Abbe is the master while we are at sea and this is his ship but once we are on the river and heading inland it will be my turn to act as guide and you will all be grateful to have me on board. When we reach the territory of my people you will be even more grateful."

"Maybe," Veda sniffed. "But he does not think much of you," Veda continued his gaze settling upon Abbe. "Our captain says it was not your fault that you were born a Thuringian. He pities you."

"Ha!" Walaric exclaimed. "Abbe is a Frisian. What can you expect from such people. The Frisians are the tightest of all the tribes. They will never give you anything for free. Everything must be paid for even if you are a close friend or relative. Being born a Frisian is to be cursed with a tight purse and a mean heart. The only people worse than them are the Franks."

"You don't like the Franks?"

"I hate them," Walaric said his face abruptly darkening before he looked away. "Don't get me started. There is a blood feud between my people and the Franks. We cannot stand each other. Death to the fucking Franks."

"So the enemy of my enemy is my friend."

"Yeah, something like that," Walaric replied composing himself. "The Franks raped my wife, killed my dog and stole my cattle. So you see the scum do not only raid Roman land. They attack ours too. I have sworn an oath of vengeance on the altar of Woden - that I will never be a friend of the Franks."

"Good. Then we have something in common," Veda said nodding, looking serious. "When I was still a boy I too was attacked by a Frankish raiding party. They killed my younger brother."

"I am sorry to hear that," Walaric said looking away. "My people - we do not like kings or emperors for that matter. The Franks will soon have a king to rule them but we remain true to the old ways. Among us every man and woman is equal. We choose the best men to lead us. We are free. Our women accompany us into battle, to remind us what is at stake. That is our way and before the coming of Rome we did not seek material goods. We had no notion of these luxuries that now flood into our land. But Rome corrupted us and all the other tribes and now we lust for what you Romans have. We crave gold, wine, we want all the fine things that your empire produces. We may be a free people but we are bound to

Rome like a baby sucking at its mother's teat. It is not going to end well."

"So you blame Rome for corrupting your society?" Veda asked. "Are you trying to excuse these war bands that cross the Rhine to plunder Roman land. If so that is a pretty pathetic excuse."

"Raiding and war have always been part of our way of life," Walaric replied with a shrug. "A man must make a living after all. The strongest take what they want. The weak suffer what they must. But among us Thuringii there are also honourable men. Honour is not something that we have had to import from Rome. We should talk now, you and I - like such men. Like honourable men."

For a moment Veda said nothing as he looked down at the deck.

"Laelian is the boss, our paymaster," Walaric said lowering his voice and turning to warily eye the legate who was sitting inside the ship's cabin. "Without him none of us get paid so he must be kept alive. He is noble born but he is not noble. My dog had a nobler heart than that man. They say that he is a personal friend of Postumus which is probably how he got this job in the first place. They say that he is a genius, a rising star within the empire but I don't think so. From time to time I hear things. The rumour back in Portus Itius is that Laelian lost a lot of his wealth on a trade deal that went badly wrong. He is an ambitious man but in need of money. He uses these diplomatic missions and the contacts he makes to strike private business deals on the side. Mostly amber, slaves and mercenaries in exchange for manufactured Roman goods. My people," Walaric said with a little quiet chuckle, "we call him Greedy Fingers."

For a moment Walaric paused.

"Hulmu is the one to watch out for," Walaric said shifting his gaze from Laelian to the mercenary leader who was out on the mudflats. "He used to be a centurion. Foederati. Until the army kicked him out. Dishonourable discharge, apparently. I don't know the full details but he is a superstitious man and also a killer. We all kill when we have too but he enjoys it a little too much. The others fear him which is why they follow him. Don't get on his wrong side. You see that pouch he wears around his neck. I think it contains something that is precious to him. He is forever touching it - as if it gives him some sort of power. As for Hannibal," Walaric continued a note of disgust entering his voice, "he is a sexual predator. He preys on children and he thinks it is easier to do so beyond the Roman borders. He caused some problems last year with my people. So stay away from him too. He is a mental case. And as for the rest of them," Walaric added observing the bodyguards, "they are all ex-speculatore, special forces, apart from Thiemo who served in the 2nd Batavian cohort. They are in this for the money, like myself."

For a moment Veda remained silent taking on board what had just been said. Then he turned to Walaric. "Why are you telling me this?"

Taking a deep breath the German paused.

"Listen," Walaric said changing the subject. "Abbe tells me that you were making inquiries about Jonas. You wanted to know what happened to him?"

"You know what happened to him?"

"A little, yes," Walaric said lowering his eyes. "My tribal elders appear to have a lot of faith in me for this is the second time that they have asked me to escort the Roman legate to our territory. I was there last year too at the Thing at Thor's Oak with the same crew as we have today except for Abbe and you who are new to this mission. It is dangerous work for me as we must cross hostile territory to reach my homeland. The tribes they do not like each other much. There is constant friction and warfare. We only band together if we are threatened by an outside power. But you Romans know that too. If we are captured our enemy will most likely ransom you lot as you are Romans, but for me only a most painful death would await. They would probably sacrifice me to one of their gods."

For a moment Walaric paused.

"You need to understand," Walaric continued giving Veda an appraising look. "The Thuringii - we are a free people and it is the elders of my tribe who give me this task which I am at liberty to refuse. The Roman legate does not command me, although he pays me. Now Jonas," Walaric said before hesitating, his eyes suddenly gleaming with something unspoken. "Jonas was a good man. I liked him. He took his job seriously just like you and I respect that. So what I am about to tell you - I do for him. So listen closely. You should know that on the way back to Roman territory, after we had completed our task, Jonas and the legate quarrelled. I don't know about what exactly but I think the legate wanted Jonas to do something or agree to something and that Jonas refused him. We were then in the territory of the Semnones. After that he left the ship and he was murdered soon thereafter."

"So I have been told," Veda said raising his eyebrows as he studied the Thuringian guide. "But how can you be sure that he was murdered? I am told they never found his body. Jonas worked for the same bank as I do and the bank says that officially Jonas is still missing."

"Missing," Walaric said looking amused. "No my friend. Jonas was murdered. He was crucified. Nailed to a tree and left there for all to see. I saw him with my very own eyes. They tortured him before they killed him. It was pretty brutal. Someone even cut off his balls and cock and took them away. I swear on all that is sacred that this is what I saw."

"I don't understand," Veda said hurriedly, frowning in confusion. "Why did you not tell the bank about this last year? There was an official inquiry into Jonas's death. Did they not ask you about him? Laelian stated in his report that they never found his body but that it was a Semnonian war-band who killed him. I saw his report with my own eyes."

"The gold was delivered as promised. The agreement between my people and Rome was not affected. As for the official inquiry. No one asked me any questions afterwards," Walaric said with a shrug. "So maybe they did not care or they forgot. The legate is in charge of this mission and submitted his report on the matter. But we all saw Jonas's body. All of us. We left him there. Nailed to that tree. The legate would not allow us to give him a proper burial."

"Laelian would not let you bury his body!"

"He said there was no time and that it was too dangerous," Walaric said nodding solemnly. "He said the Semnones may return at any moment. We had to go and we did."

"Fuck," Veda swore softly as he abruptly looked away, his expression darkening. "So the bank either did not know about this, about this evidence or they deliberately lied to me."

Taking a deep breath Walaric once again hesitated.

"Maybe the bank were also lied too," he said in a careful voice. "I don't know for sure who killed Jonas. I did not myself witness his death for I was told to stay on board. I am making no accusations for I have no proof and only a fool makes accusations without proof. The legate claims it was the Semnones who murdered Jonas. But I doubt it was the Semnones. We were alone that day and Jonas was not gone for long. When Jonas left the ship Laelian sent his men after him in order to bring him back. Draw from that your own conclusions."

Staring back at Walaric it was Veda's turn to hesitate. Then slowly he turned his eyes towards the cabin where Laelian and Hannibal were finishing their breakfast. For a moment he remained silent before his gaze shifted to Laelian's five bodyguards who were messing about just outside the ship. The men laughing as they struggled to free Atticus from the deep mud.

"Why?" Veda said abruptly. "Why was Jonas murdered? Was it to do with the gold?"

"Why else," Walaric said quietly.

Once again Veda remained silent, his mind working.

"I was never one of them," Walaric said quietly gazing at the bodyguards. "They leave me alone because they need me just like they need you and Abbe. But I was never their friend. Laelian, that secretary of his and the bodyguards - they are a tight knit group who stick together. They are something apart. Close to each other as a war-band. The seven of them - their association is an old one going back many years. The rest of us are outsiders to them. They don't trust us and they don't let us in on their secrets. Those men - they are not your friends. I just thought I should warn you."

"Why are telling me this?" Veda snapped.

"Because what happened to Jonas was not right," Walaric said as he stiffly got back to his feet. "It was not right. It offended me."

Chapter Thirteen - Stuck on the Mudflats

The line of armed men were a score strong and were heading straight towards the spot where the 'Glory' was still stuck in the mud waiting for the tide to come back in. Coming from the direction of one of the dune covered islands the experienced locals were plodding across the mudflats with a distinctive gait. One foot always raised high out of the mud, so as not to get stuck. The approaching men were armed with harpoons, small hide bound round shields, hunting bows and hand axes and some were dragging fishing nets behind them. Their intent unclear. No one speaking. No banners on display. No horns. Watching them from the barge a strange silence had settled upon the crew as all had stopped what they had been doing to stare at the newcomers. Trying to figure out what they wanted. Then shattering the ominous calm Abbe's voice rang out, loud and frantic.

"To arms! They mean to attack us you fools!"

Swearing out loud as pandemonium abruptly broke out aboard the barge, Veda threw himself onto the deck as an arrow went whizzing over his head. The missile was followed swiftly by another. Pulling his pugio knife from his belt he hurriedly crawled to the side of the hull where Caledonus had taken shelter. The unarmed freedman staring at him with large eyes, clutching his backpack as another arrow thudded into the mast of the 'Glory'. But before Veda could speak or act a great triumphant roar rose up from the newcomers. The noise coming from horribly close by.

"They are storming the boat," Felix bellowed as Atticus hurriedly tossed him a legionary shield from the ship's hold. "Here they come!"

Swearing out loud again Veda pulled Caledonus back down into cover as the freedman tried to raise his head to take a peek over the side of the hull to see what was going on.

"Find a weapon, anything!" Veda yelled at him.

Spotting Laelian and Hannibal rushing into the safety of the cabin Veda's expression darkened as the two men slammed the door shut behind them. Their flight followed moments later by the frantic noise from inside the cabin of someone barricading the doorway. At the bow of the barge the five bodyguards led by Hulmu were shouting instructions to each other as they prepared to meet the assault. The soldiers bunching together in a tight military formation for all round defence and hurriedly arming themselves with proper swords and large oval shields.

Suddenly Veda heard voices on the other side of the hull. Just a foot away. The men were speaking German in their coarse northern accents and a moment later a pair of hands appeared close by. The fingers gripping the edge of the hull as if someone meant to haul themselves up and over into the barge. But just as Veda was about to make his move Jorina appeared and raising her hammer she swiftly and brutally brought the iron down hard on the fingers. The blow shattering the bones with a horrible cracking noise and making the owner scream in pain - the hands abruptly vanishing from view. Then she and Abbe had thrown themselves down into the shelter of the hull beside Veda. Abbe armed with an old sword in one hand and a knife in the other. The expression on his face like thunder. The old man's chest heaving. Jorina silent as a mouse. And a moment later they were joined by a red faced Walaric armed with a Frankish hand axe. The fat man panting from the unexpected exertion.

"Defend the other side," Abbe yelled turning to Veda. "We will take this side. They must not be allowed to board us. Kill anyone who tries!"

"These are your people! What the fuck!" Veda shouted back at Abbe in a mixture of rage and confusion as nearby something heavy and powerful suddenly thudded into the wooden hull, the massive and furious blow shaking the barge and making Jorina yelp in shock.

"They are not having my ship!" Abbe bellowed. "Move!"

Gripping his knife Veda did not argue as he snatched up Caledonus's backpack. Hurriedly slithering and rolling across the barge to the opposite side he banged his head into the protective wooden hull. The raiders were here too however. Just feet away from him on the other side of the hull. The men mustering as they sought to board the 'Glory'. The Frisians crying out to each other in harsh, excited voices. Moments later Caledonus came crawling across the deck - the young freedman armed with the ship's iron frying pan as he threw himself onto the exposed chest of gold that was sitting out in the open. Caledonus hugging the chest as if it was the most precious thing in the world. But there was no time to call him back. Suddenly a fishing net came sailing over Veda's head. The meshing dragging across the deck as if to catch him in its folds. Frantically flinging the net aside Veda swore as close by Caledonus clung to the chest for dear life. Then three Frisian raiders were heaving themselves over the side of the hull. Tall men with fiercely blond hair - just like Abbe and they were armed with spears and axes. But just as the first of them prepared to attack the crew Walaric's axe came whirling through the air and embedded itself smartly in the raider's chest. The blow sending the man staggering backwards and crashing back onto the deck.

With a howl of aggression Veda launched himself at the second man. Catching him in a low tackle that sent both of them sprawling and rolling over the deck as an arrow went whining over their heads. And for a few moments the two men struggled with each other. Grappling. Trying to land the killer blow. A desperate and frantic fight to the death. Grasping. Biting. Hitting. Snarling. The Frisian however was big and strong and was starting to get the upper hand when Caledonus suddenly hit him over the head with his iron pan. The blow knocking the raider off balance and as he lay on his back on the deck gasping for breath, Veda's eyes widened as he saw Jorina finish off the man by repeatedly smashing her hammer straight into his face. Blood and bone fragments splattering her face and clothes.

But there was no time to thank his freedman. A moment later a sharp cry of pain rang out and Walaric sank to his knees on the deck with an arrow sticking out of his back. The Thuringii guide grimacing in pain. Rolling over onto his side Veda snatched up his knife from where he had been forced to drop it. Then leaping back onto his feet he was attacking the third Frisian who was locked in hand to hand combat with Abbe. The two men were still on their feet as they grappled with each other. Grunting and shoving. A desperate fight. From the corner of his eye Veda noticed two more Frisians clambering over the side of the hull. But there was nothing he could do about them.

Catching the man who was attacking Abbe from behind, Veda's left arm went curling around the man's neck, gripping him tight, before he stabbed him in the back. His knife arm pumping with furious energy as he repeatedly drove his pugio into the man's exposed flesh until he was no more. Allowing the corpse to collapse onto the deck Veda swiftly turned to face the new threat but as he did he gasped in shock as a Frankish throwing axe went hurtling past him. The blade narrowly missing him but not Jorina who was struck in her thigh. The axe embedding itself in her flesh and bringing her down onto the deck with a shriek. Her hammer falling from her hand and clattering onto the wood.

Glaring at three more Frisians who had made it onto the deck, armed with just his knife and only Caledonus in support, Veda's chest was heaving with exertion as behind him he heard Abbe's distraught cries. The captain rushing over to his daughter. A still Walaric lying on the deck with the arrow protruding from his back. He was not going to make it Veda thought with sudden clarity of mind as he stared at the Frisians. He was going to die on this deck, right now. The raiders were too many and too well armed for him to take on.

Beyond the raiders at the bow of the barge Hulmu and his men however were still in the fight. The professional soldiers standing back to back, crying out to each other. Their shields overlapping and forming a tight wooden wall. The corpses of four raiders lying around their position. Another wounded man trying to crawl away and leaving a trail of blood in his wake.

"Clear this fucking deck!" Hulmu roared suddenly in his coarse eastern accent. "Protect the legate! On me!"

The bodyguards did not need to be told twice. Sticking close together the five soldiers began to advance towards the stern. The soldiers knowing what to do. Their training and experience showing. The blades of their swords stained with blood. The men protected by their large military shields. And as they advanced towards Veda the remaining Frisians seeing they were about to be caught hastily abandoned the ship. The raiders leaping over the side and joining the survivors as they fled back across the mudflats.

"Good work lads! Let them run! Protect the legate! That's our job," Hulmu bellowed as next to him Thiemo stooped and calmly slit the throat of one of the wounded Frisians who had been unable to get away.

Gasping for breath, clutching his knife Veda stood on the blood stained and corpse strewn deck staring at the fleeing raiders out on the mudflats. The Frisian numbers were sharply reduced. The fight was over and on-board the 'Glory the only noise suddenly came from his own heavy breathing and Abbe's cries of distress. Catching his eye Hulmu gave him a cold murderous look. Then the mercenary leader turned his attention to the cabin where Laelian and Hannibal had sought safety, calling out to them, and as he did Veda turned around and slowly blew the air from his cheeks in relief.

Towards the stern of the barge Caledonus had once again flung himself protectively on top of the chest of gold. The freedman clutching his frying pan - watching Veda with large haunted eyes. Not knowing what else to do. Close by Walaric was lying on his stomach not moving and not making a sound. While Abbe was cradling his daughter in his arms. His face ashen. The axe was still embedded in her thigh and the girl was bleeding heavily. Her eyes were closed and her face was pale. For a moment Veda stared at the scene unable to move as if stunned. Then springing into action he hurried over to Abbe - calling out to Caledonus to check on Walaric.

Kneeling beside the father and daughter Veda bit his lip as he hurriedly cut a strip of cloth from his cloak and began to bind the tourniquet around the girl's upper thigh. Working in silence to stem the loss of blood he avoided Abbe's gaze. Then just as he had finished he wrenched the axe from her flesh causing the sixteen year old to cry out in pain and her body shudder. A moment later Caledonus was at his side. The freedman excitedly gargling, thumping his chest and raising his thumb indicating that Walaric was still alive.

"Find something to disinfect and bind the wound," Veda snapped turning to Abbe and speaking in German. "Vinegar would be best, fresh boiled water will do. The tourniquet will slow the loss of blood but the greatest danger is infection. The wound must be cleaned regularly. And she needs to rest. That is all I can do for her. Caledonus," Veda said sharply turning to him and switching to Latin. "Help the captain carry Jorina to the bed in the cabin. Then come back and help me with Walaric."

Staring back at him for a moment Abbe was unable to speak. The captain's face ashen. The man looking shaken. Then at last gathering himself he nodded and reached out to grip Veda's arm. "Thank you," Abbe said quietly in a tight and suddenly dignified voice. Colour returning to his cheeks.

"They were after the gold!" a voice suddenly boomed - full of rage and frustration. Looking up Veda saw that Laelian and Hannibal had emerged from the cabin. The legate, surrounded by his bodyguards, standing on the blood stained deck was gazing at the gory and bloody scene with a frown. Hannibal holding his hand to his mouth as if he did not want to breath in the infected air. Then Laelian turned to stare at Veda.

"Those raiders wanted to take our gold," the legate bellowed. "But how did they know we had the gold in the first place? How did they know we were carrying such a valuable cargo. Did someone tip them off?"

Staring back at the legate Veda did not reply.

"No one tipped them off about the gold," Abbe suddenly cried out rising to his feet as he turned to confront Laelian. "If you need someone to blame then blame me. These raiders they were Frisians. They were my people. I knew there was a risk that we could be attacked but I hoped we would be gone before they could organise themselves. I was wrong and my daughter may now die because of my mistake. But no one was after your precious gold. The locals around here they see a ship stranded out here on the mudflats and they think it belongs to them. They take what they want from their neighbours and foreigners alike. It is our custom. In all likelihood they did not know about the gold we were carrying."

"Oh that's great. So your own fucking people attacked us!" Laelian shouted shooting Abbe a contemptuous look. "What a traitorous bunch of barbarians you are. This whole mission could have ended right here if not for the skill and bravery of my men. Do you know the consequences that our failure will have on the empire. Postumus's whole German containment policy would be in tatters if we lose the alliance with the Thuringii."

"But they didn't take the gold and we are still here, so why don't you pipe down," Veda growled rising to his feet as he came to Abbe's defence. The two of them gazing back at the legate.

"You!," Hannibal cried out pointing at Veda with an outraged finger. "You will not talk to the legate like that!"

Ignoring the secretary Veda's eyes met with those of Laelian and for a brief moment the two of them stared at each like stags decided whether to rut. Then at last Veda turned away and moving across the deck he crouched down beside Walaric who was still lying motionless upon the deck. Reaching out he gently touched the man's shoulder and was rewarded with a faint groan.

"Tide is coming back in Sir, " Felix called out.

Chapter Fourteen - Dangerous Waters

Standing at the stern beside Abbe who was holding the tiller, Veda gazed out across the sea as the 'Glory' pushed on across the waves. His poncho hood drawn over his head against the constant sea spray that came crashing over the side of the hull. The barge's square reddish sail was bulging in the wind. The blood stained deck pitching, rolling and creaking as the breeze carried them towards the east. The taught mooring ropes groaning. The salty scent of the sea cold and refreshing. While to the south the coast was a hazy grey line.

It was afternoon and towards the bow of the barge Laelian and Hannibal were standing talking quietly between themselves. The men holding onto the mooring ropes to steady themselves. Hulmu and his men were sitting around the cabin in the centre of the boat, gambling as usual. The mercenaries competing for the pile of belongings, clothes, boots, weapons and ornaments that they had taken from the dead Frisian raiders. Their eager laughter and excited cries out of kilt with the sombre mood that gripped the others.

For a while neither Veda or Abbe spoke, the two men content in the silence. The Captain looking grim. As if he had decided the only thing he could do was endure the present circumstances in silence. Gazing across at Caledonus who was sitting on top of the iron chest out on deck Veda sighed. Then he turned his eyes towards the cabin inside which they had laid their wounded. Jorina was showing signs of recovery from her axe wound but Walaric was not. The fat German was suffering from a fever. His condition steadily deteriorating.

"How long before we reach the mouth of the Albis?" Veda said at last turning to Abbe.

"Maybe another day," Abbe replied keeping his eyes on the horizon. "If the wind holds and there are no more storms."

"Good. If Walaric does not recover will you be able to navigate us upriver until we reach the territory of the Thuringians?"

"I should be able to," Abbe grunted.

Nodding Veda said nothing. His expression thoughtful.

"I should never have taken this job," Abbe snapped, his face darkening. "It was a mistake. All the gold in the world is not worth Jorina's life. We should have stuck to working the limes. This whole job - its fucked up. But I cannot go back now. The legate over there would never allow it and his men - they are killers. They would not hesitate to murder me if the legate gave the order."

"Then do this job for me," Veda said turning to look in Laelian's direction. "Jorina will recover and we will get this done. Do it for me if not for the money."

Standing holding the tiller Abbe remained silent for a moment. Then at last he glanced at Veda.

"They should have put you in charge right from the start and not the legate," the old Frisian growled. "But your Roman system. It promotes the high born. It rewards hierarchy and ignores those with true skill and merit. Among my people we have no kings. We choose our leaders from among the best men. Every man and woman is equal in the eyes of our gods."

"So I hear," Veda said with a thoughtful look. Then reaching out he laid a hand on Abbe's shoulder. "Jorina will recover. We will make it," Veda said with a sudden smile. "We will complete this job and then afterwards we shall have a good laugh about it all. Stay optimistic. If not for yourself then for the others. You are the only captain that we have got."

And with that Veda left his position and made his way across the deck to the spot where Caledonus was sitting upon the chest of gold staring out to sea. Crouching beside his freedman Veda frowned as he fished around for something in the folds of his cloak. Then producing the Frankish throwing axe with its distinctive arch-shaped head he handed it to Caledonus who accepted it in silence.

"That was the second time that you saved me," Veda said gazing at Caledonus with an earnest expression. "So I thought it was time that you had a proper weapon. It's Frankish. I took it from one of the dead raiders. They throw it at their opponents. So learn how to use it."

Examining the blade and the axe Caledonus remained silent. Then at last he looked up at Veda and nodded clenching his hand into an encouraged fist. Before with a grin the youth opened his cloak to reveal a liberated Frisian knife hanging from his belt.

"Good man," Veda said rising back to his feet looking pleased.

"Veda," a sharp authoritative voice suddenly cried out. Turning around Veda saw that at the bow Laelian was beckoning for him to come over. The legate looking serious. The wind tugging at his poncho.

For a moment Veda hesitated as the legate once again beckoned to him.

"Listen Veda," Laelian said as Veda came up. The legate speaking in a softer and gentler voice, his eyes appearing sincere. "This conflict, this tension between you and me. It's not good for the success of this mission. So it has to end. I think you and I have got off to a false start. I may have been too harsh with you and for that I would like to apologise. Hannibal here too is sorry for any misunderstandings between us and any offence he may have caused."

"I am sorry," Hannibal said gazing at Veda with eyes that said he was not sorry.

Ignoring the secretary Veda hesitated. "That would be the second time that you have apologised to me now legate," he said.

"So it is," Laelian said grandly, forcing a smile onto his lips. "But I am not a man to hold a grudge. That is not permissible in my line of work. I am a diplomat. I make deals with all kinds of men."

"What do you want from me?"

"A new start," Laelian replied. "A fresh slate between you and me Veda. For the sake of our mission. For the glory of Rome and the safety and prosperity of our peoples living along the frontier. We should be friends you and I. We should and can work together you and I. Would that not be a good thing?" For a moment Laelian paused as he examined Veda. "I can help you," the legate said at last licking his lips. "I can help you get on in life. Make you rich. Famous. A hero. Whatever you desire and want."

Gazing back at the legate Veda said nothing, his expression unreadable. Then at last he turned to look out to sea.

"If Walaric dies we will have a problem," Veda replied. "The Thuringians will be upset and suspicious at the loss of their man. It may even endanger our mission. Walaric knows the Albis like no one else on-board this ship. He knows the ways of his people better than all of us. His advice would be missed. So if I were you," Veda said turning to Laelian, "I would start doing everything possible to keep him alive. We need the fat bastard."

***

"Ship. Ship. Ship!" Thiemo yelled suddenly pointing out to sea. It was afternoon and in the overcast skies the sun had vanished from view as the 'Glory' headed eastwards along the coast on the strong breeze. Turning to stare in the direction the mercenary was pointing Veda frowned as behind him he suddenly spotted the single white sail in the distance. The longship appeared to be on a pursuit course and was moving fast. As if to catch up. Oars protruding from its sleek, elegant hull. The sailors on-board working the sea in conjunction with the square sail. It's high curving prow ending in the wooden carving of a great serpent's head that rose and plunged through the waves.

Standing on the deck beside Veda, who was holding the tiller and steering the barge, Abbe was clutching a taught mooring rope with one hand, his other resting on Jorina's shoulder. The wounded teenage girl had her eyes open and was sitting on top of the chest of gold with one leg stretched out straight. A blanket drawn around her shoulder. Her cheeks retaining some colour. The axe wound in her thigh tightly bandaged with fresh cloth.

Spotting the longship Abbe's face abruptly grew pale. His eyes widening in silent dismay before the captain hurriedly turned to look up at his own sail. Then the sea. Then the coast line to the south. His mind working furiously as if he were making some calculations. Then he shifted his attention back to the longship. His concern deepening. His breathing quickening.

"Trouble?" Veda asked noticing Abbe's expression.

"Yes," the old Frisian growled. "They mean us no good. They are pirates. They intend to capture us."

"How do you know? Could they not be traders?"

"Everyone out on these seas is a pirate," Abbe replied. "Trust me. They mean us no good."

"Your people? Franks?"

"Saxons," Abbe snapped his mouth curling in disgust. "Saxon sea pirates most likely. We are entering their territory. They will show us no mercy. Those people are so stupid that they will not even bother trying to ransom you Romans. They will take Jorina as a slave. They will take the ship and all our belongings and throw the rest of us overboard."

"We will fight them," Veda said in a determined voice. "We drove off those Frisian raiders. We can do it again."

"No," Abbe said, his eyes fixed on the longship. "There are too many of them. Count the banks of oars. These men they will be proper experienced warriors. Unlike those opportunistic locals we met on the mudflats. These Saxons make their living from piracy. No. All we can do is flee. We must run. It will be dark in a few hours. Our best hope is to try and lose them in the darkness. And pray that this wind will hold. For if it doesn't we are done for. They have three times the number of oars as we do. They are moving faster than us."

Taking a deep breath Veda held onto the tiller as he stared at the pursuing longship.

"Legate," Abbe roared catching Laelian's attention. "Get your men to man the oars. Tell them to row for their fucking lives! Your freedman too," Abbe added turning to Veda with a deadly serious look. "We need every bit of power that we have got if we are to escape."

Standing out on deck staring at the distant longship Laelian hesitated for a moment. Then he was bellowing instructions to his bodyguards. The deck a sudden hive of frantic activity.

"What instructions did your bank leave you with," Abbe said, his eyes fixed upon the longship, "in case of impending capture by the enemy?"

"They told me to hide the gold," Veda replied with a shrug as he held onto the tiller. "But if we are in danger of being seized then I will throw the chest overboard. They are not going to get the gold."

Saying nothing as Caledonus poked his head out of the hold, where he had been sleeping and hurriedly took his place at the oars, it was Abbe's turn to take a deep breath. His grip on his daughter's shoulder tightening.

"Promise me this Veda," the Frisian said, his expression suddenly growing cold. "If they take over my ship and I am no longer capable of doing it myself. Then kill my daughter and send her to join me. Death is preferable to being captured by these men. I will not allow them to defile Jorina."

"They are not going to take the 'Glory'," Veda said avoiding Abbe's gaze. "We are going to get away."

Standing beside him Abbe remained silent. Then once again he turned to look up at his sail and the sky as if checking something.

"What can I do?" Veda said quietly.

"Keep her steady on this course," Abbe snapped, "and pray to your gods that the wind holds and that darkness comes sooner than usual. It's going to be a damn close run thing. They are gaining on us but they are not going to have us without a fight. The Saxons are not the only ones who know how to sail a boat. Curse their filthy souls!"

***

The wind had died down to a whisper as the 'Glory' crept through the darkness. The sea becalmed. As if it were holding its breath. The waves slapping gently against the hull of the flat-bottomed barge. The night was pitch black and in the skies overhead there was no sign of the stars or moon. Standing at the stern still holding the tiller Veda peered into the darkness. The crew crouching along the deck. Weapons in hand. No one speaking a word. The tension growing. The night still as a mouse except for the sea and the soft creaking of the ship's timbers.

"They are close," Abbe whispered. "To our right. A hundred paces or so I think. I can smell the bastards. They are searching for us. Keep the ship steady on this course. I have got an idea on how to lose them."

Saying nothing Veda kept his hand on the tiller and did as asked, turning his head to try and see what Abbe was doing in the darkness. But whatever the captain was up to he was not saying and the night revealed nothing of his plan. Quietly pulling something from a storage box Abbe was a dark shape in the darkness. Moments later Veda heard a soft, quiet splash as something entered the water. Then Abbe reappeared. The old Frisian clutching a long coil of sturdy rope, one end of which he hurriedly tied to an iron mooring hook attached to the deck. The rope playing out and slipping over the side of the hull like a thief in the night, as if it were attached to something in the water. Then subtly at first Veda felt the 'Glory' start to slow as if the ship had suddenly grown heavier to handle.

Finishing his task Abbe appeared once more at Veda's side. The captain's breathing audible. For a moment no one spoke until at last with a little grinding noise the rope attached to the deck went taught.

"We're slowing down," Veda whispered. "What did you do?"

"Good," Abbe said quietly. "That's the idea. I deployed our storm anchor. The drogue will slow us down. An old trick I learned from a north-lander who used it to steady his boat in a storm. Hopefully those Saxon bastards will not notice and continue to drift right on past us. The sea current will take us eastwards. Then north. We cannot fight the current without power from our sail or the oars but right now there is no wind and the oars will make too much noise. So we will just them let them drift on past and get ahead of us before we change course and slip away."

Veda was about to say something when to his right he heard the sudden splash of oars and the voices of men calling out to each other. The Saxon voices were harsh and confident. The noise was coming from barely a hundred yards away - the Saxon ship hidden in the darkness. Then to Veda's horror - to his left a solitary lamp suddenly appeared in the night. The light blinking on and off. Then remaining on. A pin prick of light in the night. The unexpected appearance of the light followed by a few loud cries of greeting.

"Father - a second ship!" Jorina whispered from her position close by where she was sitting on top of the iron chest.

"They are searching for us," Veda muttered.

Swearing softly Abbe did not move. The crew tense like the mooring ropes that secured the mast. Staring at the lamp across the water Veda tightened his grip on the tiller. Feeling his heart pounding in his chest as the seconds slipped on by. Each feeling like an age. But as they did and nothing happened it became clear that neither ship had spotted them in the darkness. And slowly, ever so slowly, the two longships on either side of them began to pull ahead. The light growing dimmer and dimmer and the noises out on the water fading away until at last they could no longer be heard and seen.

"They have gone father," Jorina said at last in a relieved voice.

"Maybe," Abbe murmured.

"The darkness will not cover us forever," Veda said quietly exhaling with relief. "Once it grows light they will find us again. If we want to get away we must make our move now while we still can."

"Yes," Abbe said quietly. "Turn her to the south. The coast is to the south and not far away. We will try and hide among the salt marshes and hope that these Saxon bastards lose interest in us. It's not ideal but it is our best chance."

"But I can't see anything," Veda protested. "The night is pitch black. We do not know where we are. If we head for land now the chance is high that we will simply get stranded on another mudflat waiting for the tide to come back in. And you know how that worked out for us last time. In daylight anyone will be able to see us from miles away. We would be sitting ducks."

"Father," Jorina whispered.

"Not now Jorina," Abbe snapped sharply silencing his daughter. "Listen," the captain continued turning to address Veda in a patient voice. "This is our situation. We are close to the mouth of the Albis. We are close to the river now. The marker we need to find is a small island that sits guard just outside a wide bay. My people call the island Nige O. Once we find the island we enter the bay. The mouth of the Albis lies inside this bay. But we need daylight to spot Nige O or else we will sail straight past without realising it is there. Normally I would have spent the night ashore and waited until daylight before resuming our journey. But with those pirates out there we cannot now do that. My guess is that those Saxon bastards will be lurking around the entrance to the bay. They will be preying on any shipping trying to enter or leave the Albis. So if we can't approach in daylight our next best option is to find a spot along the coast where we can hide up and wait until those Saxons lose interest in us and move on."

"If we head for the coast now it is more likely that we will blunder into a mudflat or sandbank and get stuck at low tide," Veda replied shaking his head. "That will leave us exposed and vulnerable if those pirates return. I have a better idea. Instead of turning south for the coast we turn north-west. We head out into the open sea and hide out there."

"Are you mad," Abbe hissed from the darkness. "Head out into the open sea! What happens if we are struck by a storm. The 'Glory' cannot handle heavy seas. We will get swamped and sink."

"Which is precisely why those pirates won't expect us to do that," Veda countered. "They won't think of looking for us out there. They will expect us to stay close to the coast. One of my ancestors - his name was Marcus," Veda continued. "A hundred and fifty-five years ago he sailed all the way to the land of the Hyperboreans and back. He sailed right across the ocean and he survived. He spent weeks out on the sea without sighting land. I read his account of his journey. If he can do that, we can do this. We should turn towards the open sea and hide there. I have no fear of the sea."

"It's madness," Abbe hissed again. "And you should fear the sea - boy. If you are right in the head you should fear her."

"Father," Jorina said suddenly refusing to be silenced this time. "There is another way. We could make for the isle of Hallig. I know it is not far away. We would be safe there among mother's people."

"The isle of Hallig?" Veda whispered, frowning. "Where is that?"

At his side Abbe however had gone still. The captain's expression hidden by the darkness.

"I don't want to go there," Abbe said at last in a quiet voice. "I swore that I would not set foot on that island again."

"Father," Jorina said speaking in a tired but insistent voice. "You always told me to speak my mind when I believed something was right. Well this is right. We should make for Hallig. We will be safe there and it is less than a day's sail from the mouth of the Albis. Maybe mother's people can help us. They are still Frisians, father. They are still our people."

"Your wife's family? They live on the island?" Veda asked.

Once again Abbe remained silent, a dark brooding shape in the night as he appeared to be thinking it over.

"My wife and I," Abbe said at last in an unhappy voice, turning to address himself to Veda. "We did not get on so a few years ago we agreed to separate. She would return to Hallig which is where she is originally from. She would take our son with her and I would stay in the delta with our daughter. We divided our children. That was our divorce agreement and I have not seen her or my son since she returned to her home island."

"You don't get on with your wife and her family?"

"No," Abbe growled. "I do not. My wife and I do not get on and her family are nothing more than a bunch of crooks and cheats."

Chapter Fifteen - An Unexpected Stop

As the 'Glory's anchor plunged into the sea Veda stood on the deck of the barge gazing across the short stretch of water at Hallig island. Taking in the steep cliffs and spectacular sea stacks that soared two hundred feet straight out of the water. The cliff tops, ledges and rock formations crowded with flocks of noisy birds, some resting, some circling overhead. A cacophony of life. The tiny island - just a half a square mile of land amid the German sea - treeless but stained green with moss and grass. The sandy beach a dirty yellow. The sea grey. The sky blue.

It was morning and along the narrow beach that lay at the base of the cliffs the gaggle of women and children who were out searching the flotsam that had been washed ashore - collecting stuff from the shoreline in wicker baskets - had stopped what they had been doing to stare at the newly arrived ship. No one calling out. No one appearing alarmed.

"What are they doing?" Veda asked turning to Jorina who was sitting guard on top of the chest of gold. The girl was looking stronger now that her wound was starting to heal. Her keen eyes were fixed on the islanders as if she was searching for someone among their ranks.

"They are looking for and collecting amber," the girl replied without taking her eyes off the islanders. "Sometimes the amber washes up on the beach after a storm. They sell it to the traders from the south."

"Amber!" Veda said raising his eyebrows as Abbe came stomping past, the captain's demeanour brooding and unhappy. "Then this must be a rich island. Amber is as precious as gold in Rome."

"It's not rich. The islanders are dirt poor," Abbe growled as he folded his arms across his chest and paused to stare at the gaggle of women and children. "They are dirt poor because they are stupid and ignorant. Because they are bunch of backward peasants. They may own the amber but they don't know how to get it to the Roman markets. So they allow others to do the trade for them. Those traders who dare venture this far north must brave storms and pirates and it is they who pocket all the big profits. The islanders get a pittance."

"It's a living," Veda said with a shrug.

"I hope you like fish," Abbe snapped crossly. "The herring catches around here are plentiful. The islanders - they don't serve up much else. Stinking fish for breakfast, lunch and dinner!"

"Abbe," Laelian called out as he approached. The legate looking concerned. "I understand the necessity to hide here for a while from those Saxon pirates but I do not want to stay here for long. We have a mission to complete and time presses us so complete your business with the locals as fast as possible and then we should be on our way again."

"Oh I am not setting foot on that island," Abbe replied in a defiant mood, turning to Laelian and shaking his head. "You misunderstand me legate. I have no business to conduct with these peasants. I am staying right here on-board my ship. I intend to remain anchored here until the time arrives for us to leave and head southwards again."

Frowning Laelian stared at Abbe in confusion. But before anyone could speak Jorina suddenly raised her arm and pointed at someone approaching along the beach. "Father," she called out tempering the excitement in her voice. "Look! It's grandfather. He has come. It is him! I am sure."

Gazing across the short stretch of water that separated them from the beach Veda too had noticed the small group of men. The young warriors were carrying round shields with tiered centres and spears and as they approached he spotted a much older man among them. The man appeared to be in his sixties and was clad in a cloak made of black bear's skin, long reindeer hide boots and a round hat made from brown rabbit fur.

"I want to go ashore," Jorina said quickly turning to her father. "I am going ashore to greet grandfather. It has been years since I last saw him."

Not responding to his daughter, Abbe's face was like thunder as he kept his eyes upon the approaching warriors.

"I will go with you," Veda said quickly.

Watching her father Jorina waited for an answer but none was forthcoming. Then with her youthful face set with sudden resolve and determination she tried to rise to her feet and as she struggled Veda swiftly caught her arm, helping her up. The girl grimacing with pain and leaning against him for support.

"Here take this," Veda said handing her an oar. "Use it as a crutch."

Accepting the oar Jorina paused as with its help she was able to stand upright on the deck. Then she turned to Abbe with a final questioning look.

"Father?"

"I will stay here on-board my ship," Abbe growled, his expression defiant. "I will stay with Walaric. He will need me. He is not doing so well. You go. You too legate."

Watching her father, Jorina hesitated. Then she turned away and staggered towards the side of the barge.

Wading through the shallow surf and up onto the beach, Jorina led the way as Veda and Caledonus followed her carrying the heavy iron chest between them. The freedman additionally burdened by the backpack containing their personal belongings that was slung across his back. While behind them, as if in procession, Laelian, Hannibal and their bodyguards brought up the rear. The Romans observing the party of barbarians waiting for them on the beach with wary, suspicious eyes. No one speaking. The islanders, clad in their simple plain animal skins, were gazing back at the strangers with the hard, dirty faces of people used to grinding poverty and hard labour. The women and men's dress indistinguishable. But as Jorina came up to the group of silent, waiting people the old man suddenly threw back his head, raised both his arms and roared in delight and moments later he advanced towards the girl and swept her up in a great bear hug. And despite her wounded leg a shy smile appeared on Jorina's face as she was lifted off her feet.

"Jorina! It's you! You came back! This is a surprise. Look at you now. All grown up!" her grandfather roared. His old face filled with happiness. "This is a good day. No. This is a great joyous day!"

With Jorina conversing with her grandfather, Veda came to a halt on the beach and not taking his eyes off the barbarians he, together with Caledonus, lowered the chest full of gold coins into the sand. But the locals did not appear hostile. The tension had vanished as soon as it became clear who Jorina was and as they stood about an excited stir swept through the ranks of the islanders. Glancing around Veda saw that Laelian and his men too were not sure how to handle this situation. The Roman legate had remained standing in the gentle surf, frowning with Hannibal at his shoulder. The five bodyguards clustered in a defensive posture around their principal. Their hands resting idly on their sword handles. Their other hands gripping large infantry shields.

"Romans," Jorina's grandfather exclaimed at last breaking away from Jorina and turning his attention to the men standing waiting on the beach and in the water. And as he did his pleased joyful expression became guarded. For a long moment the old man with his white hair remained silent as he studied the faces gazing back at him. Then at last he nodded and with a graceful and respectful gesture he inclined his head towards Laelian, welcoming him.

"Rome is welcome on our island," the old man called out speaking German in his thick regional accent. "If my granddaughter does not mind travelling with you then neither do I. My name is Helmuth. I was born on this island amid a terrible storm. Come ashore, my friends. You have nothing to fear from us. We are humble fishermen but we remember the customs of our ancestors. All who come in peace are welcome on our island."

"Tell him," Veda heard Laelian say behind him in Latin as the legate turned to his secretary, "that we are grateful for his hospitality but that we do not wish to impose ourselves on him or his people. We are only here because we seek shelter from Saxon pirates who threatened to attack us earlier. We will be on our way again as soon as we can."

But as Hannibal began his translation, speaking in German, Helmuth interrupted him with a good humoured wave of his hand. "No, no my friends," the old German cried out raising his voice. "This is a great day and a great day must be celebrated with a great feast. Please I insist. Tonight you are my guests. Tonight we shall feast the return of my beautiful granddaughter. All are welcome. You are not allowed to say no," Helmuth added booming with laughter at his own joke. "Our law on hospitality to strangers forbids us from turning you away without a proper feast. So please come. All of you - come and lets enjoy ourselves. You have brought my granddaughter safely back to me and for that I am grateful."

Looking uncomfortable Laelian took a deep breath. For a moment he hesitated. Then at last he nodded in agreement and started to wade the final few yards through the surf and onto the sandy beach. His bodyguards following in silence.

And as he did so Jorina turned and spoke to her grandfather. Her words too softly spoken for Veda to hear but as she spoke the old man's expression once again turned serious. Shifting his attention towards the 'Glory' anchored just offshore and the solitary man who was watching from her deck, Helmuth paused.

"She is not here!" Helmuth boomed at last in a loud voice addressing Abbe from across the water as he fixed his eyes upon the captain. "My daughter is on the mainland with your son so you don't have to meet her! So stop sulking. Get off that ship of yours and come and join us for a proper feast!"

***

It was evening and outside the large Frisian longhouse it was pouring down. The rain pelting the dark land. There was no one about. The island still, undisturbed and peaceful. Inside the longhouse however sixty or so noisy and boisterous people had gathered. Men, women and children. Their voices raised. Laughing, talking and singing. Flutes ringing out. The mood jovial and relaxed. The islanders were sitting on the earth floor or standing about in groups drinking beer and mead from jugs and simple wooden cups that they freely dipped into two large barrels. The Frisians were clad in their simple animal skins. Most of them were barefooted. Some of the women were wearing bead and colourful amber necklaces around their necks and small whale bones in their hair. Others were carrying their new born babies in their arms. Their naked breasts on full display as if this were normal. While shaggy hunting dogs moved about in between the humans growling and snapping up the fragments of food that had fallen to the ground.

The middle of the longhouse with its high sloping thatched roof was lit up and warmed by a great log fire, set inside a ring of stones, over which a whole pig was slowly roasting suspended on a pair of iron fire dogs. The smoke from the fire escaping through a hole in the roof. The animal's juices and fat were leaking into the fire making the inferno spit, hiss and crackle. The flames casting eerie leaping shadows against the wood and clay walls of the longhouse that made the younger children shriek with excitement.

While sharing the space with the humans, in a separate fenced off section, the farm animals, several cows, a horse, chickens and pigs were watching the party in stoic silence. The pong of the animals and their excrement mixing with the heady aroma of fish, unwashed bodies and wood-smoke. But no one seemed to mind the smell or the terrible singing Veda thought, as clutching his cup of beer, he observed the feast with a good natured smile.

Sitting together in a tight group among the mass of Frisian revellers the Roman party were silent as they drank their frothy beer. Caledonus perched on top of the iron chest. Looking about with a curious expression. The five bodyguards wary and unhappy that they had been asked to leave their weapons outside. Only Laelian appeared to be enjoying himself Veda thought as he turned to observe the legate and his secretary who had been given a place of honour beside Helmuth. The old man laughing heartily as he appeared to be telling Laelian a joke. The Roman diplomat leaning in towards him and listening with practised, professional bemusement as Hannibal translated between the two men.

Jorina was sitting at her grandfather's other side. One of her grandfather's arms resting paternally across her shoulders as if she were his pride and joy. Her youthful face looked pale in the flickering firelight. The girl was doing her best to enjoy herself but she could not quite hide her look of disappointment. She had to still be suffering from her wound Veda thought as he observed her. Or else it was her father and mother's absence.

Then Veda's gaze came to rest upon a hunched and hooded figure sitting quietly in a chair arranged just behind Helmuth and as he did he was suddenly aware that the others in the crowded and noisy Frisian hall, either out of fear or respect, were avoiding the person. As if the figure was not there. As if they did not exist. Frowning Veda stared at the stranger. Clutching a wooden cane with a silver knob the seated figure was the only person in the longhouse who had been offered a chair and the only one to be wearing a hood. The mysterious hooded figure was clad in a long flowing and finely crafted white woollen cloak. Their face concealed in the shadows and it was impossible to see whether they were a man or a woman. But from underneath their hood Veda suddenly sensed that he was being watched. And as he gazed across the crowded room at the stranger Veda felt a sudden chill run down his spine. As if he had been touched by a ghost.

Sitting cross-legged at the hooded figure's feet was a young woman clad in a similar long and loose fitting white garment. An amber amulet depicting a wagon drawn by heifers hanging from around her neck. The girl could be no older than eighteen. With long blond plated hair that tumbled to below her shoulders and she was gazing out across the feast with a disciplined expression. Refusing to participate in the merriment and fun while next to her a plate of food and a beaker of drink appeared to remain untouched.

Wrenching his eyes away Veda quickly looked up as Jorina came limping over to him walking stiffly with the aid of the oar he had given her. The girl sitting down beside him and edging Caledonus aside as she forced the freedman to share the top of the iron chest. For a moment the two of them said nothing as Veda took a sip of beer and they gazed at the feast.

"You don't look too happy," Veda said at last turning to the girl. "Are you disappointed that your mother and brother are not here?"

In response Jorina simply nodded, biting her lip. Blushing.

"He is not happy either," she exclaimed at last nodding with her head at a sour faced unsmiling man who was standing by the fire tending to the roasting pig. Turning to gaze at the man Veda saw that she was right. As the man turned to look around at the feast Veda saw that he looked distinctly unimpressed by the whole affair. "He is not happy," Jorina continued, gazing at the man, "because this is his home and we are eating his food and drinking his beer."

"This is his home?" Veda exclaimed sounding surprised as he stared at the man tending to the roasting pig. "But I thought this was your grandfather's house. He is the one after all who invited us to this feast."

"No, this is his neighbour's house," Jorina replied. "And that man is our neighbour. My grandfather is too poor to be able to lay on such a feast like this. But our laws of hospitality mean that a man cannot turn strangers away if they arrive asking for help. And if a man cannot provide he is entitled to go to his neighbour and ask them to provide in his place. No one is allowed to ignore the law. It is disgraceful to do so. The whole community must help if necessary."

Looking surprised Veda stared at the girl. Then he turned his attention back to the unhappy looking host and as he did he smiled. "All right. Now I understand why he is not happy," Veda said. "This feast. It was not his idea. These are not his guests but he is ending up paying for it all. Your people sure have strange customs. This would never happen where I am from."

"It is our way," Jorina said with a shrug. "It has always been this way. The legate is an important man. We are a hospitable people. It is a matter of honour but it goes both ways. It is forbidden for anyone to take advantage of this hospitality. And at the end of the feast it is customary for the guests to offer their host a gift if the host asks for it. So be warned. The nature of the gift will reveal to everyone present the nature of the man giving it. The gift must be chosen wisely for if it is not done properly it can cause great offence and upset."

"A gift," Veda said gazing at the owner of the longhouse with a sudden thoughtful look. "I see. I wonder whether the legate is aware of the custom. Will our host ask us for a gift?"

"Most certainly yes," Jorina said studying the owner of the longhouse. "He is a tight bastard that one. But he does not deserve any of your gold. He is wealthier than most because he was lucky to once find a wrecked ship on this island. Some say he helped wreck the ship in the first place. I just wanted to warn you. He will ask you Romans for a gift at the end of the feast and my people will judge you by what you give him."

"I will think of something," Veda said nodding.

"My father respects you," Jorina said boldly, her face suddenly deadly serious. "As do I. The duty of a wife is to share her husband's fate. To share with him in all the danger of war and work. That is our custom. You are a good man Veda, despite the fact that you murdered your father. I will not hold that against you if you were to choose me," she added before swiftly rising to her feet and limping off back to be with her grandfather.

Staring after the girl Veda looked surprised. Then he groaned and turned to look away. It was not his custom to say no to a woman but Jorina was only sixteen and far too young for him.

"You! Yes you!" Helmuth bellowed pointing across the crowded hall and suddenly Veda was aware that the old man was addressing him. "I can't help but notice that you and your man carried that heavy chest all the way from your ship to this house," Helmuth cried out. His face red from drinking too much beer. "Why? What have you got hidden inside that chest that is so important?"

For a moment Veda did not reply as a few heads turned to stare at him and he caught Laelian's sudden look of alarm.

"You are right Sir," Veda shouted back, an amused smile playing across his lips. "The contents of this chest mean a lot to me. They are the reason why I am here in the first place. So I must keep my eyes on this chest at all times. You want to know what is inside? The ashes of my father, Sir. I am carrying them to his final resting place. It is my duty as his son to do so."

"Your father's ashes," Helmuth roared. "So you respect your father?"

"No, he was an abusive bastard," Veda replied smiling again. "I killed him."

For a moment Helmuth hesitated as he stared at Veda. Then the old man threw back his head and roared with laughter. His laughter proving infectious and setting off the people around him as if they had just heard a good joke.

Smiling back at Helmuth Veda raised his cup of beer in a toast before the old man lost interest and turned his head away. Moments later Veda felt a slight disturbance in the hall, as if a blast of cold air had suddenly entered the longhouse. Then abruptly Abbe sat down beside him. The captain looking troubled. His head and cloak drenched by the rain. His unhappy, brooding eyes fixed upon Helmuth, his father in law.

"Walaric is dead," Abbe said. "He died an hour ago. We will need to give him a proper funeral."

"Shit," Veda muttered turning to look at the captain.

"His people, the Thuringians," Abbe continued, his moody eyes fixed upon his father in law. "They will not be happy that their man is dead. There are going to be consequences. They may even think we had something to do with Walaric's death. This could complicate our mission. He knew the course of the Albis and the Marsh rivers, the interior of Germany, better than any of us. Walaric's task was to help and advice us on our journey. To get us safely to his peoples Thing. To Thor's Oak. To aid the legate in the renewal of our alliance with his people. Who is going to do that job now? His death is a fucking disaster!"

"I will speak to the legate," Veda said quickly turning to gaze across at Laelian. "Without Walaric we will just have to improvise. We will just have to share his responsibilities as best as we can. If you can navigate us up the river I will try and act as our mediator with these Germans."

"Or we could just go home?" Abbe growled.

"No," Veda said shaking his head. "That is not an option. We carry on as planned."

"I thought you would say that," Abbe said sounding displeased. "All right Veda. Have it your way then. I shall follow your star - well for the moment at least."

"Oh so you decided to stop sulking. You came at last!" Helmuth roared as he suddenly noticed Abbe sitting beside Veda. The old man's nose a bright red from too much drink. Turning to stare at his son in law Helmuth paused, his mind working on what to say as Abbe glared back at him. The ominous silence between the two men lengthening.

"You have nothing to say to me?" Helmuth bellowed at last and as he did the hall quietened down, heads turning to stare at the confrontation.

"What? What do you want me to say to you," Abbe retorted.

"Well you could start with an apology," Helmuth barked. "Your treatment of my daughter was a disgrace!"

"No it wasn't," Abbe shouted back as the hall abruptly went silent. "You just don't like me. You never wanted me to marry her in the first place. I have known that from the beginning.

You made it hard for both of us because you thought I was not good enough for your daughter! You wanted her to marry another."

"She returned home here to this island in tears!" Helmuth yelled back. "That was your doing!"

"What happened between me and my wife is our business. Not yours!"

"Well what do you expect," Helmuth bellowed glaring at Abbe, "Yes I wanted her to marry another. Your wedding gifts to her - to my family - were shit. They were an insult. You gave us a queer cow that refused to get pregnant. Roman coins that are now worthless."

"And you gave me a second rate sword that bent and broke on first use," Abbe retorted, his eyes blazing furiously.

"That sword had served me well for a long time," Helmuth roared jabbing an accusing finger at Abbe. "Maybe you just did not know how to use it."

"You are a backward and ignorant peasant," Abbe shouted back. "You refuse to open your eyes to the new things in this world and the new ways of doing things. That is why you are still so poor that you can't even pay for this feast and you have to go begging to your neighbour for help!"

"What?" Helmuth roared angrily as he staggered to his feet in a drunken rage, his eyes blazing. "Say that again and I will finish you here right now boy with my bare hands!"

"Enough!" a female voice suddenly yelled - her voice filled with authority and as Veda turned his head in astonishment the hooded figure slowly rose from their chair and drew back their hood revealing the face of an old woman. Her face tattooed with strange runes and symbols. Her skin shrivelled and aged but her eyes clear and fierce like those of a hawk. Clutching her silver topped cane the woman glared at Helmuth who was looking taken aback before she shifted her steely gaze towards Abbe. The longhouse suddenly silent except for the roar of the fire and the pounding of the rain outside.

"Have you both forgotten where you are!" the old woman cried out in an accusing voice that carried across the longhouse. "Has the drink gone to your head! This is a feast to welcome guests and no violence is permitted here. Not tonight. Not in my presence. You dare shame the earth goddess."

As the old woman finished speaking an awkward silence settled across the crowd. Helmuth suddenly looking sheepish. Abbe's grim eyes fixed upon the ground refusing to look up at the woman.

"Offence has been given, high priestess," Helmuth called out at last turning towards the old woman. "It must be answered. Abbe here insulted me. My honour has been questioned. All heard him speak. His insult cannot be allowed to stand without a response. I want to fight him. Single combat."

"And indeed it shall not go without a response," the priestess replied staring back at Helmuth. "But you shall not be the one who will decide what to demand from the one who insulted you."

"Then who will?" Helmuth called out, looking confused.

"The Roman," the priestess cried out and as she did Veda was suddenly concious that her eyes had turned towards him. "The Roman who boasts of killing his father will be the one to say what redress you may seek for this insult to your honour. His decision will settle this."

Suddenly Veda was concious that everyone was staring at him. The hall quiet and expectant. For a moment he did nothing. Then slowly he rose to his feet. His gaze switching between Abbe and Helmuth before settling upon the old priestess. Their eyes meeting.

"Helmuth has had too much to drink," Veda exclaimed speaking in German as a little smile appeared across his lips and he turned towards his audience. "Abbe is pained by his friend's recent death. Neither are themselves right now. The words they speak are not their own but those of mischievous spirits who turn grown men, who really should know better, into bickering children. And none should pay much attention to the words of children. So no decision on redress will be made until the morning has come and they are themselves again."

As Veda sat down again he was aware of the priestess watching him. The longhouse around him still as a mouse. Then as if released from a spell people began to move again and talk among themselves and within a few moments the feast had resumed. Taking a sip of beer from his mug Veda coolly exhaled before turning to glance at Abbe.

"Children, seriously," the captain murmured looking displeased. "Could you really not have come up with something better than that."

"I bought us time," Veda said quietly raising his cup of beer to his mouth again. "After the feast is over we will slip away back to the Glory and sail out to sea. We can be gone by dawn. I would have left you behind to fight your father in law in a duel but we need you to captain the 'Glory.'

"I will fight that old prick any day," Abbe hissed. "I am not afraid of him."

Suddenly Veda was conscious that Helmuth had risen from his seat and was approaching. The old red faced man looking annoyed and swaying lightly on his feet. His hand clasping a cup of beer while behind him Laelian was rooted to the spot looking on in horror at the unexpected turn of events.

"Listen, as you seem to be in charge here," Helmuth snapped addressing himself to Veda and ignoring Abbe. The old man's breath stinking of beer. His hand trembling slightly. "I will make an agreement with you. I will drop this whole matter. This insult to my honour on condition that you and your crew leave tomorrow and that you take the high priestess with you. She has overstayed her welcome and we islanders are anxious to get rid of her. So she will depart with you tomorrow and I shall forget all about this matter. Agreed?"

Chapter Sixteen - The High Priestess of Nerthus

Hidden in the narrow, shallow inlet among the salt marshes the 'Glory' was just another dark shape in the night. Her solitary mast poking up above the marshes. Her sail furled. The white sand dunes and the broad tidal mudflats that stretched away along the edge of the wide bay were quiet and deserted. The night air was cold and still. The sea was lapping gently against the wooden hull of the ship. The timbers creaking quietly. While the soft high-pitched call of a solitary hunting sea bird could be heard overhead.

Out on the deck, sitting on top of the iron chest, Veda was gazing at the ship's cabin, inside which the high priestess, her young acolyte, Laelian and Hannibal were conversing together in quiet voices. While standing in the doorway to the cabin, Abbe was listening in. The captain leaning against the side of the wooden hut. His arms folded across his chest. The small cabin was lit up by a single glowing oil lamp that hung suspended from the ceiling.

The priestess and her young acolyte had barely said a word to him since they had come aboard Veda thought as he observed the quiet meeting that was taking place within the cabin. Laelian had been immediately enthusiastic about accepting the priestess on to the ship pointing out that she could be useful to the mission. For who would dare attack a vessel carrying a high priestess of the earth goddess. Abbe however had grumbled. The Frisian unhappy with the prospect. Referring to her as a sorceress but he had been overruled. His objections dismissed by Laelian. And now the legate appeared to be warming even more to the woman, actively seeking her advice.

Looking on Veda fidgeted with the rings on his fingers. Suddenly uncertain whether he had done the right thing. Abbe had told him that the old woman was called Ganna and that she was a famous high priestess of Nerthus. The earth goddess whose cult was worshipped among many of the German tribes. As a priestess of Nerthus the mother goddess, Ganna was inviolate. Her person sacred. A feared and revered woman who the tribes believed had the power of prophesy. None were allowed to touch her or do harm to her and wherever she went all were compelled to cease making war on their neighbours. Such was her reputation and power over the tribes Abbe had told him that the strongest warriors did not dare challenge her. That even kings would seek her advice. That her word was law. Such sorceresses were holy among the tribes Abbe had explained. Such women would travel around among the people adjudicating between conflicts, disputes and acting as peacemakers and judges in wartime.

Turning his head towards the spot at the bow where Laelian's five bodyguards were resting Veda frowned. The priestess's presence on-board had certainly managed to unnerve Laelian's bodyguards he thought. The soldiers had taken to muttering uneasily to each other and he had caught them now and then shooting the priestess guarded looks. Their dislike and fear of the holy woman palpable. And the fact that no one knew what she wanted or where she wanted to go had not helped lift the sullen suspicious mood. For when the day before he had asked her where she wanted to go the priestess had simply answered that she would go where she was needed.

Hearing Caledonus clambering out of the barge's hold Veda rose to his feet, swapping places with his freedman, who swiftly sat down on top of the chest to start his shift, guarding the gold. Approaching the cabin to listen in to the conversation that was taking place Veda paused as Abbe turned and glanced at him. Sitting on the bed with her acolyte down on the floor by her feet like a dog, the high priestess was wearing her bright white cloak. The hood of which was lowered around her shoulders. Her aged face and shrivelled skin making it impossible to tell how old she was. Her finger nails black, long and shaped like knives. The runes and strange symbols tattooed to her forehead visible in the weak reddish light. While leaning against the inner wall of the cabin with Hannibal at his side Laelian was on his feet, gazing at Ganna with a serious and respectful look. Hannibal translating his words quickly and effectively into German.

"Abbe tells me that we are less than a mile from the mouth of the Albis," Laelian said quietly addressing Ganna. "The sea pirates have gone. So tomorrow I intend to enter the Albis and row upstream. To penetrate the river far to the south-east. Our destination is the confluence of the Albis and the Marsh rivers where the territory of the Thuringians begins. We are heading for Thor's Oak. We have important business to conduct with their tribal leaders."

"I know why you are here, " Ganna replied, her voice hoarse as if she were suffering from a cold. Her clear hawk like eyes gazing back at Laelian. "Nerthus is both male and female. She sees both ways. She sees all. She sees into men's hearts. You have come to bribe the Thuringians. To buy their aid in your war with the Franks. Nothing escapes Ganna."

Hesitating Laelian frowned.

"You carry valuable cargo. In that iron chest over there," Ganna continued with a little cackle as her eyes came to rest upon Veda. "Guarded by the one who murdered his father but shows no remorse for the deed. But do not worry. I am not interested in your gold. I am Ganna. Seeress to King Hadugato of the Saxons. The most famous priestess in all of free Germany. You have helped me escape from that cursed island so now I will help you."

"So you say," Veda shot back in German folding his arms across his chest, "but how do we know that we can trust you?"

"Trust," Ganna replied with another little cackle. "Oh you can trust me. Once long ago I accompanied my king to Rome to meet your emperor. You Romans treated me with honour and

I was allowed to return home afterwards unscathed. I shall treat you in the same manner. I have influence with King Hadugato. He will listen to me. I can help you."

"Indeed," Laelian said politely. "Which is why I now ask for your advice, priestess. From where we are anchored right now it is two days upriver to Drusus's old fort on the island at Treva. To the place where the amber road from the east crosses the river on its way to Roman territory. Last year the Saxons were friendly to us and let us pass unhindered. Is that still the case? And what can you tell me about the country beyond the old station at Treva? I have not received any reports on that area for a while now."

"If you wish to travel south and upriver," Ganna replied in her hoarse voice, her eyes gleaming coldly in the soft warm light. "King Hadugato of the Saxons will welcome you if you come to trade but not if you intend to cause trouble. He has no quarrel with Rome. These days in his old age he is easily misled and craves your gold and silver too much. But the other tribes will be less welcoming of Rome. Be aware of them. They share the Franks lust for Roman blood. The Saxon Thing will take place at Treva in three nights time and the king will be there. The river will be busy. Many will come to listen to the words of their leaders and to decide on what to do about their problems. It is a good time for exchange. You should go to Treva and seek an audience with the king."

"The Saxon Thing!" Laelian exclaimed as Hannibal translated for him, the legate looking surprised. "It is happening in three nights time? Then they are early this year."

"They are early," Ganna said nodding solemnly in confirmation. "They have had much to discuss and many worries since I left them. But to the south beyond the territory of the Saxons there is war between the Semnones and Langobardi. There is fighting all along the river. It will not be safe for you legate and your crew to venture into the midst of that war alone. Better to go to Treva and stay there and seek an audience with King Hadugato. I can help negotiate and arrange safe passage for you down the Albis through Saxon territory and an armed escort for beyond. All I ask in return is that you take me to Treva."

"Maybe," Laelian said frowning with sudden concern, "but I was not planning on visiting and staying at Treva. We avoided Drusus's old fort last year because they said there was plague there. And we do not have unlimited time either. I must reach the Thuringian Thing at Thor's Oak by the full moon on the fifth month."

"You must choose," the priestess barked, her fearless hawk like eyes gazing up at the Roman legate. "There is no plague at Treva and you will be attacked if you take the river south beyond Saxon territory. You have asked me for my advice. I am seeress to King Hadugato. You should head for Treva and seek an audience with the king. I can ask the king for help on your behalf. There are other Roman traders already at Treva. Men who come searching for the amber and slaves too. You will be safe among the Saxons. They will not harm you and your men while you are under my protection."

"I don't know," Laelian muttered suddenly looking torn. "Those Saxon sea pirates certainly weren't friendly."

"We do not have to visit or stay in Treva, legate," Abbe suddenly exclaimed turning to Laelian. "There is an alternative. The sorceress may say that it is safe but men can be easily excited and we carry valuable cargo. If it became widely known what we carry it could cause problems for us. Hear me out," Abbe continued raising his hand to forestall any protests. "The Albis is very wide, close to its mouth. Two miles wide in certain places. A better idea would be if we simply found a hiding spot along its banks and wait it out there, while one of us goes to Treva to make inquiries as to the state of the river further south. I know the mouth of the Albis a little, legate. It is lined with marshes, sandbanks and thick forests. The river bank is a good place to hide a ship."

"Ah the Frisian speaks," Ganna cackled before anyone else could answer. Her contemptuous gaze turned towards Abbe. "So like his kin. So arrogant in his certainty. So purposeful in his contempt. But he should know better than to question the earth goddess. He should know better than to question Ganna. You Romans belong to me now and I shall make certain that none of you is harmed. King Hadugato will listen to me. I have influence with him. As long as I remain on this ship the earth goddess will protect you."

"Legate?" Abbe said in a questioning voice, refusing to look at the high priestess.

"I don't know," Laelian replied frowning, looking undecided. "Treva is at least two days up the Albis from here. We have to pass the old station anyway but stopping there was not part of the plan. I can certainly take you to Treva, priestess," the legate said turning to Ganna with a little respectful and professional nod. "But let me think about your offer to meet with the king. I will make my decision when we are closer to the old fort. Thank you priestess. Your advice is appreciated and I shall take it under consideration."

As the meeting broke up and everyone started to return to their sleeping places Abbe made his way back to the stern of the barge where he had taken to sleeping beside the tiller. Settling down beside Jorina who was already asleep the captain took a deep unhappy breath as he reached for his blanket while nearby Veda turned to look out across the darkened salt marshes that were dimly outlined by the moonlight.

"I would not normally say this," Abbe grumbled turning towards Veda, "but I miss old Walaric. It should have been him offering us advice just now but instead we are now accepting the advice of a sorceress. He may have been a Thuringian but I would have trusted Walaric's counsel. He was an honest man. Damn it - why did he have to die! The legate is a fool to trust her. I don't like her Veda. I don't like her one bit. That sorceress. She is trouble."

"No it is you who is the fool. You know nothing Abbe!" Laelian said angrily as he suddenly appeared from out of the darkness. The night hiding his face. "You heard her just now," the legate snapped. "Ganna is King Hadugato's seeress. I have dealt with such powerful women before. She is right when she says she has influence with the Saxon king. These priestesses are a powerful political force. When dealing with these barbarian tribes we must always take their opinions into account. So if one of them is our friend and offers to help us then I am seriously tempted to accept that help. We are far from home. We need every bit of good fortune we can get. From my experience no diplomatic negotiation can be conducted without taking the opinions of these women into account. That is the reality of doing business with these Germans."

"She is a sorceress and no good will come from taking her advice," Abbe growled stubbornly from the darkness. "I am not wrong about that woman."

Chapter Seventeen - Trouble on the Albis River

A thick eerie mist hung over the Albis as the 'Glory' slowly crept upstream. The mile wide river estuary placid. The afternoon air still. The barge's six oarsmen quietly and rhythmically propelling the ship onwards through the stillness. The gentle plop of their oars dipping into the water the only noise. Standing at the stern holding the 'Glory's' tiller Abbe was trying to peer ahead through the fog. The captain looking concerned while standing right beside him Veda was gazing in the direction of the riverbank where gaps in the mist revealed glimpses of the dark dense forest that came right up to the water's edge.

Nearby, sitting on top of the chest of gold, Jorina was repairing one of her father's socks, working with thread and needle, while right at the front of the barge Laelian was standing bolt upright without moving; his back turned to the rest of the crew. The legate peering upstream as if he had become the ship's wooden figurehead. Shifting his gaze to Walaric's corpse which had been laid out on deck, wrapped up tightly in a woollen blanket, Veda took a deep breath. His expression brooding. Thoughtful. Then his gaze came to rest upon the high priestess and her young acolyte. Ganna and the young woman were sitting together in the middle of the barge near to the cabin. Ganna reclining upon a chair as if she were a queen, gazing silently out into the mist. Her young attendant settled at her feet, busying herself by rubbing an ointment into her mistress's skin. The young woman working with a silent and dutiful solemnness.

"This is Saxon territory," Abbe said as he held onto the tiller. "The legate may think they are friendly but I do not. Never trust a Saxon bastard my grandfather used to tell me. No this is dangerous country, my friend. Tonight I think we had better anchor in the middle of the river for safety. Just in case. The river is very wide here so we should be all right."

"Well I can see fuck all in this mist," Veda murmured.

"You know how I know we are now in Saxon territory," Abbe went on. "Can you not smell the stench?" the captain said glancing at Veda with a little crooked smile. "This is Saxon land all right. The Saxons they never wash you see. You can smell them coming from a mile away."

Grinning at the joke Veda gazed out across the river, the wisps of mist enveloping the barge. The river silent.

"What do you know about this place, Treva?" Veda asked. "The legate claims that it is an old Roman military post founded by general Drusus two hundred and seventy years ago. From the time when the emperor Augustus tried to conquer Germany east of the Rhine. But I did not know such places still existed. Surely there cannot be any Romans there?"

"I have been there once," Abbe replied holding onto the tiller. "There is nothing Roman about the place apart from its name. It's a Saxon settlement now but traders do visit the harbour from time to time. Treva exists because its on one of the amber roads. If the Saxons cannot steal Roman goods then they will settle for the next best thing which is to trade for them. Never trust a Saxon. That is what my grandfather used to say."

"So are you still concerned about heading over into Treva?" Veda said lowering his voice, glancing across at the captain.

"I am biased," Abbe grumbled. "I don't like Saxons. Reserve Frisians we call them. So yes if we can avoid Treva that would not be bad. Their Thing, their tribal assembly, it means there are going to be thousands of people gathered together in one place. And where there are such great crowds there is always trouble. The legate may not be looking for trouble, but trouble has a habit of coming looking for you."

"You don't like anyone, father," Jorina said sighing refusing to look up from her needle work, her eyebrows raised. "You don't like Franks, Saxons, Goths, grandpa and the mother goddess...You don't like fish sauce. You don't like mother. You didn't like Walaric..."

"Like I said I am biased, girl," Abbe interrupted glancing at his daughter. "But I have a good reason to be so. All those people you mention, all of them can kill you and make your life miserable."

"Mother would never kill you," Jorina replied with another sigh. "The others, maybe."

"But will Ganna not offer us some protection?" Veda said, frowning. "You heard what she said last night. She can help us. If she can convince the Saxon king to give us an armed escort would that not be a good thing? If she is as sacred as you say she is then who would dare attack us? I think Laelian was right when he said that the opinions and friendship of these women matter."

"Don't allow yourself to be fooled like she has fooled the legate," Abbe murmured, his smile fading away. "The sorceress may be sacred among the tribes but these women have their own motives. They are not neutral observers. They only ever work to further their own interests and they always demand payment for their work. You think she only wants us to take her to Treva. Think again. No. She wants something else from us. Something which right now she is concealing from us. I hate to say this but Helmuth was right when he said the islanders of Hallig had had enough of her. Hosting one of Nerthus's sorceresses can become an expensive burden. I am sure that they were glad to see the back of her and now it is our turn to be stuck with her. That old bastard must be laughing into his beer right now. We chose badly by agreeing to take her on-board."

For a while Veda said nothing as he pondered on what had just been said.

"Talking about stink," Abbe growled, gesturing with his head at the corpse lying out on deck wrapped in the woollen blanket. "What do you want to do with poor Walaric? We can't leave him out here forever. He will start to decompose long before we reach his homeland."

"You are right. We will cremate him tomorrow," Veda said lowering his eyes, "and I will hand his ashes and his personal belongings to his relatives if they are present at the Thing when we get to Thor's Oak. He was a decent man. He deserves to be given a proper send off."

***

It was just after dawn the following day when a hand shook Veda awake from where he had been sleeping out on deck. His body covered by a blanket. His head resting upon the iron chest which was covered by another blanket. Abruptly sitting up Veda blinked in alarm as Abbe was suddenly crouching beside him. The captain's weathered face looking unhappy.

"We have a problem," Abbe murmured as he turned to look down the length of the barge where the others were preparing for the start of the day. "Last night someone robbed Walaric of all his earthly possessions. They stole everything. His rings. His knife. His money. The lot."

"What?" Veda exclaimed, frowning. "Are you sure?"

"I couldn't sleep," Abbe said lowering his voice to a whisper, his face darkening with anger. "Stealing from a dead man is a disgrace. It offends me. It was Felix. He was on guard duty last night but I saw him going over Walaric's body. He thought no one noticed him but I did. He has hidden Walaric's things in his marching pack. I am sure of it. What do you want to do?"

Swearing softly Veda turned to gaze down the length of the barge to where the five bodyguards were sitting together chatting and preparing a cold breakfast. The soldiers weapons and shields lying nearby within easy reach. Then his gaze shifted to Laelian who was sitting inside the cabin waiting for Hannibal to finish serving him a bowl of porridge.

Without saying another word Veda rose to his feet and started down the deck towards the soldiers. And as they noticed him approaching the five men fell silent. Stooping Veda snatched up Felix's marching pack and before anyone could stop him he had turned the satchel upside down scattering its contents across the wooden deck.

"What the fuck!" Felix yelled in protest angrily rising to his feet.

But Veda was not watching him. His eyes were upon the items lying scattered across the deck and among them was Walaric's knife and a few of his finger rings. Abbe had spoken the truth. The evidence exposed for all to see. For a moment Veda did not move. Then slowly he looked up at Felix and as he did the rest of the mercenaries swiftly rose to their feet in support of their comrade and turned to confront Veda in a menacing manner. Aware suddenly that Abbe was standing behind him, backing him up, Veda's face darkened.

"You piece of stealing shit," Veda snarled. "You would rob a dead man of his belongings."

"So," Felix said with an indifferent shrug, standing his ground. "He did not need them any more. He was just another fat tribesman. What do you care?"

"He was one of us your prick!" Veda roared. "He was a good man. He deserves our respect. Are you stupid? This whole mission is about maintaining and renewing our friendship and alliance with the Thuringians. What are his relatives going to say when they discover that you stole all his personal belongings?"

"They will only know that I took them," Felix snarled as he took a menacing step towards Veda, "if you tell them. So what are you? A snitch. You thinking of betraying us now?"

"Betrayal," Veda snapped, his expression hardening. "That's a good one after what happened to Jonas last year."

"What are you saying?" Hulmu suddenly butted in, staring at Veda with growing anger.

But just as Veda was about to reply to the ex-centurion, Jorina appeared and with everyone turning to look at her in surprised silence, she bent over and calmly started to collect Walaric's possessions, before limping away with them back to the stern of the barge. No one making a move to stop her.

"You watch yourself!" Hulmu hissed at last raising a threatening finger at Veda. "Accidents happen all the time out here."

"They do," Abbe said sharply as he stood behind Veda, the captain's face dark as thunder as he glared back at Hulmu, "but this is my ship. So if there are going to be accidents then they are going to happen to you and your men. Got that you Goth bastard."

"All right. All right. Break it up!" Laelian cried out as he quickly moved to insert himself in between the two parties. The legate turning to Hulmu and then to Veda with a disapproving expression. "We are one crew. I will not have us quarrelling among ourselves. That will not do. You," Laelian exclaimed hurriedly pointing at Veda, "and you," he added turning to Hulmu, "you two will stay away from each other. That's an order. I do not want any more trouble."

"Sir, talking about trouble," Hannibal suddenly called out. "Look! Out there on the water. They are heading straight towards us."

And as everyone turned to stare in the direction in which the secretary was pointing Veda spotted the approaching dugout. The simple canoe was moving towards them from the far bank. The two men inside the dugout were alone and furiously digging their paddles into the water as if they were afraid of arriving too late. And as they drew closer to the Roman ship one of them hurriedly raised his hand signalling that he meant no harm. The two Saxons examining the Roman vessel and its occupants with curious, expectant and excited looks.

"Trade!" One of the men called out grinning disarmingly, holding up some fish he had caught as the dugout glided closer. "Romans! We wish to trade with you."

***

The Saxon village was set in a muddy clearing amid the forest, a hundred yards from the river. The score of longhouses, workshops and their attendant agricultural land forming a cluttered circle of human habitation. The longhouses with their steep sloping roofs of dark thatch and walls made of clay and wood, were arranged around a central granary that had been raised above the ground on stilts. Wisps of smoke were rising from smoke holes while chickens were wandering about freely and several dogs were standing about barking at the party of Romans. Their warning barks going unheeded. While from inside the houses which they shared with the humans, cattle were mooing, waiting to be milked.

Finishing his barter with the old man, a spare pouch of Roman surgical instruments in exchange for a piece of orange amber, Veda looking pleased, slipped his new acquisition into his pocket before turning to look around at the village. The trade with the Saxons had been completed and a short distance across from him Laelian and his bodyguards were relaxing. Standing around drinking beer which the villagers had offered them. No one appeared to be in a hurry. The atmosphere in the village relaxed and friendly. Examining his newly acquired medical surgery kit the old Saxon looked up at Veda and nodded in gratitude.

From inside a workshop close to where Veda was standing the blacksmith had resumed his sweaty work. Hammering away at a piece of iron. The man's face covered in soot. His leather apron singed. The smell of coal smoke from his furnace hanging in the air. While from the doorways to their homes a few women, tall and fair-haired, clad in animal skins and cloaks fastened by clasps at the shoulder were still peering stern-faced at the party of Romans. Their arms folded across their chests. Some clutching infants to their breast, but most had vanished back inside - resuming their work and tasks. The excitement at the Roman arrival in their village already receding. Only the children remained. Large groups of them standing gathered together gazing silently and curiously at Laelian and his bodyguards. Many of the children were barefooted. The swarms of youngsters so great in number that they easily outnumbered the adults.

Sensing Hulmu watching him with a dark unfriendly look Veda ignored the ex-centurion, staying where he was and refusing to join the legate and his men. The tension between them still raw. In contrast - looking relaxed and at ease - Laelian was conversing quietly with his men. The party of Romans relaxing now that business had been concluded before they would return to the ship. The food and beer which they had bartered from the villagers in exchange for Roman iron cooking pans, wine and terracotta pottery, lying stacked up nearby waiting to be carried back to the 'Glory'. There was no sign of Hannibal who appeared to have gone off on his own. Abbe, Jorina and Ganna had remained behind on the 'Glory' as had Caledonus who he had left behind to guard the chest of gold and for the moment Veda was alone.

Turning to one of the Saxons as a man brought him a cup of beer, Veda nodded his thanks, accepting the beaker. The villagers were Saxons but they appeared peaceful and friendly. So unlike their feared reputation he thought. So unlike the Frankish war-band who had attacked him and his brother all those years ago. Taking a sip of the beer Veda once more turned to look around. The villagers he had noticed had been particularly interested in getting their hands on Roman technology. They seemed oblivious to the true value of the piece of orange amber, which he had bartered from them. Oblivious to how much they could have got for it if they had sold it in a Roman market. Ignorant to the world beyond their village. Willing to massively overpay to satisfy their craving for Roman manufactured goods. They were a people ripe for exploitation he thought as he glanced across at Laelian, recalling what Walaric had told him about the legate's business dealings on the side. About his greed and his need for money. And as he studied the legate Veda reached up to rub his chin with a careful, appraising look. There was money to be made in free Germany and the legate would be all to aware of that. Had Jonas been murdered because he had got in the way of one of the legate's business deals?

Suddenly the peacefulness of the village was rent by a high-pitched scream. The noise swiftly followed by an outraged bellow. The sound had come from inside one of the longhouses. For a moment nothing further happened. Then a panicked yell rang out and moments later Hannibal appeared, racing towards the spot where Laelian and his bodyguards were standing about drinking their beer. The secretary was being pursued by a man and a woman. The man clutching an axe. The woman screaming in fury. Swearing to himself as Hannibal fled, finding safety amid the group of Roman soldiers, Veda hurriedly downed his beer before hastening towards the legate who was suddenly facing down an enraged German couple. The man raising his axe menacingly in the air. The woman spitting fury as both tried to get at Hannibal who had found shelter behind his boss. And as Veda reached his comrades more villagers appeared, drawn by the furious outraged yells. Some running. Some looking alarmed. Others armed. The men and women rapidly converging upon the small Roman party. Dogs barking wildly. The mood abruptly souring. The peace gone. To be replaced with the threat of violence. The Saxons calling out to each other.

"Fetch the priestess. Now! Hurry!" Laelian shouted hastily turning to one of his bodyguards as he tried to keep the growing mob at bay. The Saxons pressing around him trying to get their hands on Hannibal.

"All right. All right. Calm down," Veda yelled in German as he hurried over. "What is going on? What is this about?"

"Your friend!" the enraged Saxon clutching his axe yelled rounding on Veda with a furious look. "He tried to force himself upon my daughter. He tried to rape her! I want justice!"

"She is just eleven years old!" the woman screamed turning on Veda, spittle flying from her mouth. Her face dark with savage rage. "I caught him trying to force himself on her!"

"All right calm down, all of you, we can settle this," Laelian cried out in Latin as he and his men, together with Hannibal, were forced back and trapped against the wall of one of the longhouses. The legate holding up his arms as he desperately tried to contain the growing mob of furious villagers who were pressing around him. The Germans shouting back at him.

"He is not my friend," Veda yelled in German as he too tried to hold back the enraged mob. Then before anyone could act, before the riot got completely out of control, Veda turned and swiftly catching hold of the cowering Hannibal he dragged the man out from behind Laelian and flung the secretary onto the ground. Moments later, his boot pressing down on Hannibal's back forcing the squirming man into the dirt, Veda' pulled his knife from his belt. Holding up the blade he turned to the baying mob angrily pushing back a man who tried to attack the secretary. "Stay back!" Veda roared. "Stay back. You will get justice. I promise. But this will be done properly. Stay back all of you!"

"I want his blood! He attacked my daughter. He tried to rape her!" the father holding his axe bellowed as he came marching up to Veda, flinging aside the villagers who had got in his way. The man pausing only when he was nearly head to head with Veda. His eyes blazing. While lying on the ground pinned beneath Veda's boot Hannibal howled in growing terror.

"And you will get your justice," Veda snapped as he stood his ground, facing down the enraged father. "But it will be done properly. So back off. No one will touch this man until then."

"And who are you to deny me," the father roared giving Veda a violent shove that Veda accepted without response. "Who are you Roman to deny me justice. I want that man's blood!"

"Are you going to give us justice!" another man suddenly cried out as half a dozen angry villagers were suddenly crowding around Veda. Glaring at him. Threatening to overwhelm him. Violence just a heartbeat away. The situation rapidly spiralling out of control. The Roman party was now in mortal danger. But suddenly the mood of the mob changed. The people abruptly quietening down. Then backing away and as he turned to see what was going on Veda spotted Ganna, her acolyte and Abbe hurrying towards him. Ganna was hooded and clad in her white cloak but the villagers had recognised who she was.

"Justice, high priestess," the girl's father called out lowering his axe as Ganna approached. The villagers moving aside for her in respectful silence. "This man tried to rape my daughter. I want his blood. It is my right."

Coming to a halt Ganna did not immediately reply. Then at last she drew back her hood and slowly twisted her head to take a look at Hannibal who was lying face down in the mud, pinned there by Veda's boot. Before turning to gaze across at the mother who was resting her hands protectively upon the shoulders of a young girl who looked no older than eleven. The girl trembling with emotion. Her face pale as milk.

"And justice you shall get," Ganna exclaimed. "But you shall not be the one who decides. Nor will anyone touch the Romans. They travel with me. They belong to the earth goddess. He will decide," the priestess of Nerthus cried out gesturing at Veda. "He will give you justice."

Among the crowd of villagers her words were met with shocked silence. Then to Veda's surprise some of them started to mutter angrily among themselves. A few of the people crying out in protest. Others raising their fists in the air and it was suddenly clear that Ganna's authority was not total. Some of the villagers shouting insults at her.

"The Roman will give you justice," Ganna cried out again unperturbed by the protests. "He knows the cost of murder. The shame of the murderer. The earth goddess wishes him to decide. That is her will."

"Veda," Laelian called out urgently but Veda was not listening to him.

Staring at Ganna, Veda frowned before he shifted his gaze to the furious mother and father. His eyes eventually slipping to their young daughter before he turned to look down at Hannibal who was cowering in the dirt beneath his boot.

"Did you try and rape this girl?" Veda asked addressing himself to Hannibal in Latin.

"She was asking for it," Hannibal whined. "It was consensual."

"She is eleven years old, you arsehole!" Veda cried out, angrily pressing his boot into Hannibal's back and making the secretary squirm. "She is a child. Damn you man! Damn you and your lies."

"What is your verdict Roman?" an angry voice cried out from the crowd. "What justice?"

Taking a deep unhappy breath Veda turned to look at the mob. Sensing that all eyes were upon him. An ugly expectant mood taking hold. Then his gaze shifted to the high priestess. Why had she picked him out to deliver judgement? Why did she not deliver justice herself?

"Veda, I need Hannibal alive!" Laelian cried out hurriedly in Latin. "He is not to be harmed. I will not allow it."

"All right, all right," Veda called out in German raising both his arms in the air in an attempt to calm the mob. "Silence. Shut up all you! Is this the man who tried to rape your daughter?"

"That's him," the young girl said pointing at Hannibal. "He attacked me when I was milking the cows."

And as she spoke an angry swell of emotion swept through the assembled villagers. But none made any attempt towards violence. The presence of the high priestess preventing blood from being shed.

"You said this man attempted to rape your daughter but he did not complete the act?" Veda said hurriedly addressing himself to the parents.

"What difference does it make," the father shouted. "His intention was clear."

"All right I accept this man tried to rape your daughter," Veda replied in German. "He is guilty of that but the act was not completed. So he will live. You will not get his blood."

"What!" the father roared, enraged.

"Instead this man will pay you compensation," Veda said standing his ground as the mob howled in protest. "Blood money. A hundred Roman silver coins. And once he has done so this matter will be closed. That is fair. That is justice."

"Silver," the father growled but it was clear that Veda's words had taken some of the sting and anger out of his voice.

Nodding Veda gazed at the man for a moment longer as he ground his boot harder into Hannibal's back making the secretary groan in pain. Then at last the father nodded in agreement and Veda quickly turned towards Laelian, his expression like thunder.

"Hannibal will live but you will pay this man compensation. A hundred denarii! That is the agreed price," Veda shouted. "Do it now! Then get this piece of shit out of here before they change their mind and slaughter us all. We need to go. Now legate! Now!"

Staring back at Veda Laelian looked shocked at being told what to do but nevertheless he did as Veda had told him to and as the money was quickly handed over Veda released his grip on Hannibal's back and swiftly hauled him back up onto his feet. The secretary's look of relief instantly shattered as Veda's fist slammed into his stomach, making him double up and cry out in pain. Then shoving the groaning Hannibal into the arms of Felix and Atticus, Veda was done with him. Turning his back on the secretary with a furious, contemptuous look.

As the party of Romans beat a hasty retreat through the forest towards the spot where the 'Glory' sat moored along the river bank, Veda was concious that Abbe had suddenly joined him. The Frisian looking troubled. His eyes darting about as if he feared attack. The two of them bringing up the rear, followed closely by a large group of sullen, angry villagers.

"I don't know why Ganna keeps asking me to act as a judge," Veda murmured, "but its beginning to piss me off. What is her game?"

"It seems to be her style," Abbe muttered. "Instead of making judgements herself she lends her authority to those she considers wise. Maybe she is testing you."

"Yes well I am not wise and next time she can ask you all right," Veda grumbled turning around to quickly glance at the posse of villagers who were following him back to the river. "That prick Hannibal nearly got us all lynched."

"Did you notice how some of those villagers openly insulted her," Abbe said with a frown. "That was unexpected. I have not known that to happen before. It was as if they were challenging her authority. Not everyone it seems respects the sorceress or the earth goddess any more. Oh how times change. I have even heard it said by some," Abbe added his face darkening, his voice suddenly sounding uneasy, "that the decline of the old gods has something to do with that new god you worship in the Roman territories. The god of the Christians. They say that the Christian god is gaining in popularity."

"Christians are persecuted within the empire," Veda said quickly. "And I doubt that their religion has yet spread across the frontier. But you are right. I noticed the protests too. Maybe that is what Ganna is worried about. Losing her popularity to these imported foreign Gods. Maybe she fears the threat they pose to her own power. I don't know. The fact however remains that if Ganna had not showed up we would all be dead right now. Ganna - she saved us back there. She prevented that mob from turning violent. They held back because of her. Did you see how their mood changed as soon as they recognised who she was. Like it or not we owe her our lives I reckon. The question is why? Why is she doing this? Why is she helping us? I can't figure it out."

"Veda!" Laelian called out hurrying back to him as the party reached the river bank with the 'Glory' anchored close by. "My gratitude. You handled that well."

"You should thank your priestess," Veda replied with sudden scorn. "She saved us, not me."

"You are right," Laelian said looking rattled. "You both saved us. Well done."

"You are wrong to trust her, legate," Abbe said lowering his voice as he came up to Laelian. The captain looking deadly serious. "Ganna is a sorceress and practised in the ways of deception and witch craft. She is fooling you. She twists men around her finger like they are pieces of rope. That is her whole job! Tell me. Why has no one asked her what she stands to gain from introducing us to her king? Why is she willing to do this for us? We should part ways with her immediately. She is only going to bring us trouble."

"Are you mad!" Laelian retorted, glaring back at Abbe. "That woman just saved us back there in that village. She is our friend. No. You have just convinced me. I have made up my mind. We shall head for Treva and seek an audience with the Saxon King Hadugato like she suggested. That is the right thing to do. If we can get the King to agree to provide us with an armed escort for our journey up the Albis then so much the better."

"You really are a stupid man!" Abbe retorted raising his voice.

"And I am done with you!" Laelian responded crossly, raising his finger in warning as he glared back at Abbe. "When we get back I will make sure that your contract with us is not renewed. You have proved to be a poor replacement for last year's ship's crew."

"Good! For I was not going to do this a second time anyway," Abbe said angrily. "Screw you and your offer of easy money. I will complete this mission and then I am done. This is not worth it any more."

"Veda," Laelian said turning to him and giving up on Abbe, "regards what happened with Hannibal and that child. I hope that it goes without saying that you will not mention this episode in your report if we make it back. No one would benefit from this. It would be best for all concerned if everything were to be forgotten. So can I count on you not to mention this?"

"Your man nearly got all of us killed," Veda said coldly, turning to Laelian. "He's a child molester so off-course it is going into my report. Everyone is going to know what a monster he is when we get back. I am going to ruin his reputation. So if you were wise you would sack him the moment we get back."

Staring at Veda Laelian's face appeared to tighten through several levels of displeasure. His lips curling angrily. His eyes blazing with fury. His nose twitching. His cheeks blushing. Then without saying another word the legate turned and stomped off in a huff.

For a moment Veda watched the legate go with an amused smile. Then suddenly he felt Abbe tugging gently at his sleeve.

"He's an arrogant prick that one," Abbe said quietly holding onto Veda and turning him to face away from the others as they prepared to board the 'Glory'. "That is just who he is. But enough. We have a bigger problem. A word of warning, my friend," Abbe continued. "Don't be so sure that she saved us. The sorceress is not on our side. She is only ever on her own side. These women. They have their own ambitions. They are not your friends. They care only about power and how to hold onto it. They are a bunch of lying, manipulating bitches. And this sorceress is no different. She will never do anything that is not in her interests and she will have a plan. I don't know what it is but I know it involves us and I don't like it one bit. We should leave her behind," Abbe added fixing Veda with another imploring look. "We should part ways with that sorceress right now. Damn it Veda. My daughter could get hurt. This is not only about you and me. I just can't shake this feeling that something terrible is coming our way."

"I hear you," Veda said taking a deep breath and lowering his gaze. "But unfortunately the legate is still in charge and you heard his answer just now. Laelian is not going to leave Ganna behind just because you don't like her and we cannot force the issue. Hulmu is already itching to stick a knife in my throat. So we have no choice but to go along with him."

"It's bollocks!" Abbe said angrily. "This whole job is so fucked up!"

Chapter Eighteen - The Saxon Thing

Rising from the middle of the broad waters of the Albis estuary the small island divided the river into two. The marshy banks covered in tall yellow reeds, beyond which poked the sloping thatched roof's of the German longhouses. The core of the Saxon settlement of Treva however was clustered around the harbour. A solitary wooden jetty that led to a muddy beach. It was afternoon and smoke was rising from numerous cooking fires - the village teeming with people and activity. Cattle mooing loudly. Dogs barking excitedly. Geese cackling in their pens. A bell tolling away from somewhere out of sight. While the approaches to the small harbour were crowded with a vast number of dugouts. The simple one and two man log canoes lying beached in the mud or converging on the island from every direction. Their occupants using paddles to power themselves through the water. The craft were dangerously overloaded with trade goods, baskets containing live poultry and other supplies.

The Saxons were gathering for their Thing, their tribal assembly, Veda could see as he stood gazing at Treva from the bow of the 'Glory'. Thousands appeared to be coming. Each Saxon community sending representatives. The Roman barge joining the armada that was heading straight for the harbour. Laelian's bodyguards and Caledonus were working the oars in two banks of three but among the dugouts out on the water no one was paying them much attention. As if the locals were used to the sight of Roman merchant ships in their waters.

Gazing at Treva Veda frowned. There was no sign of the original Roman military camp which Drusus had erected on the island so long ago. Treva was decidedly Saxon in character. The only hint to its origins the old name that continued to live on. But among the swarms of dugouts there were larger sea going ships too. A couple of galleys that looked like they could be Roman traders and as he peered at the boats Veda's frown deepened. Lying at anchor inside the harbour was another ship sporting a curved prow that ended in a great serpent's head. The vessel looked very much like the Saxon sea pirate vessel that had tried to overtake and attack them just a few days earlier.

Gazing at the anchored pirate ship Veda took a deep breath. Looking unhappy he turned towards the bodyguards sitting upon their rowing benches. The soldiers pulling at their oars in practised unison. Pirates and hostile barbarians were just one part of the threat. Matters were not good on board the Glory. The mood and cohesion continuing to deteriorate. The crew increasingly divided. Abbe and Laelian had stopped talking to each other after their row and he had been forced to act as a go between the two men. And as he gazed at the bodyguards Hulmu noticed him. The ex-centurion glaring back at him before silently reaching up to draw a menacing finger across his throat.

Ignoring Hulmu, Veda's eyes came to rest upon Ganna who was sitting upon her chair out on deck. The priestess gazing across the water at Treva with a patient expression that revealed nothing. Her young acolyte sitting nearby preparing some food. Ganna's presence was an enigma. She had helped save them back in the Saxon village but the tension between her and Abbe was troubling. Abbe was right about one thing. The priestess was up to something Veda thought as he quietly observed her. He could sense it - but what? What was she planning?

"Veda!" Laelian said as he approached, raising his hand and giving him a quick, guarded look. The legate looking grumpy. "We have a big day tomorrow and I don't want any fuck-ups. So we will anchor in the harbour tonight before going ashore tomorrow. Now I have spoken with the priestess," Laelian continued. "Ganna tells me that last night she had a dream. A vision in which everything was on fire. She said the whole world was burning. She says that before she takes us to meet King Hadugato tomorrow she wants to pay a visit to the shrine of Nerthus. There is one on the island, just beyond the village. She says her dream tells her that the earth goddess is angry and must be appeased with a live sacrifice. I thought it prudent to agree."

"I see," Veda replied looking unimpressed. "So we are doing what she wants. So is she in charge of this mission now?"

"No, I am," Laelian growled. "I am the legate. But the priestess is proving useful to me. If she can win us the favour of the King and an armed escort, our journey upriver will become a lot easier. Look," Laelian said taking a step towards Veda and lowering his voice. "I am not stupid. I know what and who she is. But we use the priestess to get what we need and then afterwards when she is of no more use to us we will get rid of her."

"You don't think she knows that too," Veda shot back. "What do you think she wants in return for helping us? Have you considered that? There will be a price to be paid for her help."

"We're not having this conversation. You heard me! Inform Abbe about my instructions and tell him that no one is to go ashore until the morning. That will be all," Laelian said brusquely before turning and stomping off back towards the cabin where Hannibal was watching Veda. The secretary's lips curling into a sneer as their eyes met.

Ignoring Hannibal, Veda lowered his gaze.

"So what did the arsehole want?" Abbe murmured as Veda came to stand beside him at the tiller. "I saw him talking to you just now."

"The arsehole says that you are to anchor the 'Glory' in the harbour for the night and that we are not to go ashore until tomorrow," Veda replied. "He says that the priestess wants to conduct a live sacrifice at the shrine to Nerthus before we go and meet King Hadugato."

"A sacrifice, I see," Abbe said. "Well Jorina and I will stay onboard my ship. I do not need to meet any King or set foot in Treva for that matter. You can tell the arsehole that I am staying right here. He will just have to do all the arse kissing himself but then he is oh so good at that."

"Caledonus will join you," Veda said quickly. "He too will stay behind to guard the gold. I will go with Laelian."

"I could poison his food," Abbe said darkly as he shifted his gaze towards Laelian. "No one would know."

"No," Veda said quickly. "We don't make our move until I say so."

For a moment Veda paused. Then he looked away.

"When we were on Hallig island," Veda said abruptly turning back to Abbe with a sudden thoughtful look. "Did your father-in-law ever tell you what Ganna was doing out there in the first place? On the island I mean. It just strikes me as an odd place for a high priestess of Nerthus to visit. There is nothing there. The island is tiny and there were only a handful of people. Why was she there?"

"No he did not have much to say to me before we left," Abbe responded with a brooding look. "I don't think Helmuth and I shall see each other again. If we do it will only be to fight each other to the death."

Once again Veda looked away. "Right," he said at last in a quiet voice. "While we are on the island tomorrow I want you to keep the 'Glory' in a state of readiness. Just in case things go wrong and we have to make a hasty retreat. I want to be able to move fast if we have too."

"Sure. That is the first sensible thing I have heard said all day," Abbe replied. "You can count on me."

Chapter Nineteen - Treva

Wading ashore onto the muddy beach, feeling uneasy Veda turned to look around. His pugio knife concealed beneath his cloak. It was morning. The sky was a clear blue. The spring weather warm and comforting. But in the village the masses of Saxons going about their business appeared unconcerned by the appearance of the small party of Romans. No one confronting him. Some of the barbarians glancing at him curiously as they past on by. Most ignoring him completely. Only one man showing open hostility by pausing to spit onto the ground just in front of Veda before moving on without saying a word. Treva itself was crowded with new arrivals. Many of whom it seemed had spent the night out in the open. But there was no denying the mood of excitement that gripped the village. A good natured excitement, revealed by the laughter and joyful shouts as groups of friends and relatives met up. The chance to do business with their peers, to arrange marriage alliances, to barter for goods or just to catch up with the news and old friends was too good to be missed. The Thing one of the annual highlights in the barbarian calendar.

Coming ashore with Veda, slipping out of the dugouts that had transported the crew to the island from the 'Glory', which remained anchored in the harbour, the others appeared wary and uneasy too. Laelian sticking close to Ganna. Hannibal staying close to Laelian and the five bodyguards, armed with their long spatha swords and their large Roman infantry shields forming a loose protective formation around their principal. The professional soldiers prepared to fight. Their faces hard as iron as they searched the crowds for trouble. Only Ganna, hooded and clad in her fine white cloak, looked completely at ease. The old woman clutching her silver ended cane as she started up the beach and into the village. Her head held high as if she were returning victorious from the battlefield. Her pace measured and dignified as if she were not in a hurry.

But where was the priestess's acolyte Veda thought as he vainly turned to look around at the crowds. The young servant girl had been missing since dawn. She had vanished without explanation and no one knew what had happened to her. The girl must have slipped away during the night he had concluded. It was an inauspicious start to the day.

As the priestess started out into the village, leading the party of Romans, the Saxon tribesmen, recognising her, hurriedly got out of her way. Men shooting her wary and respectful glances. Women hurriedly calling out to their children, gathering them close as all turned to stare at the priestess and the Romans who were accompanying her. The happy laughter and joyful reunions suddenly dampened as people became aware of the presence of the holy woman in their midst. The children staring at Ganna and the Romans in curious silence while at the entrance to one of the German longhouses an old man stiffly got down on one knee and reverently bowed his head to the priestess as she past on by. But as swiftly as the crowd had quietened down the excitement and joyful chatter returned, reviving rapidly as Ganna moved away.

Pushing deeper into Treva the small party had reached an animal pen filled with noisy mooing cattle when their path was suddenly blocked by a brawl. A group of men were wrestling with each other. Hitting, kicking and punching at each other in a frenzy of violence. Bodies rolling over the ground. Voices shouting, howling and crying out. The fight not a playful jest but deadly serious. While standing to one side a bunch of women were screaming encouragement. Another group of women yelling at the first group. The fight threatening to spill over to the women as insults were hurled at each other.

Avoiding the commotion Ganna calmly turned away and as the party past the last longhouse, beyond, in the fields at the edge of the village, Veda suddenly caught sight of a large fire-pit filled with wood. The pit was on fire. Great roaring flames leaping upwards, sending a plume of black smoke towering into the clear blue sky. Gathered around the fire-pit were a few people, some down on both knees praying while others were throwing small personal items, rings, clothing, knives and ornaments into the fire.

Approaching the fire-pit Ganna came to a halt before the great fire, slowly lowering her hood and as she did Veda realised that the fire *was* the shrine to Nerthus and that the people gathered around it were not throwing things away but making offerings to the earth goddess. Standing beside Ganna at the edge of the pit, Laelian turned and caught Veda's eye but said nothing. Of-course Veda thought as he remembered. The German tribes did not honour and worship their gods in temples and buildings like everyone else did. Instead they believed that the Gods lived in sacred groves, rivers, mountains and the wild forest. The Gods were free - like men. Turning to look around with a thoughtful gaze Veda reached up to rub his chin. Apart from the fire pit there was nothing else here. No opportunistic temple touts trying to sell cheap trinkets and mementoes. No temple whores looking for clients. No farmers selling live offerings. No lawyers or bankers trying to drum up business. Just the faithful, an empty field and the blue sky.

Standing at the edge of the fire-pit Ganna did not move or speak. Her head bowed to the flames as if she were waiting for the earth Goddess to reveal her presence. The small party of Romans were clustered around her. Unsure of what to do. The men waiting in silence for her to start the sacrifice. Then abruptly Ganna tilted her head backwards and raised both her arms to the sky. Her eyes were closed. The heat from the flames blasting her body. Her mouth working - speaking silent and secret words.

Observing the old woman Veda too remained silent. Then he turned away and as he once again looked around the empty field he frowned. Something appeared to be off but he could not quite put his finger on it. The thought niggling away at him frustratingly just out of reach. Then Veda grunted in surprise.

Among the handful of people gathered around the fire-pit he suddenly noticed a Roman. The man was definitely Roman, wearing a Roman cloak. His features darker and more Mediterranean than German. Leaving his position at the rear of the Roman party Veda strode over to the man who had just finished his prayers. Noticing his approach the man gave Veda a little guarded nod.

"You are Roman?" Veda said speaking in Latin as he came up to the stranger. "What are you doing here?"

"Yes. I am a trader," the man replied in good Latin. "Out of Portus Itius. Been coming to Treva for several years now. To trade for amber and slaves."

"Then I saw your ship down in the harbour," Veda said nodding with a little relaxed and friendly smile. "Good. I am with them," he added hastily gesturing in Laelian's direction.

"With the priestess?" the Roman trader replied with a guarded look. "I saw you arrive earlier."

"Yeah with the priestess," Veda replied. "We are travelling upriver. A long journey. Listen," Veda continued quickly not allowing the trader the chance to interrupt him. "I was told that there is trouble further south along the Albis. That the Langobardi and Semnones are at war. That the river is not passable for traffic right now. Do you know anything about that?"

"War you say," the trader said with a sudden frown. "I don't think so. One of my trading partners just came down the river and he had no trouble. There is no war between the Langobardi and the Semnones. Whoever told you that does not know what they are talking about."

Staring at the Roman trader Veda had gone very still. The blood slowly draining from his face. Then slowly he turned around to stare at Ganna and, as if sensing him, the priestess's silent prayer recital abruptly came to an end. Opening her eyes she turned her head towards Veda fixing him with a strange triumphant look. Her eyes blazing with sudden religious fervour. Her mask slipping. As if she knew he knew.

"Legate!" Veda cried out in alarm. Then Veda froze in shock. Beyond the fire-pit from between the cluster of longhouses at the edge of the field a large group of armed men had appeared. The host were walking straight towards him. The men in no particular hurry. The newcomers were led by a warrior riding a horse. The old man's head was adorned with a magnificent gilded helmet that was only ever worn by a King. And escorting the King across the field towards her mistress and the fire-pit was Ganna's young acolyte.

For a moment Veda was unable to move. Staring at the host of armed men who had appeared out of nowhere. His stomach threatening to throw up its contents. Shock robbing and delaying him. Then swearing out loud he was rushing back to his companions.

"Legate!" Veda roared as some of the faithful around the fire-pit started to hurry away and the rest hastily began packing up. "We have been betrayed. The priestess - she lied to us. There is no war to the south. It was a lie to get us to come here! The bitch betrayed us!"

But Laelian appeared not to be listening. His face was turned towards the newcomers. The legate staring at the approaching host of armed warriors in shock. His bodyguards hurriedly turning to face the threat. But it appeared hopeless. The Saxons outnumbered them fifteen to one.

"Legate!" Veda bellowed frantically as he came rushing up to him but Laelian looked stunned. Unable to speak or move. Swearing out loud at the man's indecision, Veda hurriedly turned towards Ganna and saw her watching him with a look of triumph from the edge of the fire-pit. Her savage joy and cruel delight revealing itself. Then she laughed. And as she did Veda realised what had been bothering him earlier and he groaned in despair. Fear shooting up his spine.

"I will talk to them," Laelian called out in a shaky voice as he stared at the approaching host of warriors who appeared to be in no rush. "I will speak with the King. Maybe you are wrong Veda. Maybe we have not been betrayed. Maybe I can reason with him."

"You can't!" Veda roared. "The sacrifice! You said she wanted a live sacrifice but where then are the sacrificial animals? They are not here because *we* are the sacrifice! She intends to offer us to the earth goddess. To Nerthus! We are to be a human sacrifice. They are going to throw us into that fire-pit and watch us burn! That is her plan. She lured us here so she could sacrifice us to her goddess. That was her plan all along."

But Laelian was unable to handle the situation, just silently shaking his head in response. His bodyguards clustering around him. The soldiers staring at the approaching Saxon horde with resigned acceptance. The fight was not one they could possibly hope to win. Then with a snarl Veda was at Ganna's side and before the old woman could protest he had seized her. Yanking her nearly off her feet Ganna yelped as Veda turned to face the Saxons, grasping the priestess before him like a shield. One arm wrapped tightly around her neck. The other holding his knife close to her face.

"Stay back! You come any closer and she dies!" Veda shouted in German. "I will kill your priestess!"

"Then you will die a most painful death," the lead warrior retorted, his face grim but instead of continuing his advance the man brought his horse to a halt and the host of warriors with him too came to a stop. The mass of hard faced, bearded men bristling with shields, spears, swords and axes. The Saxons glaring at the small party of Romans. The hostility palpable. The tension rapidly rising. The situation on a knife's edge.

"Maybe," Veda shouted as he began to back away dragging Ganna with him. His knife hovering close to her face. "But I am expendable. No one will miss me. I am already promised to hell and the gods of the underworld so you see I don't really care. I will take your priestess with me if you attack. I mean it. If I die, she dies. We go down together."

"I am King Hadugato. King of the Saxons," the man on the horse called out looking unhappy at the stand-off. "This is not Roman land and Ganna is my seeress. She belongs to me. So let her go unharmed and I promise you that we will give you a swift and clean death before sending you into the flames."

"Fuck you!" Veda cried out as he continued to fall back. "You attack. She dies!"
But before anyone could speak or react, Ganna's acolyte suddenly shrieked in rage and charged towards Veda intent on freeing her mistress from his grip. But as the young woman came rushing up, Hulmu stepped in. The ex-centurion catching the girl by her arm and with a powerful bellowing roar he dragged the startled woman with him before sending her flying into the blazing fire-pit. The acolyte screaming as the flames swiftly started to consume her. Transforming her into a human torch.

"Stay back! Stay back!" Veda roared raising his knife as howls of outrage swept through the ranks of the assembled warriors. The acolyte's terrible high-pitched shrieks ringing out as she burned to death. For a moment it seemed the Saxons would attack but the threat to their high priestess's life appeared to be working for despite their mounting anger none of the Saxons made a move. The warriors holding back. Unsure of what to do. Veda's threat just enough to keep them at bay.

"Where do you think you are going?" King Hadugato bellowed, looking shocked as he stared at Veda.

"Back to our ship," Veda roared as he fell back towards the village, dragging Ganna with him. The small party of Romans clustering around him for protection as the mass of Saxons started to follow. "We were lured here on false pretences," Veda shouted. "Your sorceress, she lied to us. I will let her go unharmed once we are back at the river. You have my word."

"Kill him! What are you waiting for! I am not afraid to die," Ganna suddenly yelled directing herself towards King Hadugato. "If you are a real man. You will kill them all and honour Nerthus. The Romans belong to the earth goddess. They are pledged to her. Do this and Nerthus will grant good fortune to all Saxons. There is no higher and greater sacrifice than that of living beating human hearts. Nerthus demands their blood…"

But Ganna's words ended in a scream of pain as Veda unexpectedly bit her in her ear before he clamped his hand across her mouth muffling her voice.

Falling back through the village with King Hadugato and the mass of Saxon warriors following closely behind in a tense moving stand-off, Veda led the way back towards the harbour. The crowds of people gathering for the Saxon Thing falling silent at the unexpected sight as the tight group of Romans came hurrying on by. No one making an effort to intervene. The only hostile act a solitary throne stone that clattered into Thiemo's shield. Clamping his hand around Ganna's mouth Veda at last exhaled with relief as he spotted the muddy beach and the armada of dugouts lying drawn up on the shore. And beyond, a short distance across the water, the 'Glory' was still riding at anchor in the harbour. Peering at the Roman barge Veda spotted Abbe dashing about on deck and Caledonus hurriedly raising the anchor. His companions appeared to have recognised that he was in trouble.

"Take those dugouts!" Veda hissed turning to his companions as he hastened towards the water's edge. "Get back to the ship. Hurry!"

The Romans did not need to be told twice. Hastily freeing one of the dugouts and dragging it into the river Laelian and Hannibal clambered into it. The two men frantically paddling back towards the safety of the Glory. Entering the river, still dragging Ganna with him in an iron grip - one hand clamped around her mouth. The other holding his knife, Veda hurriedly turned around to face the mass of Saxons who were following closely behind led by their King on horseback. Then as Thiemo came splashing past him pushing a dugout into the river Veda once again sank his teeth into Ganna's ear making the sorceress yelp in pain. Taking advantage of the distraction Veda together with Thiemo bundled her into the dugout. Then quickly Veda scrambled into the craft as the bodyguard remained in the water and continued to push them out into the river. Thiemo struggling onwards until his head was barely above the water. Grasping hold of Ganna, Veda savagely yanked her head backwards, exposing her throat and turned to face the Saxons who had come to a halt along the shoreline. The distance between the two parties starting to widen. No one making an effort to follow them into the river.

"You said you would let her go when you reached the river," King Hadugato bellowed, his face suddenly red with anger. "You gave your word."

"Well I lied didn't I!" Veda shouted back as beside him in the water Thiemo spluttered, lost his footing and started to swim. The Batavian closing the last few yards to reach the Glory, one arm swimming, one dragging the dugout with him. "You will get your priestess back alive and unharmed once I am sure that there is no pursuit," Veda roared. "I will drop her off on the other side of the estuary and then we will be on our way."

From the beach there was no immediate reaction but the crowd was growing increasingly noisy and unruly. Their voices raised, crying out with growing fury. Then the dugout was bumping into the Glory's wooden hull and as he quickly turned to look up Veda saw Abbe peering down at him and a moment later a sturdy rope net tumbled down the side of the Glory's hull.

"Climb up! Get on-board now!" Abbe yelled. "We have to go!"

Scrambling up and over the side of the hull Veda cursed as he hit the deck with a painful thud. The Glory was already moving and as Veda staggered to his feet Jorina came limping past, the ship's main sail rapidly unfolding in her wake. The square sail flapping around, then holding fast and bulging in the breeze. The mooring ropes tightening. The timbers creaking. Standing at the tiller Abbe was already plotting a course out into the estuary. Grasping hold of Ganna, Veda hauled the priestess back onto her feet and turned to stare at Treva's beach. Most of the Saxons were still standing where he had left them but to Veda's consternation one group of men had broken away. The men piling into one of the larger merchant ships while others had taken to the water in their small dugouts. The warriors paddling frantically to catch up with the Glory.

"They are coming after us!" Hannibal shrieked, pointing.

"What the fuck happened back there Veda?" Abbe yelled from his position at the stern, holding the tiller.

"You were right!" Veda shouted as he retained a tight grip on Ganna. "She betrayed us. She was never going to help us. The priestess was going to offer us all as sacrifice to her earth goddess. She was going to feed us to the flames right in front of her King. She was planning a spectacle."

From the direction of the tiller there was no immediate response. Then a howl of fury and rage, so deep and strong, rose up that it startled everyone, making them stop and turn to stare at Abbe in shock. Glued to the tiller, unable to leave his post, Abbe looked like he was about to explode. Once again Abbe opened his mouth but instead of words only a torrent of noise came pouring forth. Red hot rage as if a thousand voices were all yelling at the same time.

"You arsehole!" Abbe screamed turning towards Laelian as at last he managed to calm down. "I warned you! You piece of shit. You nearly got us all consumed by fire! I am going to throw you overboard the moment we are out of here. You are going to get the fuck off my boat!"

"Be quiet man," Laelian roared as colour shot into his cheeks. The legate recovering from his earlier indecision. "We're not out of this yet. Look! They are coming after us. They are not going to let us get away."

Looking out across the water Veda saw that Laelian was right. Racing after them in pursuit as the Glory began to head down stream and into the wide estuary, was a solitary merchant ship crammed with warriors escorted by a small fleet of one man dugouts. The Saxon paddles furiously pounding the water. The warriors shouting to each other. Their intent clear.

"We are not going to get away," Laelian yelled his face darkening in alarm. "They are gaining on us. We are going to have to fight."

"Why?" Veda snapped as he brought his head close Ganna's. "Why us? What had we done to you to deserve the fate you had in store for us?"

"You belong to the earth goddess," the sorceress hissed. "She demands your blood. Roman blood that came to her fire willingly. You were the price that had to be paid for her continued blessing. And the goddess will not be thwarted. She will get what was promised to her. You will all burn in her holy fire. If not now, then on another day. You are all marked. You cannot escape your fate."

"You know what I think," Veda snapped as he held his head close to hers. "I think you were on Hallig island because you were exiled. Perhaps one of your prophecies did not work out. You were there because you had fallen out of favour with your King Hadugato and he sent you away. And this human sacrifice. Our lives. This spectacle that you were planning. It was just about you trying to regain the King's favour and respect. A demonstration of your power. You just needed the right audience. Well lady it is not going to work out like you wanted. Screw the earth goddess and her holy fire. I piss on your goddess."

"Prepare to be boarded," Laelian screamed.

Grimacing Veda looked up as the Saxon merchant ship suddenly loomed into view. The deck of the ship lined with armed men. Then he was dragging Ganna with him into the shelter of the Glory's cabin just as Caledonus appeared, rushing up carrying his pack slung across his back. The freedman armed with the Frankish throwing axe Veda had given him. The iron chest containing the gold was already inside the cabin placed their in advance by Caledonus. But there was no more time to prepare. With a sharp bump that nearly knocked them all off their feet and onto the floor the Saxon ship made contact and a moment later with harsh savage cries the Saxons came leaping onto the Roman deck.

"Give me your axe!" Veda yelled turning to snatch Caledonus's weapon from his hand. "Watch her! If I am dead, then kill her."

As the first of the attackers came charging at Veda, from the doorway Veda sent a man stumbling backwards with a well placed kick. Leaping onto his opponent Veda finished him off with his axe, nearly decapitating the man with a furious blow that sent a flood of blood surging across the deck. Stumbling backwards to defend the door into the cabin Veda yelped as a throwing axe went hurtling past him. Narrowly missing him and thudding into the wood beside the door. The attack was followed by a woman's scream. But there was no time to see what was going on. Fending off another jabbing attack by a man armed with a spear, Veda snarled like a cornered animal. Refusing to be lured out from the relative protection that the cabin entrance offered. Then another Saxon came at him. A giant of a man with a full black beard and holding a huge two handed axe in his hands. The warrior screaming insults as he swung his heavy weapon at Veda threatening to cut him in half. Falling back into the cabin with a terrified cry Veda was just in time as the heavy axe struck the side wall instead making the whole cabin shake. Then before the warrior could pull the blade free from the wood Veda's own axe had sunk straight into his skull. Killing him in one blow.

Kicking the corpse to the ground Veda sprang forwards, his bloodied axe raised. His action forcing a couple of Saxons to retreat. The men suddenly watching him with wary looks. Snatching a look around the corner of the cabin as he heard Jorina scream again, Veda gasped as he saw that the rest of his companions had fortified themselves at the stern of the barge. Abbe at the tiller. Jorina at her father's side. Laelian and Hannibal crouching nearby armed with long spatha swords. But it was the bodyguards who were doing all the fighting. Arranged across the three yard wide deck, their flanks secured by the ship's hull, Hulmu and his colleagues had formed a solid shield wall. The five ex-special forces soldiers crouching behind their large infantry shields. Their swords jabbing and stabbing at the Saxons, cutting them down with cold, brutal professionalism. The deck around them littered with bodies of the dead and the dying.

Then Hulmu was shouting orders to his comrades and as he did the five bodyguards began to move forwards as one. A moving wall of shields from behind which deadly sword points punched and jabbed into their opponents. Sinking into any exposed flesh. The bodyguards starting to drive the remainder of the attackers back towards the bow of the barge.

Retreating into the safety of the cabin as another throwing axe thudded into the deck nearby Veda gasped. Then stooping he quickly picked up a discarded Saxon shield and prepared to face the next attack. But it did not come and moments later Veda saw that the remaining Saxons had abandoned the fight and were scrambling back onto their own ship. None willing it seemed to face Hulmu and his heavily armed comrades. The fight appeared to be over. The Saxon ship and the Glory slowly separating. The Glory starting to pull ahead and put distance between them. The swarm of dugouts losing heart.

Emerging from the cabin clutching his bloodied axe and Saxon shield Veda's breath was coming fast. His chest heaving from exertion as he quickly turned to check around. The deck of the Glory was a mess. Covered in blood, bodies and abandoned weapons - the groans and cries of the wounded ringing out. But there were no more Saxons. The enemy had been swept clean off the barge and appeared to have given up the pursuit. Pausing as the bodyguards began to move about finishing off the wounded and to inspect their bloody and effective work, Hulmu caught Veda's eye. The tough ex-centurion looking hard as nails. The brutality in his eyes remaining even as he stared at Veda. As if Veda was just another opponent to be despatched. Turning away, concealing his own contempt, Veda took a deep relieved breath as he saw that Abbe and Jorina appeared to be unhurt. Jorina looking pale. Laelian and Hannibal looking around at the carnage in disbelief. They had done it. They had seen off the attack.

Turning away Veda re-entered the cabin and a moment later he reappeared dragging Ganna with him. Moving her towards the stern where the fighting had been the fiercest he finally paused, forcing the priestess to look at the bodies strewn across the deck.

"There is your blood! There! See what you have done!" Veda cried out angrily. "They are all dead because of you. It did not have to be this way, but this is your fault! Is that enough blood to satisfy the bitch you serve."

In response Ganna said nothing. But suddenly she rounded on him. Furiously sinking her teeth into Veda's hand. Biting him as hard as she could and making Veda roar with pain. Yanking back his hand and acting on instinct Veda caught hold of the priestess and before anyone could stop him he had pushed her to the side of the barge and tumbled her overboard. The priestess landing in the water with a scream and a great splash. Watching her from the side of the Glory as her head re-emerged from the water, spluttering, her arms flailing in the Albis, Veda shot her a dark departing look. His mouth working a silent curse. Then as the Glory continued on down stream he turned his back on her.

Chapter Twenty - We have a Job to Do

It was a sunny morning and sitting on top of the iron chest out on deck Veda was repairing Caledonus's leather boot. While seated at their oars the five bodyguards plus Caledonus were slowly propelling the 'Glory' upstream. The barge steadily advancing through the placid waters, leaving ripples in her wake. The river had narrowed considerably after they had left Saxon territory behind and had started to penetrate ever deeper into the heart of free Germany. The banks of the Albis were lined with the thick and apparently endless forest and apart from a few birds hovering high overhead and a curious otter poking up from the water there was no one about. The land quiet and still. The river deserted.

Pausing his repair work Veda lifted his head to take a look around. Feeling the sun warming his face. The Saxon round shield and heavy two handed battle-axe which he had liberated from the dead attackers, lying on the deck within easy reach. It had been several days since they had been attacked outside Treva in the estuary but since then there had been no sign of pursuit. No indication that King Hadugato was coming after them and their journey up river had been largely uneventful. No one barring their route. There only contact with the locals a few tribesmen who had come out onto the river to do barter trade and try and sell them some fish. It was just as well Veda thought as his eyes came to rest upon Abbe who was sitting in Ganna's old chair beside the tiller. The Frisian resting a sword across his lap. A deliberate and provocative act. Abbe's expression brooding and dark as the night while at his side, still not fully recovered from her leg wound, Jorina was holding the tiller, steering the barge up the river. Her long blond plaited hair snaking away down her back. A throwing axe stuffed into the belt of her tunic.

The tension on-board the 'Glory' was becoming intolerable Veda thought. The crew now firmly divided into two camps. Both sides confined to the barge, their circumstances forcing them to co-exist. The silence between them now pregnant with growing hostility and suspicion. Abbe and Laelian were now not only not talking to each other but they also had to be physically kept apart. The threat of violence between those two had become real. Laelian and his men had taken to sleeping at the bow of the barge while he, Abbe, Jorina and Caledonus had taken to occupying the stern. Nor could the crew agree on a guard duty roster or even eat together. It could not last Veda thought as he lowered his eyes turning his head towards the two handed axe lying out on deck. The only thing they had been able to agree upon was that they had a job to do. The mission to deliver the gold and renew the alliance with the Thuringii would continue.

Finishing his repairs to Caledonus's boot Veda stiffly rose to his feet and after handing the boot back to his freedman he came up to Jorina and silently took over the tiller allowing her a break. The girl swapping places with him and sitting down on the chest containing the gold.

"I am going to kill that arsehole," Abbe murmured darkly from his chair. His hand resting upon the sword in his lap as he glared along the deck towards the spot at the bow where Laelian was sitting urgently scratching notes into a soft wood letter with a iron pointed stylus. While sitting opposite the legate, Hannibal appeared to be talking to him in a quiet voice. "Laelian reckons we are just another a day away from the confluence of the Albis and the Marsh rivers," Veda replied ignoring Abbe's comment. "Once we reach the confluence we should be in Thuringian territory. Friendly territory. The legate says that we will go ashore at the junction of the two rivers and continue our journey from there on foot until we reach Thor's Oak."

"He thinks that does he!" Abbe snarled, his mouth curling in contempt. "And what does the legate know about these inland water ways or this country? Walaric should have been here to guide us towards his people. He knew the way better than any of us. If he had been here we would never have taken that sorceress on-board nor got into that fight. I was right. I was fucking right about Ganna!"

"Walaric is dead, father," Jorina retorted sharply from where she was listening in to the conversation.

"Listen," Veda said looking grave as he held onto the tiller, his eyes fixed upon the river ahead. "Laelian says that from the confluence of the rivers to Thor's Oak should be a three day walk at most. We are to meet our allies at Thor's Oak on the day of the full moon of the fifth month. It coincides with the Thuringian Thing which is normally held there too. Laelian says that Thor's Oak is a sacred grove containing the ancient tree. The Thuringii believe that the god Thor sometimes resides within the tree. It is a holy place for them."

"I know what Thor's Oak is," Abbe snapped, scowling. "The question is does the legate know how to get there without a proper guide? I think he is just making things up as he goes along."

"We will find our way there," Veda said with a sigh. "But you are right. It would have been better if Walaric was here but we should be able to cope. Maybe we can get some of the locals to show us the way."

Muttering something under his breath Abbe remained unhappy. Then he rose to his feet grasping his sword and turned to gaze out across the water at the dense forest beyond.

"There is something else," Abbe said at last, frowning as he peered at the deep forest. "I can't shake this feeling that we are being watched. Someone is following us."

"Watched! Followed!" Veda exclaimed as he hurriedly turned to gaze at the thick forest that lined the shore. "By who? King Hadugato and his men?"

"I don't know," Abbe grumbled. "Call it an old sea dogs sense but I just can't shake the feeling. We are being watched. Someone is following us," he said raising and pointing his arm at the shore. "Someone is out there in the forest tracking us."

For a moment Veda said nothing as he stared at the forest. But along the shore he could see no one about. The woods still and quiet. Then he shifted his gaze to Abbe and then to Jorina who simply rolled her eyes.

***

It was afternoon when Veda heard Laelian calling out to him. The legate beckoning for him to come on over. Rising from his spot where he had been sitting on top of the iron chest Veda frowned as he made his way over to the cabin in the middle of the barge where the legate was waiting for him flanked by Hulmu. What did the man want from him now? Halting before Laelian Veda folded his arms across his chest ignoring the ex-centurion's cold, menacing stare. Gazing back at him Laelian was sporting a strangely resigned look as if he had come to a decision from which there would be no going back.

"By tomorrow we should reach the confluence of the Albis and the Marsh," Laelian said. "We are not too far from our destination. Thor's Oak is only a few days walk from here. So the time has come for me to issue you with your instructions. Once we get to the mouth of the Marsh we will need to find a suitable hiding spot where we can anchor the ship. I want you to tell Abbe that he and his daughter shall remain behind to guard the ship and await our return. You," Laelian said pointing a finger at Veda, "and your freedman will accompany us to the meeting. You will need to carry the gold. Like I said I expect it will be a three day walk but we should be in friendly territory."

"All right, I will inform the captain," Veda said stiffly.

Facing Veda, Laelian hesitated and as it was clear that there was something else on his mind. Something weighty. The legate once again regarding him with that strange look of resignation. As if something momentous was about to take place. Something irrevocable.

"We need to talk," Laelian said at last lowering his voice. "There are things that you need to know and things I need to know."

"Really?" Veda said a little amused smile crept onto his lips.

"When we get to Thor's Oak I shall conduct the negotiations with our allies," Laelian said raising his chin, his eyes gleaming. "I shall agree the renewal of the treaty of alliance and you must do all the things that your bank has instructed you to do. That is why you are here. That is your job."

For a moment Laelian hesitated. Then he continued.

"Now I am going to be honest with you Veda. I have tried to be your friend. I have tried to be kind to you but now I have run out of time. You will discover the truth sooner or later anyway so it is better if it comes from me now. So here it is. I will let you into a secret. The conditions of our alliance with the Thuringii," Laelian said smoothly, "which I negotiated with them, state that Rome pays an annual subsidy of fifty pounds of gold coins. That is the deal."

"Fifty pounds of gold," Veda exclaimed as a little colour shot into his cheeks. "But I am carrying sixty-six pounds of gold. The bank has paid you sixty-six pounds of gold. What do you need the…"

Veda's words abruptly ended as he stared at Laelian. Then Veda looked away sharply as he understood.

"We take all the risk getting here," Laelian said with a little shrug. "We deserve some of the spoils. It's simple. The

Thuringii get their fifty pounds of gold subsidy. The bank and the authorities believe that the subsidy costs sixty-six pounds. The excess money, all sixteen pounds of gold, is divided up between myself and my men. Each gets a cut dependent on their rank. And I am going to cut you in too Veda," Laelian continued watching him carefully, "at the same payment level as Hulmu here. The only thing you need to do is never tell soul about this arrangement. And as for your report to the bank, we shall write that together you and I. So what do you say? Do we have an agreement?"

Staring back at Laelian Veda remained silent.

"Is that what happened to Jonas?" Veda said at last. "You offered the same deal to him. To cut him in on your little scam but he refused and you murdered him in order to keep him from exposing your corruption?"

Taking a deep breath Laelian turned to look out across the river with a sudden faraway look. "What happened to Jonas was unfortunate," the legate replied. "He was stubborn and too honest. He threatened to report the matter to the bank on our return and well," Laelian said with another little shrug, "he left me with no other choice. He had to be silenced."

"I see," Veda said coldly. "But did you really have to torture Jonas? Walaric told me that he was nailed to a tree. That someone even cut off his cock and balls. Was that really necessary?"

"Yeah someone did that," Hulmu said glaring at Veda with a challenging look as he reached up to touch the little pouch that hung suspended from around his neck. "I keep them here. His cock and balls. Jonas's power is now mine. I have taken away his manhood. He belongs to me now."

Staring at Hulmu Veda's mouth curled with disgust and fury but he restrained himself from taking a step forwards and punching the ex-centurion. For a moment Veda did not speak.

Then he turned his head and saw that Abbe and Jorina were silently watching him from the tiller.

"It's fraud," Veda said at last turning back to Laelian. "It's corruption. You are stealing money from the state. From my bank. From Rome."

"So we are," Laelian said smiling. "But do you really think we are the only ones who are stealing from the state? Grow up Veda. Everyone is stealing what they can from Rome. Come on Veda. Don't act like you don't know that it is going on. Like I said, we all take the risk. We are owed our cut. No harm done eh."

"So are you in with us or not?" Hulmu snapped with sudden impatience as his hand dropped to rest upon the hilt of his sword.

Lowering his eyes Veda hesitated. It was clear that the offer was not an offer at all but an ultimatum. For if he refused the offer Laelian would have him killed. Hulmu appeared to be already itching to get on with it. And then when he was dead they would probably murder his companions too. To get rid of any witnesses. Laelian would invent another tragic story. A report would be filed and everyone would forget about it and move on and no one would ever know the truth. He really had no choice Veda thought.

"All right. Screw it," Veda said looking up at Laelian with a sudden amused smile. "I agree and I want my cut and afterwards we will write my report together like you suggested."

"Good man," Laelian said looking not completely convinced as beside him Hulmu appeared disappointed. "So you will keep your mouth shut about our little arrangement, right? I don't want you even speaking a word of this to that freedman of yours or Abbe and his daughter. Got that?"

"Of-course. I understand. I will keep it to myself," Veda said smiling at the legate. "Because if I don't I know Hulmu here is more than keen on sliding a knife under my ribs. I won't say a word. I want to live and grow old."

"Good," Laelian said nodding, scrutinising Veda with a careful look. "I am glad to hear it. But if you fuck me," the legate snarled suddenly, his face darkening as he took a menacing step towards Veda. "I will not only have Hulmu cut out your heart while you are still alive. I will send him to pay your family a visit too. You don't want to make an enemy out of me!"

Watching Laelian and Hulmu returning to the front of the barge Veda's smile slowly vanished. Then he took a deep breath and lowered his eyes. "Was this how it happened to you, brother?" he muttered to himself as he recalled the soldiers the Praetorian prefect Balista had sent to his home on the isle of Vectis. The soldiers who had come bearing instructions to arrest him and his whole family and burn down his estate because of something, Corbulo his older brother had done in the east. An act of collective punishment.

Taking over the tiller from Jorina, Veda said nothing, aware of Abbe and Jorina waiting for him to speak. His eyes fixed upon the river up ahead.

"Just give the order," Abbe said suddenly in a quiet voice. "And I will kill them all while they are sleeping."

"They murdered Jonas," Veda replied quietly at last. "Laelian is stealing public funds to line his own pocket and that of his men. Sixteen pounds of gold. He made me an offer to cut me in exchange for keeping quiet about it and filing a false report with the bank and I agreed. I had no choice."

Swearing softly to himself Abbe looked down at the deck.

"Tomorrow Laelian reckons we will reach the mouth of the Marsh river," Veda continued. "From there we continue on foot to Thor's Oak. He says that you are to remain behind and guard the 'Glory' and await our return."

"Veda," Abbe said speaking in a soft and paternal voice, "they are going to kill you. Once you are alone with them the legate will kill you. At some point he is going to realise that you are just too great a risk. He is going to figure out soon that he cannot trust you."

"I know," Veda replied coolly. "So tomorrow we are going to part company with these murderers. Prepare yourselves," he said turning to Abbe. "Tonight we sleep with your weapons close. I will take the first watch."

Chapter Twenty-One - Fracture

Anchored alongside the bank just below the confluence of the two rivers, the 'Glory' was a hive of activity. The crew moving about on deck gathering their possessions together as they prepared to continue their journey on foot. Felix and Hannibal were down in the hold handing up supplies to the others. While Hulmu and Thiemo had already gone ashore and were guarding the landing site. Weapons drawn. The soldiers clutching their shields. Watching the forest.

It was afternoon and drizzling. The sombre skies overcast and the men were clad in their ponchos. Their hoods pulled down around their shoulders. While the current gently tugged at the "Glory' trying to coax the Frisian barge back down river, back home. Strapping the heavy two handed battle-axe across his back, Veda paused to quickly look around. The Marsh river was less than a third of the width of the Albis which even this far in-land was still some two hundred yards wide. The placid waters flowing northwards from their source in the Giant mountains. The tributary true to its name. For its banks were swampy, waterlogged with snow melt and lined with tall reed beds among which he could hear and see nesting birds. While beyond the flat uninspiring country was covered in thick virgin forest that appeared endless. The land still and quiet.

Finishing checking and securing his heavy backpack Caledonus quickly caught Veda's eye as some unspoken message past between them. The freedman was looking tense. His axe was stuffed into his leather belt. Saying nothing Veda turned towards Abbe and Jorina who were watching the preparations in silence from their position beside the tiller. Making no effort to help. Abbe with his arms folded across his chest. Jorina looking strangely tense as she fidgeted with a small Frankish throwing axe. For a moment Veda's eyes met Abbe's prompting a resigned look to appear on the Frisian's face.

"Veda!" Laelian called out as he came up to him. "We are nearly ready to go. Get the chest onto the land and then wait for me onshore. You and your freedman will have to carry the gold to Thor's Oak unless we can find you some transport. Atticus! Come here and give them a hand and for god-sake do not drop that chest into the water! You hear me!"

"Sure," Veda replied without bothering to look at the legate. Gesturing at Caledonus he moved over to the spot where the iron chest containing the gold was sitting out on deck together with a long iron slavers chain. Leaving his backpack behind Caledonus hurriedly joined him and together they lifted up the chest by its handles. Shuffling across to the edge of the barge Veda quickly placed the chest back down on the deck. Then just as Atticus was about to clamber over the side of the hull and down into the dugout that was floating in the river below Veda pushed the mercenary out of the way.

"My job," Veda growled as he hurriedly slipped over the side of the boat and lowered himself into the dugout. Looking up as Caledonus and Atticus began to carefully and slowly lower the heavy chest down to him using the iron chain, Veda grasped hold of it, guiding it, before securing the chest at the bottom of the simple craft. His freedman hurriedly retrieving the chain. Atticus slipping over the side of the Glory and into the water. The mercenary gasping at the cold as he caught hold of the dugout and steadied it. For a moment sitting alone in the dugout waiting for Caledonus to join him, Veda looked pensive as he gazed at the elaborately designed chest with the proud logo of the B&M Brothers banking house engraved into it. Then at last with the two of them and the gold crammed into the dugout he turned towards the shore and using his paddle he covered the short distance between boat and river bank before the nose of the dugout got stuck in the soft marshy ground. Emerging from the river next to the dugout Atticus shook himself, water streaming from his clothes as Hulmu appeared on the bank above.

"Get the chest onto higher ground," Laelian called out from the deck of the Glory as he observed the work. "And Atticus bring back the dugout. We are going ashore."

Saying nothing Veda did as asked and together with Caledonus he carried the chest up onto the bank and into a small field beyond before setting it down in the long green grass. Straightening up Veda once again turned to look around as Hulmu stood guard nearby, with Thiemo positioned closer to the edge of the forest. The two armed soldiers watching the woods for signs of trouble. And for a moment, standing gathered around the chest, the three of them were left alone as they waited for the others to join them. The ex-centurion was silent. Then Hulmu turned to Veda, his eyes gleaming with sudden malice.

"You owe me Veda. Because of you all of us are now getting a smaller share of the gold. If it were up to me," the Goth hissed. "I would not have shared anything with you. You don't deserve anything. You are fortunate that the legate is a generous man."

"One day I am going to cut your throat," Veda replied calmly. "And then I am going to cut off your balls and feed them to the pigs for what you did to Jonas. That is a promise."

"Ha! You think that you are the first man who has tried to kill me," Hulmu said smiling cruelly as he reached up to touch the small pouch that hung around his neck. "Join the queue. I don't care. I would have let that priestess burn you alive. It would have been cheaper for all of us. Know this Veda," Hulmu added taking a step towards Veda. "I do not forget a face or an insult. Anyone who gets in my way finds an early death. You had better watch yourself when you go to sleep tonight. Now that too is a promise."

Turning towards the Glory anchored alongside the river bank Veda remained silent, ignoring Hulmu as the three of them waited for the others to join them. Spotting Abbe standing at the stern Veda abruptly raised his hand in a sombre farewell gesture which was immediately reciprocated from the deck of the Glory. Then Veda turned to look at the iron chest and as he did he sighed. While at his side Caledonus was looking increasingly nervous.

Finally Laelian and the others appeared ashore. The legate and his staff leaving Abbe and Jorina behind on the Glory. No one bothering to say goodbye to each other. The two parties glad to be rid of each other. Relieved that they no longer had to share the boat. Jorina retrieving the dugout from the deck using the iron chain which had been attached to it. Bearing a stern look Laelian approached the spot where Veda and Caldonus were waiting with the gold. His men carrying their weapons, personal belongings and supplies in Roman army marching packs that were slung across their backs.

"Let's go!" Laelian called out gesturing towards the forest. "We have a three day walk ahead of us to Thor's Oak and only four days before the full moon. The Germans may not be a punctual race but I am. We are not going to be late for the meeting. So let's go. Let's go!"

"Hang on," Veda suddenly called out. "Caledonus has forgotten his pack. It's still on the Glory. We will need to go back and get it. It's got all our belongings inside. We won't be a moment."

"Wait!" Laelian called out sharply, frowning. "Your freedman will go and fetch it. You Veda will stay here."

"It's a heavy pack Sir," Veda protested. "It would be better if both of us went. He will need help. It won't do if it were to fall into the water and get wet."

"No. Stop wasting my time Veda," Laelian growled refusing to budge. "Your freedman goes. You stay here. Now tell him to get a move on. You are holding us up!"

Swearing silently to himself it was Veda's turn to look annoyed. But left with no choice he turned and gestured to Caledonus that he should obey and get going. The freedman starting out towards the river bank as if he had been expecting to do so. Idly turning to gaze at the Glory anchored out in the river Veda took another deep breath.

"Run! Run! Now!" Veda suddenly bellowed at Caledonus as without warning he broke away from the others, sprinting towards the river. And Caledonus too did not need to be told twice. The young freedman abruptly joining the mad rush towards the water's edge. The two of them running for all they were worth. His heart pounding in his chest. Gasping for breath. The heavy two handed axe strapped across his back slowing him down, Veda did not look back as he heard a sudden yell before he threw himself headlong into the water. His head going under and into a green watery world full of bubbles. Then he surfaced. His arms flailing and frantically slashing through the water as he battled towards the Glory.

Behind him he suddenly heard more yelling. Then Laelian's booming outraged voice.

"Bring him back! Bring him back!"

Grasping hold of the netting that hung over the side of the Glory, Veda turned his head and was just in time to see an axe come hurtling towards him. The blade thudding into the hull next to his head while just a short distance away Hulmu stood on the river bank. The Goth gasping for breath as if he too had been running. His cruel eyes fixed on Veda. The man pulling free his knife as he prepared to enter the river in pursuit and finish the job. But then as Felix came rushing up to support his colleague an arrow suddenly buried itself in his stomach. The impact stopping Felix in his tracks. A look of surprise and astonishment appearing on the bodyguard's face as he staggered backwards before sitting down on the ground.

"Stay back!" Stay back you scum!" Abbe roared from the deck above Veda's head. The captain training his bow and arrow at the men ashore. And as if to reinforce the message Jorina appeared and with a fierce and furious cry she flung an axe at Hulmu which the ex-centurion dodged. The attack however forcing him back and away from the river's edge. Grasping hold of the netting, his body half submerged in the river, Veda groaned. On the land Laelian's men had caught Caledonus before he had been able to reach the water. And as he looked on Atticus hauled the young freedman back to his feet as Laelian came marching up. The legate looking furious as he spotted Veda clinging to the Glory's hull.

"What is the meaning of this?" Laelian roared. "What do you think you are doing?"

"Just say the word Veda," Abbe bellowed from the deck directly above him, "and I will shoot the bastard!"

Noticing Abbe standing on the deck training his bow and arrow at him Laelian's expression abruptly changed and he hurriedly fell back behind the protection of his men's shields as Hulmu dragged the wounded Felix back towards his colleagues. Abbe's arrow still sticking out of his stomach. The rest of the soldiers making no attempt to attack the barge.

Grimacing Veda started to clamber up the rope netting, hurriedly catching hold of Jorina's hand as she helped him clamber up and back into the barge. Once on-board Veda hastily turned to face Laelian and his gang.

"Mutiny!" Laelian shouted, his face turning red with anger as he glared back at Veda from the shore. "This is mutiny Veda! You are going to be punished for this! You have gone too far."

"No it is you who has gone too far," Veda roared back. "It is you Laelian who has lost your way. When I get back I am going to make certain that everyone who cares to listen will know about you. About what you have done. About the corrupt man you are. I am going to destroy you!"

"Big words!" Laelian jeered. "But I have your man and I have the gold. You have nothing. Do you think I make idle threats Veda. You and your family are dead if you speak so much as a rude word about me. And even if you were to make it back no one will believe you. It would be my word against yours and who do you think people are going to believe."

Gazing across the water at Laelian Veda exhaled, steadying his breathing, controlling himself, his clothes soaked. Then his eyes came to rest upon Caledonus who was being held captive by Atticus and Thiemo. The freedman forced down onto his knees with a knife at his throat.

"All right. You have the advantage. You have the gold," Veda shouted. "But I have the only key that unlocks that chest. Good luck trying to open it without my key. That chest is state of the art. It was built to be unbreakable. You won't be able to open it. Only I can with this key," Veda added pulling the iron key from around his neck and holding it up in the air for all to see. "So I will make a deal with you Laelian. I will swap you my key in exchange for my freedman. Return him to me alive and unharmed and I will give you the key. Then after that we can all go on our merry way. You have the gold. You can complete your mission."

For a moment Laelian stared back at Veda in silence as he appeared to be thinking through the offer. While Hannibal turned and quickly said something to his boss. Then more silence. The river and the shore quiet.

"All right Veda, the key for your freedman," Laelian shouted. "But don't you dare trick me again! You hear me!"

"Done," Veda bellowed. "Release him now and I will give you the key."

On the shore no one moved. Then Laelian appeared to say something to his men and a moment later Caledonus had been released. Stumbling towards the water's edge with Hulmu and Atticus escorting him the young freedman hurriedly turned to look back as if he were expecting to be ambushed and struck down by an axe or spear. But none came. Laelian and the rest of his men remaining where they were and as Caledonus reached the river and hurriedly entered the water, swimming towards the Glory, Veda threw the heavy iron key towards Hulmu who caught it with one hand.

Leaning over the side of the hull Veda hurriedly pulled Caledonus up and onto the deck. The freedman soaked and shivering uncontrollably from the cold and shock.

"You all right?" Veda said quickly inspecting Caledonus with a concerned look - the freedman simply nodding in reply. Straightening up Veda turned to look across the water towards Laelian and as he did so the others did not notice the sudden subtle change in Veda's expression.

"Raise the anchor captain," Veda called out to Abbe without taking his eyes of Laelian. "It's time to leave. Do it now. Hurry."

"You gave them the gold," Jorina blurted out as she turned to stare at Veda in confusion. "Now they have everything and we have nothing."

Ignoring the girl Veda kept his eyes fixed upon the party of Romans on the shore as Laelian and his men gathered around the iron chest. Quickly Laelian inserted the key into the lock and opened the strong box. Then the legate froze. For a long moment he did not move. As if in shock. Then frantically he pushed the chest over onto its side and as he did so a heap of white sand poured out into the long green grass. Staring at the heap of white sand in disbelief Laelian's face went bright red. Before he swiftly straightened up and turned to stare across the water towards Veda. And as he did Veda turned to glance at Caledonus and the two of them shared a little secret and triumphant smile.

"You bastard! You traitorous scum bag!" Laelian roared from the shore, his arms flailing in the air in furious impotence as the Glory slowly started to drift away on the current and out into the middle of the river. "You tricked me Veda! Where is my gold! Where is my fucking gold!"

"The gold was not in the chest," Jorina exclaimed with a fierce disbelieving blush. Then she turned to stare at Veda with large confused eyes. "I don't understand. Where then is the gold?"

In response Caledonus crouched beside his back pack and opening the top he grinned at Jorina as he beckoned her over, revealing to her a mass of gold Roman coins crammed inside the pack.

"The gold was in Caledonus's back-pack all along," Veda said smiling. "All of it. It has been there from the very start. We secretly transferred the gold from the chest the night after we came aboard. A security precaution. In case of trouble. We have been guarding a chest full of sand ever since."

And as the blush on Jorina's face deepened Veda caught Caledonus's eye and the two of them began to laugh. Their laughter growing louder and louder, the sound ringing out across the placid waters of the Albis.

Chapter Twenty-Two - The Making of a Hero

It was getting late in the day as the Glory drifted down the Albis. The drizzle had ceased and the Frisian barge was heading back the way it had come just hours earlier. Heading downstream in the direction of the sea. The current propelling them onwards without the need for the oars. Standing at the tiller beside Abbe who was steering the craft through the water, Veda looked grave. His eyes searching the river bank and the water up ahead. It had been several hours since they had so abruptly parted company with Laelian and his men but there had been no sign of them. No sign of a pursuit.

"I reckon we can make it back to the sea in five days," Abbe said chatting away and looking relieved. "Faster if we were to travel at night. We could be back home within ten days with favourable weather and no mishaps. There are just four of us left now so no point in trying to row upstream any more. Not against the current. We don't have the manpower for that. And no sign of the legate!" Abbe added turning to Veda with a cheerful grin. "He's given up. Makes sense I suppose. He can see that we are heading back home and he knows that he stands no chance of keeping up with us and retrieving the gold. I reckon he is going to return to the Rhine by the overland route. Two hundred miles through Frankish territory. Good luck with that. Ha ha! Maybe those Franks will gut him and put his head on a spike. No point in him attending the Thuringian Thing either without that gold is there! No the bastard lost and I hope he dies. You outsmarted him Veda. He's going back home with his tail between his legs. He's done. He's finished."

"We're not going back home," Veda replied, keeping his eyes upon the river bank.

"What!" Abbe exclaimed looking startled.

"Not yet," Veda replied sombrely. "You are right, Abbe. Laelian does not have much of a choice now but to return to the Rhine. Without the gold he has nothing. His best course of action now would be to try and safely return to Roman territory and report his version of events to the authorities. He is no doubt going to blacken my good name but right now we have bigger problems to deal with. Even if Laelian were to ask Postumus for a new subsidy of gold and plan to return to the Thuringians at a later date, to renew our alliance, it would be too late. The Thuringians are likely to take the legate's absence at Thor's Oak as as signal that Rome is not interested in renewing the treaty. They will surely be insulted by our absence and accuse us of breaking our word. That cannot be allowed to happen. So as I do have the gold, I am going to complete our mission."

"You!" Abbe blurted out as across the deck Jorina stopped what she had been doing and turned to stare at the two men in shock.

"Yes," Veda said looking serious. "Caledonus and I are going to leave for the Thuringii tribal council at Thor's Oak and I am going to renew Rome's treaty of alliance with these Germans. I am going to give them the gold. This is why we are out here. I am not giving up now. I am going to complete the legate's mission for him."

"But is that not dangerous?" Jorina called out as she hurried over looking concerned. "There are just four of us left now."

"It's not your job," Abbe exclaimed staring at Veda with a frown.

"The treaty of alliance has to be renewed," Veda said patiently. "There is no one else who can do it. So it has to be me."

"Have you ever made an international treaty with a German tribe before? Renewing the treaty was the legate's job," Abbe said sounding incredulous. "I know he is an arsehole but Laelian was at-least a trained Roman diplomat. He knew how to negotiate treaties."

"How difficult can it be," Veda said with a little shrug. "The gold will give me all the authority that I need." For a moment Veda paused before turning to Abbe and Jorina with a sudden fond smile.

"Don't you see. Rome needs his treaty," Veda said. "The frontier communities need this alliance. People's lives and livelihoods are at stake. Anything that can help stop the Franks from raiding our land is a good thing. I have seen with my own eyes what damage these raids are doing. People are depending on us to get this done and I am not going to let them down. I have to try. So once it grows dark Caledonus and I will slip ashore and head for the Thuringian Thing with the gold. You are free to go home Abbe. I am releasing you from your commitments and I am going to pay you double the payment Laelian promised you. Consider it a danger bonus. For the risks you have both taken."

"No," Jorina blurted out hurriedly shaking her head.

Standing holding the tiller Abbe took a deep breath. Then at last he turned to Veda, with a changed expression.

"A man willing to risk his life for others who will never know what he did," Abbe said in a strained sounding voice. "A man who does his duty to Rome when others think only of stealing. A man who considers the greater good above his own. Rome it seems can still inspire greatness in men. All right Veda. I see you. I see you now. I recognise what kind of man you are at heart."

"No father, you cannot let him go like that," Jorina protested, her youthful face suddenly close to tears. "He's going to get himself killed!"

"Veda makes his own decisions," Abbe replied glancing at his daughter with a sudden fond look. "He is and always will be his own man. But I have faith in him. And he won't be completely alone. We will find a spot along the river," Abbe said turning back to Veda and nodding, "where we will hide the ship and await your return. We will wait for you for ten days."

Staring at her father Jorina said nothing. Then abruptly she turned and fled, her face averted so that none could see her emotion.

"Thank you," Veda said quietly as he watched the girl go. "But if we do not return within ten days you must leave and return home. It will be too dangerous for you to wait any longer."

"She has grown fond of you," Abbe said as he too gazed at his daughter. Then his expression hardened as he once again turned to Veda. "You be careful now," the captain said in earnest, paternal voice. "Carrying that much gold is bound to ignite the curiosity and greed of any you meet. And I still cannot shake this feeling that we are being watched and followed."

"She is just sixteen," Veda said with a resigned look as he observed Jorina. "We will be all right," Veda said turning to Abbe and laying a hand on his shoulder. "The treaty of alliance with the Thuringii must be renewed. I will see to it. I will get it done and I will get back home too. We all will."

"And the sixteen pounds of excess gold?" Abbe asked raising his eyebrows.

"I will return it to the bank. All of it. The gold rightfully and legally belongs to B&M Brothers," Veda replied. "And when we get back home I will arrange for you to be paid your double share of-course," he added with a smile. "The bank cannot complain about that."

***

The vast German forest was undisturbed as Veda and Caledonus hurried on down the narrow hunters trail that twisted away out of sight among the dense mass of trees. Tall spruces were clawing at the sky as if competing to be the tallest. Majestic beech trees with their magnificent canopies staked out their territory. Competing with ancient oaks whose thick trunks whispered of ancient times long forgotten by man. The trees towering over the heads of the two men. The thick tangled undergrowth that covered much of the ground bursting with new life. The warm, optimistic spring morning filled with the occasional rustle of small creatures, buzzing insects and the cheerful chirp of unseen birds.

The two of them were alone. Veda carrying the round Saxon shield and his two handed battle-axe strapped across his back. While following close behind Caledonus was puffing from the heavy weight of the gold he was carrying inside the pack that rested upon his back. The freedman however was showing no signs of slackening. Keeping up with Veda with youthful determination and pride. The men's hobnailed boots softly scraping across the rock and leaving a faint imprint in the soft moist ground. The forest enclosing them as if it had swallowed them up. As if they belonged to it now.

Setting the pace Veda peered ahead through the trees. Trying to spot the way. His pugio knife and a small Frankish throwing axe suspended from his belt. They had left Abbe and Jorina just before dawn. Slipping away in the darkness. The captain had found a small marshy island in the middle of the Albis where hidden by the terrain and trees he had dropped his anchor. The Frisian promising to wait for him there for ten days. Jorina had given him a fond farewell kiss. The girl making her intentions and feelings towards him clear. But Jorina was just sixteen and way too young Veda thought as he plodded along the forest trail. And he'd not had the courage to tell her so. To put an end to the girl's doomed ambition.

At last coming to a halt in a small clearing Veda peered up at the sun checking their position as Caledonus came to a halt behind him. The freedman's face covered in sweat from the heavy load he was carrying.

"Come. We have to keep going. We cannot afford to waste any time," Veda said giving his freedman a wry look. "The Thuringian tribal council takes place in three days time and I do not want to be late."

Making an unintelligible sound Caledonus quickly raised a finger and pointed towards the path. Then he opened both his hands palm upwards and gave Veda a questioning look.

"No we are not lost. We're going the right way," Veda said as he understood the question. "See I can tell which way we have to go from the position of the sun. There look. There is the sun. So that way is east. That is west. So that is south which is the direction in which we must go."

Looking up at the sun Caledonus however appeared unconvinced. Turning to Veda he quickly reached up to touch his finger to his mouth, before swiftly pointing his finger at Veda and then pointed away. Frowning Veda gazed at his companion. Then he understood.

"Yes I am sure I know the way," Veda said with an amused smile. "Come on. We need to keep going."

It was getting late in the day and it had started to rain when Veda at last came to a halt on the narrow forest path with a grim, defeated look. The two men clad in their ponchos. Their hoods drawn over their heads as the rain began to grow heavier and heavier. The tree canopies providing them with some shelter. Clouds obscuring and darkening the sky while faintly in the distance the ominous rumble of thunder could be heard. The noise of the approaching storm growing stronger with each rolling clap. Pausing beside a tall spruce tree covered in moss Veda softly swore to himself. His gaze turning to look left and then right into the forest. The path ahead had come to an end in a tangle of undergrowth.

"All right, we're lost," Veda exclaimed turning to Caledonus with a frustrated look. "Fuck knows where we are! Let's find some shelter and camp for the night. There is no point stumbling around in the midst of a storm."

Hurriedly Caledonus raised both his hands with the palms facing upwards and gave Veda a questioning look.

"Somewhere dry," Veda replied answering his freedman's question. "There must be a cave around here or else we will just have to choose one of the big trees and shelter under the canopy."

Turning back the way he had just come Veda had only gone a dozen or so paces when he came to an abrupt halt. So abrupt that behind him Caledonus nearly bumped into him. Quickly Veda raised a warning fist in the air. Then he sniffed, his nose wrinkling. For a moment he did not move or say anything.

"Do you smell that?" Veda said at last quickly turning around to gaze into forest with a puzzled frown. "I can smell smoke. It's definitely smoke. It's coming from that direction."

Staring into the forest with the rain pelting down Veda hurriedly looked up at the sky but he could see nothing among the gathering gloom, nor did the forest reveal the source of the smoke. But his nose was not lying. He could smell the smoke. Something was burning. And where there was smoke there would be fire and a fire meant people. The smoke had to be coming from close by. Leaving the path he began to carefully pick his way through the undergrowth and around the trees with Caledonus following close behind. The pair of them trying to remain as quiet as possible. Creeping through the forest Veda pulled his knife free from his belt, his eyes darting about, his nose twitching.

It was some time later when Veda came to another abrupt halt, his fist silently raised in warning to Caledonus behind him. Slowly settling down on his haunches Veda softly swore as through the trees he spotted the hut. The lonely building was nestling in a small forest clearing and from a hole in its steeply sloping thatched roof that reached nearly to the ground, a stream of smoke was billowing upwards. Peering at the hut Veda slowly exhaled. His eyes studying the home. Then quickly he shifted his gaze to the clearing and the edge of the forest but there was no one about. No other buildings. The clearing was deserted. The hut all on its own as if it were an outcast.

For a moment Veda did not move. Then swearing softly again he straightened up and started out towards the hut.

***

Sitting inside the hut huddled around the small crude table with a crackling fire burning in the hearth, Veda and Caledonus watched in silence as the old man poured the honey mead into three wooden cups. Two of which were badly chipped as if they had not been used for a long time. The German's hand trembling. The man was old. Well into his sixties with thinning grey hair and a tight drawn face that hinted at a hard life. Finishing his task the German stiffly sat back down on his stool and raised his cup in a silent toast, observing his two guests with a little puzzled expression. Returning the silent toast Veda took a sip of the mead as sitting beside him Caledonus turned to stare at the solitary cow, the goat and the dog who were watching him from the other side of the hut. The animals sharing the home with their human owner. While outside in the darkness the storm continued unabated. The wind howling and whining as it rushed around the hut and the crash of thunder and the heavy patter of the rain lashed the forest.

"Romans," the old German said looking down at the table. "I don't think I have ever had Romans come and pay me a visit before."

"We're on our way to the Thuringian tribal council," Veda replied in German as he struggled to understand the old man's thick version of German. "We have brought trade goods with us which we intend to sell there," he added gesturing at the heavy back-pack that was resting against Caledonus's legs.

"I see. I see," the man muttered nodding. Then he turned to study Caledonus with a sudden curious look.

"Thank you for your hospitality," Veda continued raising his cup. "I'm afraid we got lost in the forest today. I was hoping that you would be able to show us how we can get to Thor's Oak? We can pay you for your help? We just need to know how to get there."

"No, no need for payment," the old German said with a little dismissive wave of his hand, his eyes still fixed upon Caledonus. "I will help you. The storm will blow itself out by morning and you can be on you way then. I will draw you a map of how to get to his Oak. It's not too far away from here. You are welcome here Roman. I am just glad for your company. The animals," the man said with a sigh, stiffly turning towards the three beasts who were watching him in silence, "they are all that I have but they make for poor conversation. It has been a long time since anyone visited me. Since I spoke with anyone."

"Thank you, Sir," Veda said inclining his head in gratitude. "You live here alone?"

"Yes," the German nodded sombrely taking another sip from his cup. "Since the raiders came and murdered my wife and took away my daughters. But that was a long time ago."

"I am sorry to hear that," Veda said lowering his eyes.

"Your man," the German said suddenly gesturing at Caledonus who was watching their host with a guarded uneasy expression from across the table. "He does not talk. I see someone cut out his tongue. Has he always been like that?"

Glancing at Caledonus, Veda hesitated.

"Yes," he said at last. "Since he was still a small boy. My family - we bought him in a slave market. He is from the north of Britain and he was too young to be able to tell us why his tongue was cut out or how he ended up becoming a slave. He cannot read or write," Veda added with a shrug. "So no one knows why he is like he is but he has served my family loyally for many years."

Scrutinising Caledonus the old German remained silent. Then his face softened and he nodded.

"When a man has his tongue cut out," the German said, "it is normally because he is being punished for something he said. For instance, blasphemy against the gods or even for spreading malicious gossip. But it could also be that the boy saw something he was not supposed to see and that the guilty, the people who did this to him, they cut out his tongue so that he could not tell anyone what he had seen. They mutilated him in order to shut him up. And if that is the case then your man was not being punished. Instead he is a victim of a crime." For a moment the old German remained silent. His eyes studying Caledonus as if he were judging him. While seated at the table Caledonus had suddenly gone very still.

Sitting on his stool Veda leaned back in shock before turning towards his freedman with a frown.

"Caledonus," Veda said quietly, "is that what happened to you? You were a victim of a crime before you came to our home? Is that why they cut out your tongue? So that you could not reveal what you had seen." Pausing Veda stared at his freeman. "Is that why you are so keen to learn to read and write? Because then you can tell us what happened to you?"

Ignoring Veda, Caledonus was staring at the old German. Then slowly he reached out across the table to grasp hold of the man's arm, gripping him tightly. Their host appearing untroubled by the strange act. His friendly paternal eyes gazing back at the freedman with a mysterious, knowing look. Then pulling his knife from his belt, using the sharp point, Caledonus slowly and carefully began to draw something into the wooden surface of the table. And as he gazed at what Caledonus was drawing Veda grunted looking taken aback. At last leaning back on his stool Caledonus appeared to be done - his efforts leaving three stick men figures carved into the wood. Two small figures and one larger one. For a moment no one spoke. Then closely watching the old German, Caledonus leaned forwards again and carefully scratched a cross through the larger figure using his knife. And as he did the old man closed his eyes.

"The larger figure is his mother," the German said quietly. "Your man says that she was killed. Perhaps she was murdered."

Staring at the drawings Veda took a deep breath. Then he reached out and his finger came to rest upon the two smaller figures. "Then that must be you," Veda said turning to Caledonus," and this," he said indicating the third figure, "must be your brother. You had a brother?"

Sat at the table Caledonus refused to look at Veda as once again he leaned forwards and quickly made some alterations to the third figure and as he saw what his freedman had done Veda gasped. "A sister," he exclaimed quickly. "You had a sister."

"And she is alive," the old German said with a strange gleam in his eye. "The girl still lives."

Sitting on his stool Caledonus remained silent. His head bowed. His face turned towards the table, refusing to look at anyone as the old German softly chuckled in delight and Veda stared at his freedman in astonishment. The silence inside the hut lengthening.

"I am so sorry Caledonus," Veda said at last, abruptly lowering his gaze with a look of shame. "I never bothered to find out what your story was. Why you are like you are. I never thought to ask you. I did not think it important. None of us did. Too long we just saw you as a slave. Someone who would do things for us. And now here you are risking your life for me. The fault is mine. This is my family's fault. For that I am sorry."

Facing the table, refusing to look up Caledonus simply nodded.

"Your man wishes to go and find his sister," the old German said in a gentle voice as he raised his cup of mead to his lips. "He thinks of nothing else. But he needs your help in doing so. I too needed help once," the man continued. "To take back my daughters from the raiders but none came to help me and so they remain lost. Their fate eats away at me every day. Do not let your man become like me," the German said quietly turning to Veda.

***

Standing at the edge of the forest clearing, packed and ready to continue his journey, Veda looked troubled as he gazed back at the lonely hut. It was morning and the storm had past leaving the forest refreshed and renewed. A clear blue sky dominated and he could smell the scent of new life all around him. The forest jubilant at the return of the sun. Standing nearby, his heavy pack containing the gold strapped across his back, his knife tucked into his belt, Caledonus too was gazing back at the hut and the figure of the old German who was standing in the doorway watching them. Taking a deep breath Veda frowned. Unable to get rid of the unsettling thought that their old host had not been a man at all but a god in human disguise. Woden or Thor or even Freyr. It was not unknown for the German gods to visit the realm of men he had often been told when he was still a boy and living in the Colonia on the Rhine. And they would often come in disguise, parting wisdom to those in need or falsehoods and trickery to those less deserving. There had certainly been something strange about the old man Veda thought as he slowly shook his head. Then raising his hand in farewell to the German he turned and started out into the forest.

***

It was afternoon and sitting resting upon the boulder in the midst of a cheerful gurgling stream Veda was eating a piece of cheese while nearby Caledonus was carefully bathing his bare feet in the cold water. The two of them taking a break. The pack containing the gold resting against a tree trunk. The dense forest around them quiet and peaceful.

"You should have told me that you had a sister," Veda said at last turning to Caledonus. "You should have told me that you needed my help. And of-course I will help you find her."

Standing in the middle of the stream, the cold water coming up to his knees, Caledonus turned to Veda and quickly, using his hands, he signalled to him and in response, Veda looking sour, turned away. "Yeah I know. I don't always listen and I have not always cared. I can be a prick sometimes. You are right," Veda muttered. "Listen," he continued. "When we get back home we will start looking for her. For your sister. Maybe I can get the bank to help. Maybe we can find out what happened to her but don't get your hopes up. It's going to be a long shot. It must have been ten years since you last saw her and anything could have happened to her during that time and if she is beyond the wall in the north, well then that makes tracking her down even more difficult. So don't get too excited. Chances are that we are not going to find her."

Looking unperturbed Caledonus fixed Veda with a determined look and quickly made a sign using his hands.

"You think that she is still alive. All right," Veda said looking unconvinced. "Just like what the old man back there said then. Fine."

Emerging from the stream the young freedman hurriedly dried his feet before slipping on his boots and turning towards Veda.

"You are saying that Cata likes Senovara very much," Veda said with a frown as he tried to read his freedman's next communication. In response Caledonus simply nodded followed by a grin.

"Yeah I suppose she does," Veda said looking away with an unamused look. "That slippery banker can weasel his way into anything. He knows just how to say all the right words. He's a tricky bastard."

Veda was about to say something else when he froze. From the forest, far away in the distance he had suddenly heard a noise and as he caught the look on Caledonus's face he saw that his freedman had also heard it. The youth's face suddenly looking troubled. Then Veda heard the noise again. The barking of a pack of dogs.

Swearing softly to himself Veda rose to his feet and turned to stare into the forest in the direction from which the noise had come.

"We need to go," he said at last hurriedly gesturing for Caledonus to retrieve the pack containing the gold.

Looking over his shoulder as he heard the barking dogs again Veda hurried on through the forest with Caledonus close behind. The two of them moving as fast as they could. Weaving in and out among the trees. Their boots slipping rapidly across the earth and rocks, sending small animals scurrying away into the undergrowth. Swearing softly Veda turned his attention back to the path ahead. The sound of the dogs appeared to be closer than before. Someone appeared to be on their trail. Someone was coming after them but who and why? Had Laelian somehow managed to pick up his trail? Was the legate coming for the gold? Whoever it was they would be up to no good Veda thought darkly.

Plunging on past the trees the two of them fled. Caledonus gasping for breath burdened by the heavy load he was carrying. Veda now and then shooting anxious glances over his shoulder. The sound of the pursuing dogs would not go away. The excitement in the animal's barking now unmistakeable. They were drawing closer. They were gaining. Then from the forest Veda suddenly heard human voices shouting to each other and as he heard them a pang of fear shot up his spine. The voices were speaking in German. The men sounding excited by the thrill of the hunt. There could be no doubt now. He was being chased.

Swearing out loud Veda pushed on, now half running through the forest but Caledonus was struggling to keep up. The youth puffing and gasping for breath - his face set with determination. Sweat pouring down his face. They were never going to be able to hide or escape from those dogs Veda thought with growing despair. The beasts had his scent. His pursuers were gaining on him. What did they want? He could guess. Abbe had been right when he'd said he thought they were being watched. Grimacing, his chest heaving from exertion, Veda hurriedly turned to look around but among the forest there was no natural place for him to make a stand. The trees rustling gently in the breeze as if they were laughing at him.

"We keep going," Veda gasped as Caledonus came hurrying towards him. "We have to keep going."

Racing on through the forest the two of them refused to give up. But the barking of the dogs was now nearly constant. The beasts closing in rapidly followed by excited human voices shouting out to each other. The sound now terrifyingly close. The voices and barking accompanied by the crack of breaking twigs and the crash of bodies rushing through the undergrowth. Snatching another look over his shoulder Veda yelped as he saw a dark shape tearing towards him. The dog's legs flying. Its ears drawn back. The beast followed by a sprinting man naked from the waist upwards, clutching an axe.

Abruptly Veda and Caledonus burst from the forest and into a small sunlit clearing and to Veda's astonishment, set in the midst of the clearing, was an ancient tumulus. The circular grave mound was covered in earth and grass and surrounded by a ring of standing stones. The entrance to the ancient tomb, formed by two tall standing stones with one laid across them to form a passageway, had been partially broken open by grave robbers long ago. The narrow space beyond, dark as the night but just wide enough for a body to squeeze through. Instinctively Veda veered towards the entrance crying out for Caledonus to follow him. There was no time to think it through.

"Get inside. Into the passageway. Into the fucking grave!" Veda screamed. "We will make our stand here. Maybe they won't see us."

Gasping for breath Caledonus hurriedly slid his pack from his back and without hesitating he squeezed through the narrow opening dragging his baggage with him before vanishing into the darkness of the passage tomb. Pulling his double handed axe and Saxon shield from his back Veda quickly followed. Gasping as his body scraped painfully against the cold rough stone that protected the entrance to the tomb. Then he was inside and a cool still darkness enveloped him as he struggled to catch his breath. His boots crunching on old human bones that lay discarded across the earthen floor. The only light entering from the narrow partially opened entrance right in front of him. The tomb was silent except for Caledonus's heavy and rapid breathing coming from directly behind him.

Pulling his small Frankish throwing axe from his belt Veda waited, clutching the weapon in one hand and his Saxon shield in the other. His eyes fixed upon the narrow entrance and the sliver of daylight beyond. Unable to see anything that was going on outside.

Out in the clearing he could hear the excited barking of the dogs. The beasts had come to a halt in front of the tumulus and appeared to be waiting for their masters to catch up. But as Veda waited in the darkness one of the dogs suddenly thrust its head through the narrow gap, snarling and barking at him. Acting on instinct Veda slammed his axe into the dog, nearly slicing its head off. The body slumping to the ground. Gasping Veda straightened up. Then suddenly he heard voices just outside the tumulus and a moment later an arrow struck his shield sending him staggering backwards against the stone wall in shock. The attack was followed by silence. A strange unsettling silence. The dogs had quietened down. The human voices falling still as if something or someone had arrived. Then horribly close by, just a few yards away beyond the burial mound Veda suddenly heard a familiar voice and as he did he groaned.

"I know you are hiding inside the tomb," Ganna cried out in her cruel voice from just yards away. "You are trapped and surrounded Veda. I know it is just the two of you in there and that you have the gold. There is no way out and no one is coming to rescue you this time. So surrender now and I promise you that I will kill you cleanly before I consign you to the flames."

"Go fuck yourself!" Veda roared defiantly. "We're not coming out."

"Nerthus is patient," Ganna cried out. "But she is also hungry. Hungry for your blood and flesh. You cannot escape Veda. I promised you that I would sacrifice you on the altar of the earth goddess. You belong to her Veda and Nerthus always gets what she wants. Always. You cannot defy a goddess. You can hide inside that tomb but eventually you will run out of food and water and then you will be forced to come on out. I can wait for you. I can sit here and wait for days but you cannot wait as long as I can. You know it is true."

"No!" Veda yelled, "Not this time. You and your goddess can fuck off. We're not surrendering to you!"

Then Veda slumped to the ground and closed his eyes glad that the darkness hid his sudden and silent despair. Despite his bravado the high priestess was right. He was trapped. There was no way out and hunger and thirst would eventually force him to surrender. It was just a matter of time. "Looks like this is the end," Veda said at last turning towards Caledonus who was standing hidden by the darkness. "What do you say? We go out fighting. Take a few of them with us before they cut us down. We should die with a weapon in our hands," Veda said with sudden resolve without waiting for an answer. "That is how Corbulo would go. I am sure that is how he would want to go."

Outside in the clearing Veda could hear voices again. The priestess it seemed had settled down to wait him out. There was no need for her to try and drag him out of the tomb. She could afford to be patient. For a while he tried to count the voices, trying to establish how many men the priestess had brought with her. But it was impossible and he soon gave up. At last rising to his feet he snapped off the shaft of the arrow that had struck his shield. Then carefully he edged towards the narrow entrance and the shaft of light beyond but just as he was about to poke his head out for a quick peek another arrow came flying through the narrow gap, missing him by inches and whacking into the stone passage wall. Falling back with a startled gasp Veda steadied his breathing. There was no way out.

Swearing softly Veda leaned against the stone wall and closed his eyes. Then slowly he started to laugh. Here he was about to die in someone else's grave and with a fortune of gold coins in his possession. It was not how he had envisaged himself ending his days. But maybe this was the first step in his journey to hell he thought. To his final resting place among the furies of the underworld where he was destined to spend eternity for having stabbed his father to death. His rightful punishment for the crime he had committed.

Suddenly from outside the tumulus a startled cry rang out. The cry was swiftly followed by more shouts. The men sounding alarmed. As if something unexpected was happening. But from inside the passage tomb Veda could not see what was going on. Then abruptly a barbarian horn rang out. The deep growling and humming noise ringing out from within the forest.

Chapter Twenty-Three - Tonight is the Night

Winter 260/261 AD - Free Germany, Territory of the Franks, East of the Rhine

It was late in the evening and darkness had settled across the village beside the frozen lake. The ground covered in a thin layer of fresh snow. The only light and warmth coming from the burning bonfires. The fires roaring and crackling. The firelight silhouetting the twenty-seven German long-houses that clustered around the edge of the ice. The homes were made from wood, clay and thick thatch and were covered in a layer of fresh snow. Their steeply sloping roof's rising from just above the ground to a solitary pinnacle. But the night was not silent or peaceful. Gathered together on the communal green beside the frozen lake the whole village had turned out. The Franks were feasting. Horns were blaring and humming. Drums were beating. Dogs were barking and snarling at each, the beasts caught up in the excitement.

The women of the village, young and old, clad in their thick winter furs, were clapping, yelling, singing and chanting as they watched the spectacle. The women's voices full of excitement. Their cheeks blushing in the firelight. The crowd passing around mugs of beer and honey mead as the strong and distinctive scent of cannabis hung in the still winter air. A few of the older children were holding their wailing siblings in their arms. The children looking cross. The babies refusing to be silent. While the older men, those too old or sick to work, were holding hands with toddlers and those just old enough to stand on their own feet. The old men looking venerable and grave with their long beards. The mass of children easily outnumbering the adults. All observing the spectacle that was taking place on the green.

In the midst of the tight closed circle formed by the older warriors, a group of stark naked youths, all young men, were dancing. The naked males twisting, whirling, kicking and leaping about within the dangerous circle of razor sharp sword points that formed a perimeter around them. The older men standing motionless and holding their swords outstretched to form a cauldron of deadly iron points. The young men demonstrating their skill, courage and agility as they wove in between the unflinching weapons. Flirting with danger, injury and death. The women screeching in delight and some in fear.

Whirling dangerously along the edge of the sword wall, just about preventing himself from being impaled on their razor sharp points, Ignatz grinned in delight as he suddenly spotted Frieda among the crowd of spectators. The young Frankish woman was clad in her favourite brown bear skin cloak. The hood lowered to around her shoulders to reveal her spectacular blond braided hair. The pretty girl of twenty-two smiling back at him and whooping in excitement and encouragement as their eyes briefly locked.

Twisting away Ignatz nearly collided with another dancer. The two young men sliding awkwardly past each other in the confined, congested space. Frieda was his girl Ignatz thought as he whirled away, kicking his legs and bending his knees, and tonight he was going to have her at last. Tonight was the night he had been waiting so long for.

At twenty-four Ignatz had grown into a tall, handsome and broad shouldered young man. With a fine muscular physique that had been toughened and hardened by much hard outdoor work. His corn blond hair was tied up in an elaborate Suebian knot that clung to the side of his head and unlike many of the other Frankish youths he was clean shaven.

Dancing along the edge of the sword points, daring to get as close as possible without impaling himself, Ignatz suddenly spotted Henrik directly ahead of him and as he did his expression soured. The young man, Chlotar's son, was the same age as himself. A big lad - Henrik had relentlessly bullied him from the very first day upon his arrival in the Frankish village as an eight year old. The bullying, name calling and the constant fights between the two of them had never really stopped even when they had got older. The villagers tolerating the rivalry and bad blood as just one of those things. Henrik was not the brightest spark Ignatz thought but boy oh boy did he have a powerful right fist.

Whirling along the line of swords, stark naked, Henrik paused in front of a group of women before lewdly started to thrust his pelvis forwards and backwards as if he were having sex with them. The act provoking howls and peels of laughter and some less pleased reactions from the spectators. Then to Ignatz's disgust Henrik grinned and raised his arm and pointed a finger straight at Frieda, as if marking her out, but in response the girl's smile vanished and she quickly turned her face away, rejecting Henrik's attention. Dancing up to his rival, Ignatz skilfully inserted himself in between the big lad and the spectators, blocking Henrik's view of the women. Moving as Henrik moved, anticipating him as if they were synchronised. His dexterous display bringing forth roars of approval.

"You are in my way, slave!" Henrik bellowed angrily.

Whirling away just in time as the big lad lunged at him Ignatz grinned and beckoned for Henrik to try again as the crowd roared with laughter. The noise further enraging Henrik as the big lad set off after him and suddenly the dance had become a serious affair. A deadly contest of skill and agility between two sworn enemies. Falling back and dancing, his feet moving as Henrik came after him, Ignatz first dodged this way and then that way as Henrik tried to land a blow. The big lad missing on both occasions. The crowd, sensing a fight, had suddenly start to shout encouragement to their favourite. Whirling out of reach Ignatz once again turned to face his opponent as Henrik came after him, the big man no longer even bothering to dance. His angry eyes set on just inflicting as much pain and humiliation on his opponent as he could. Skilfully ducking and spinning away as Henrik swung a fist at him, Ignatz heard the crowd once again roar in approval and for a moment he secretly basked in their adulation. While the spectators voices appeared to be stoking his rival's anger and growing frustration. Then the people groaned out loud as Henrik roughly shoved another dancer, who had got in his way, into the sword points. The youth crying out as he cut himself.

Dancing away as he observed Henrik searching for him again, his opponent's face set with a look of savage determination, Ignatz grinned. He was starting to enjoy himself. The dancing. The heat from the fires. The drink. The roar of the crowd. It was becoming intoxicating. But as his gaze swept around the sword circle, searching for Frieda, he suddenly noticed Odo, his adopted father, gazing back at him from the crowd with a stern and disapproving look. The old warrior looking displeased with him. And as he saw the silent look of reproach on Odo's face the smile vanished from Ignatz's lips. This was no time to be picking a fight with his old rival he thought. If he ended up brawling with Henrik it would spoil the night he had planned with Frieda. It would ruin everything. And she was far more important than winning a fight with someone so unimportant as Henrik. Tonight after all was the night.

Abruptly Ignatz stopped dancing. Then pushing aside a sword he had turned away and was hastening out of the ring, abandoning the sword dance. His departure from the ritual being met with loud groans and cries of disappointment from the crowd and a bellow of frustration from Henrik.

The cave was shallow and located on a rocky ledge overlooking the frozen lake. The night shrouding the land while on the other side of the ice, some distance away, the bonfires from the village were visible. Glowing in the darkness. The noise of the feast just about audible. Alone. Inside the cave, beside a small crackling log fire and on a bed of soft animal skins, Ignatz and Frieda were attacking each other. Their hands hurriedly fumbling and ripping at each other's clothing. Hungry for each other's bodies. Tearing off her clothes, exposing her fit body and firm, nicely rounded breasts, Ignatz laid Frieda onto her back on the furs, spreading her legs as he entered her with a gasp. But the girl was not to be commanded and within seconds she had changed positions and it was Ignatz's turn to be lying on his back as Frieda started to ride him. The girl's face glowing in the reddish firelight. The cave filled with the hot scent of sex. Her hands placed on his chest. Her fingers digging into his flesh. Frieda crying out as she quickened her pace. Her naked body bouncing on top of him. Quicker and quicker she went, her gasps becoming more and more urgent until at last she threw back her head, arched her back and cried out as she came. Followed swiftly moments later by a groaning Ignatz.

For a long moment afterwards the two of them lay together not speaking, naked and entwined among the furs. Then at last Frieda raised her head resting it on her hand, her elbow in turn resting on the floor of the cave and turned to give Ignatz a little fond look.

"Are you going to ask me?" she said smiling.

"Ask you what?" Ignatz replied.

"Oh I don't know," Frieda said looking away. "A wife's duty is to share all the same hardships that her husband faces whether in work or in times of war. We share the good times and the bad. We face the challenges together. Marriage is a sacred bond. Not to be entered into lightly, never to be broken. Always to be honoured. Do you not agree?"

"I agree with you," Ignatz replied with a little smile of his own. "But I cannot afford you just yet. Your father will expect a large and expensive bridal gift and I am just a poor slave like Henrik keeps reminding me."

"Ah I see," Frieda responded as she reached out to gently run her fingers across his torso. "I remember the little blond Roman boy who first came to us all those years ago. You were eight and I was six. But I remember. The whole village turned out to see you when Odo brought you back with him. The fiery Roman boy. The slave. The boy who just liked to sulk," she said teasingly. "But you are not a boy any-more and neither are you a slave. Odo freed you and adopted you. He and Bertrada love you as a son. You are one of us now. You are a warrior of our people - of the Franks. And as for my father and the gifts you are required to give him for his approval - for our marriage," she added with a little playful smile. "Don't be so sure he will demand a high price for me. I will speak with him. Daughter to father. I will try and get you for a cheap price."

Looking serious Ignatz gazed into the flames, refusing to share Frieda's playfulness and for a moment he remained silent.

"I would give your father the world in exchange for you," Ignatz said at last. "But I have not been raiding yet and I am still poor. I have not yet proven myself. I will marry you Frieda. I have made my decision. I choose you but I must to do this in my own way. You should not make any exceptions for me. I do not want any special favours. I want to win you fairly like any other would and for that I need to become wealthier than I am now. That is how a father judges his son in law. By his wealth and status. For how else will I be able to take care of you and our children. I am my own man," Ignatz said turning to her with a serious look. "I will not be ruled by a woman. Nor by your father. No one shall rule me."

"I do not wish to rule you," Frieda said lying back down again on the furs. "And I know that you are your own man. I have always known and I would have it no other way. You are my half cast warrior and I made my choice long ago that I would marry you. But if you want to wait, then we shall wait. I can wait. I shall look at no other man while you are off raiding."

Lying on the furs Ignatz turned to stare up at the cave ceiling and for a while the two of them did not speak. Frieda's head resting contentedly on his chest. His arm wrapped around her.

"Do you think about them sometimes?" Frieda asked at last. "About your Roman family you left behind. About your brothers, Veda and Corbulo?"

"Sometimes," Ignatz said quietly. "But I do not want to go back there - I have no desire to cross the limes to Roman territory other than to raid. There are only bad memories on the other side of the river. No. Our village is my home now. This is where I belong. With you and Odo and Bertrada and all the others. And when the tribal elders call for war with Rome I shall go with them to raid across the river. I belong with the Franks now. With the sons and daughters of the northern light. That other life - it was a long time ago now. It no longer concerns me. It is in the past and I must forget about it."

"And yet I fear that it will not let you go," Frieda said with a pensive look. "You still speak the Roman language and you were old enough to remember what happened to you. Odo told my father that when you were young you would talk to yourself in your sleep in a language none of us could understand. You are different and just because everyone decided to give you a German name does not change who you are. Tell me your real name, my love. The name that your mother gave you. There is no shame in speaking it to me."

"Munatius," Ignatz said softly staring up at the cave ceiling. "I was called Munatius and I was born on the isle of Vectis, across the sea in the Roman province of Britain during the year of the six emperors. My real father was called Vennus. He was a soldier in the Twentieth Legion of Rome but he disappeared in the east a long time ago. My mother was Tadia but she died from the plague. My brothers are called Corbulo and Veda and I have a younger sister called Cata and an aunt named Helena."

Chapter Twenty-Four - Munatius

Munatius was woken by a quick series of painful slaps across his face. "Come on! Wake up," Odo growled as he stood over him, the older man already fully dressed. His worn face looking impatient. "You and I have work to do. I need you with me today."

Groaning Munatius hurriedly threw back the animal hides under which he had been sleeping and rose from his bed. The longhouse smelled of fresh cheese and wood-smoke. An iron cauldron was hanging suspended over the gentle fire that was crackling in the hearth while at the far end of the house Bertrada, Odo's wife, had just finished milking one of the cows who shared the home with their human owners. Rising stiffly back to her feet, suffering from rheumatism, the woman came up to Munatius, carrying a pot of fresh, warm and frothy milk. Her grey hair was tied back tightly and she looked her usual strict self.

"Here," Bertrada said speaking in her thick Frankish accent handing Munatius the pot of milk. "Drink it. You are going to need your strength today. Good German milk is what turned you from a scrawny little Roman boy into a tall, strapping Frankish warrior. Don't you forget it now."

"Yes Bertrada," Munatius said with a sigh as he took the milk before downing the pot in one continuous go.

"So," Bertrada said folding her arms across her chest as she examined him with a critical look. "You had some fun last night I gather up in the cave. Well. Did she say yes?"

"She did," Munatius said putting down the pot and hurriedly starting to pull on his clothes as he turned to glance across the room towards the doorway where Odo was waiting for him. "We are to be married if her father agrees to the match but first I must prove myself and gather some wealth of my own. Frieda says that she will wait for me."

"Good. Then I am happy for you," Bertrada said as the faint outline of a smile appeared across her strict lips. "Frieda always wanted to marry you. I have known that since she was still a young girl. She has only ever had eyes for you. She is an honest woman and she will make a good wife and daughter, but her father is a greedy man and he will demand a high price for her hand. It is such a shame that he must spoil everything."

Turning to a Roman legionary shield, helmet and splendid coat of chain mail body armour that hung from the wall of the longhouse, Bertrada gestured proudly at the display. "This is what Odo gave my father in order to win my hand in marriage and one day I shall give this to you," she said turning back to Munatius. "But even this magnificent display will not be enough for that greedy man. Frieda's father would prefer to sell his daughter to the highest bidder and like we discussed Odo and I have made it clear to you…"

"That you will not pay for us to be married," Munatius said smoothly taking over as he stepped up and gave Bertrada a quick, fond kiss on her forehead. "I know," he called out as he turned and headed towards where Odo was waiting. "You wish for me to make my own way in the world. To make a name for myself. If I am to afford Frieda I must obtain my own wealth and that is exactly what I plan to do. I am going to win her all by myself. I am going to make you proud Bertrada. Soon everyone will know my name."

Reaching for the woodcutters axe that was stuck into a block of wood by the door Munatius was about to pull it free but Odo shook his head.

"No," the old man said sharply, "it's not that kind of work which we shall be doing today. Leave it."

Leaving the axe Munatius shrugged.

"You are still a cheeky boy," Bertrada called out after him but as she spoke there was a strange sadness in her voice. "Fiery and defiant like the first time I set eyes upon you. Frieda is a lucky girl. Don't you forget to tell her that now."

"Love you Bertrada," Munatius called out without turning to look back at her - raising his hand in farewell as he followed Odo out of the door and into the cold and crisp morning air. Once outside Odo immediately set off without explanation. The older man was stern faced. His boots crunching through the fresh snow. Following him, Munatius turned to look around at the winter bound village. A few people were out, going about their business but the majority appeared to still be sleeping off their hangovers. The doors to their longhouses closed against the cold. While the remains of the bonfires along the edge of the frozen lake were still visible. Dark pits of ash and half burned wood in the fresh white snow. The only reminder of last night's feast and the sword dance.

Turning his attention back to Odo, Munatius frowned but said nothing as he dutifully followed the older man towards the longhouse where the priest of Woden, the village elder lived.

It had been Odo who all those years ago had led the Frankish war-band that had attacked him and his brother's party. The attack had happened far to the west of the Rhine frontier and deep into Roman territory. It should have been safe country but it had not been so. He'd been eight and Veda had been twelve, Munatius thought and both of them had been on their way back to Britain. Returning to their ancestral estate on the isle of Vectis. Sent home after they, together with their older brother Corbulo, had murdered their step father. The secret of what they had done known only by the three of them.

He could still vividly picture the attack on their convoy. Odo and his Franks had ambushed them along the Roman road. Killing the escorts and seizing everything of value to take back with them across the Rhine. Veda had managed to escape but he Munatius had been caught. And that is where his association with Odo had begun. For on that day, Odo had decided to spare him from a quick death and instead had taken him back with him across the river as a slave. And over time he had learned the ways of the Franks and Odo and Bertrada had come to see him and treat him as the son that they had never had.

"Has this something to do with planning the raids into Roman territory when the spring comes?" Munatius called out as he quickly drew level with Odo and laid his hand on the older man's shoulder.

The two of them were of the same height and build. Both tall and broad shouldered. The experienced older veteran and the young fresh and untested warrior. One blond haired. The other, black haired.

"It is likely that there will be no raiding this coming year," Odo said looking grave. "Come. The priest wishes to speak to you."

"No raiding?" Munatius said sounding startled.

Woden's priest was an old man with a bald head and he stank as if he had not washed in months Munatius thought as he and Odo were ushered into the man's presence. In the middle of the longhouse, crouching on the cold earthen floor around a cauldron that was suspended over a fire, were two young women, clad entirely in white. Their foreheads and cheeks marked by strange runes - the women only giving him and Odo a cursory look as they came in before turning their attention back to the bubbling potion they were preparing.

Guardedly Munatius turned to look around at the strange house with its even stranger things hanging arranged along the walls. The skull of a great bear, its jaws open wide. A clump of dirty and dried meat nailed to a beam which he had been told had once been a human heart. The ceremonial face mask of a Roman soldier. A strange green-brown fruit shaped like a ball with a hard furry shell which no one had ever seen before. The antlers of a great stag. As a child the priest's house had been the one place that had been completely out of bounds. The children of the village trying to frighten each other with wild stories of what went on here after dark. The house and its occupant generating a sense of doom and dread. The priest who lived here was not really the village leader. For the village had no permanent leader, but his authority as a middleman between the gods and mortals meant that on important occasions and when great decisions needed to be made, the people would come to him to ask for advice.

"Good of you to come so promptly Odo," the priest said speaking in a high weasel like voice as if someone had kicked him in the balls, Munatius thought as he sat down on the stool beside Odo, facing the holy man. "It is not the custom of our people to be punctual," the priest continued sounding weary. "They think they have all the time in the world but they do not. They think being late is confirmation that they are still free men."

"I brought my boy with me as you asked," Odo said inclining his head in a little respectful gesture to the priest. "Can we get to the point of this meeting please. I have work to do."

"Over the winter I have spoken with our tribal elders," the priest said. "They are much vexed and concerned by the attitude of the Thuringians. This alliance that the Thuringians have concluded with the Romans, it restrains us. It threatens us. It is a hostile act. It is as we feared it would be. This coming year the elders do not think they will be able to muster a large force to cross the Rhine and plunder the Roman territories beyond. Many of our men simply refuse to leave their families and homes undefended. They fear that our eastern neighbours will take advantage of their absence to attack us. Some war-bands will undoubtedly form and cross the river to attack the Romans but there can be no talk of any large organised campaign as long as the Thuringians threaten our rear."

"So. There is nothing new in this," Odo replied with a shrug. "The Thuringians and the Romans have been allies for several years now."

"Indeed they have," the priest replied, "which is why the elders have decided that the situation must change. They have agreed to send a delegation to the Thuringian Thing when it takes place on the full moon of the fifth month. Our delegates have been given the task of persuading the Thuringians to abandon their alliance with Rome and to join us in raiding Roman land together. There is enough bounty beyond the Rhine for all of us to share."

"We unite with our sworn enemies to fight against Rome," Odo said looking down at the earthen floor. For a long moment he did not speak. "Even with the Thuringians no longer menacing our rear the Romans have a new leader now. A new emperor by the name of Postumus. And I have met Postumus," Odo added looking up at the priest with a sudden gleam in his eye. "Postumus is a soldier with the strength of a Frank. The courage of a Batavian. The cunning of the Frisians and the resources of an empire that has stood against us for over three hundred years. Postumus will I fear prove to be a formidable opponent. Much more so than that soft man Gallienus who idles away his time in Italy. If you want my opinion - an attack on Rome will be a risky undertaking right now. Perhaps it would be wiser to wait until internal strife has further weakened the Romans."

"You are free to speak your mind Odo," the priest replied gazing back at him, "but the decision has been made. If we can successfully persuade the Thuringians to abandon their alliance with Rome we will launch a massive invasion across the Rhine by summer. Our men grow ever hungrier for Roman treasure. You know it is so."

Looking away Odo sighed. "Maybe," he said. "But what do you need my boy for? How does he fit in with the plans of the elders?"

"The Romans guarantee their alliance with the Thuringians by giving them gold," the priest continued as he leaned back and looked up at the roof of his home. "Rome pays them a bribe each year and every year they send an expedition to the Thuringians with the required subsidy. The Romans are adept at avoiding our territory. Instead they travel by ship along the edge of the German sea. Then up the river past Treva through Saxon and Semnonian territory until they reach Thuringian land. This year is likely to be no exception. So the Romans too will be present to press their case at the Thuringian tribal council during the spring at Thor's Oak. Your boy," the priest said turning towards Munatius, "was once one of them. A Roman. He understands their language. Their customs. So we want your boy to accompany the delegation that will be sent to negotiate with the Thuringians. We want him to use his knowledge of the eternal enemy to spy on them during the gathering. He would be ideal for such a task. No one will suspect that he understands the Roman language. For he looks just like any other of our young warriors. The elders want to learn as much as possible about the state the enemy is in before we attack them this summer."

"I see," Odo said. "He is to be used to spy on the Romans. Very well he is a free man and he can make up his own mind. So," Odo said turning to Munatius, "do you want to go to the Thuringian Thing at Thor's Oak in the spring?"

"I would prefer to go raiding," Munatius said with a little smile. "A man must be allowed to make a living and a name for himself."

"And you shall," the priest said nodding at Munatius. "But your people need your particular and unique skill right now. It would only be for the time of the tribal gathering. After which you would be free to go where you please and do what you wanted. And if you were to carry out your task successfully and to the satisfaction of the elders, your name would become known. Your fame would perhaps one day allow you to form and lead your own war-band."

Looking away Munatius hesitated.

"I do not like speaking the Roman language," he said at last lowering his gaze. "Nor do I wish to consort with the Romans. They are not my people. Their presence just brings back a host of bad memories. I am a warrior now of the Franks and I am to be married."

"And a fine warrior you shall make," the priest said leaning backwards on his stool.

"You mentioned Roman gold," Munatius said quickly interrupting as the priest was just about to say something else. "Tell me. How much gold do the Romans give the Thuringians each year?"

"The treaty between the Romans and the Thuringians says that a subsidy of fifty pounds of gold must be delivered each year," the priest replied.

"Then surely the simplest way of sabotaging the enemy treaty is by preventing that gold from ever arriving," Munatius said with a smile. "You don't need a spy nor do you need to send a delegation to the Thuringians, our sworn enemies. You just need someone bold and skilful enough who can steal the Roman gold before it can be delivered to its destination."

And as Munatius finished speaking Odo started to laugh. The noise visibly annoying the priest who raised his hand and made a sharp slashing movement in the air with his fingers.

"It is not as easy as you imagine," the priest retorted, glaring at Munatius. "The Romans are not stupid. They take precautions. We have not been able to intercept them yet. Now give me your answer. Will you accompany the delegation to the Thuringian Thing at Thor's Oak?"

Glancing at Odo who was still chuckling, Munatius hesitated again. "Sure," he replied at last turning to the priest with a sober expression. "I respect the views of our elders. If it means the difference between raiding this year and no raiding, then I shall do what they want."

Chapter Twenty-Five - The Outcasts

"You spoke well just now," Odo said as the two of them left the priest's house. The older man looking grave. "The old priest, he noticed."

"You taught me well," Munatius said looking away quickly as the two of them crunched on through the snow.

"Always listen to the tribal elders with respect," Odo said, "for you will need their approval but always remember to be your own man. Never surrender your freedom and honour. Fear nothing but disgrace and cowardice. Fight to win. Kill only if you must. Take what you need. Judge only when called upon to do so. Love life. Honour our Gods. Understood."

"Is that why you did not kill me all those years ago?"

"You were eight years old," Odo replied sternly, refusing to look at Munatius. "You were more valuable to me as a slave than dead."

"Bertrada told me that you planned to have me ransomed," Munatius said keeping up with Odo. "But that she talked you out of it. That she talked you into keeping me and adopting me as your son."

"A woman's tongue," Odo said contemptuously. "Is her primary weapon. As you will discover once you are married."

"So you never looked at another woman other that Bertrada?" Munatius said with a little provocative smile.

But in response Odo remained silent. His stern weathered face giving nothing away as to what he was thinking. For a while the two of them did not speak as they trudged back through the village but as Munatius turned towards the doorway of their home Odo shook his head and kept moving on past the longhouse and towards the edge of the snowy forest.

"No. We are not done yet. Come. There is something else that we need to take care of today," Odo called out. "Lets take a walk into the forest. I have business with Wendelin and his men."

"Wendelin!" Munatius exclaimed, turning to Odo with a frown. "I don't understand. We are going to see the outcasts?"

"We are."

"But they are a bunch of murderers and thieves," Munatius said quickly lowering his voice in a guarded manner and turning to look around to see if anyone was listening in. "No one is allowed to talk to them or trade with them," he whispered. You know that Odo. The law is clear. Those men are not permitted to remain in the village after dark. It is forbidden. Anyone is allowed to kill them if they are found in the village after dark."

"Only Wendelin is an outcast and a murderer," Odo said sounding unperturbed as he headed towards the edge of the forest. "Only he is guilty of a crime. The others. Those warriors of Wendelin's war-band who still remain with him are all honourable men. They are not outcasts. They have committed no crimes. They are simply here because that is their choice. Because once they all swore an oath to follow Wendelin to the death. To raid together. To fight together and to go to the feast halls of the gods together. They have remained true to their oath and their leader even when others have left. They have followed him into exile."

"But the elders they have forbidden any contact with these outcasts," Munatius said frowning. "You are breaking the law."

"Maybe," Odo said shrugging, "but I will not condemn good men and besides I need their help."

"You never told me that you were doing business with Wendelin?"

"You do not need to know everything."

"So why now?" Munatius said quickly. "Why tell me this now?"

"Because it is time," Odo said sharply, glancing at Munatius with a sudden resigned look, "because soon you will be leaving us to start making a name for yourself and I shall no longer be here to offer you advice. And maybe one day you will have gained enough authority and fame to form and lead your own war-band like I once did. So I want you to see for yourself what it takes to lead a band of men into battle. This is about leadership. So keep your eyes and ears open and learn something today. For it will be the last advice that I will be giving you."

Saying nothing more Munatius followed Odo as the two of them entered the forest. Picking their way past the trees and across the snow covered ground it was not long before Munatius spotted the small makeshift forest camp. The circle of ramshackle and crude one man shelters clustering around a dead fire. Some of the men's clothing and freshly caught fish were hanging up to dry from the branches of trees and beside the dead fire stood a pile of stacked firewood and a barrel of beer. The lid of which was open while a solitary goat was watching the two approaching men with bulging, fearful eyes.

Spotting Odo and Munatius approaching through the forest, five men swiftly rose to their feet from where they had been sitting about on newly felled logs drinking and finishing a cold meal. The bearded warriors were in their late twenties and early thirties. Tall strong looking and experienced men clad in an assortment of Germanic and foreign clothing. All of them armed to the teeth. Their eyes gazing back at the visitors with the hard and silent looks of men used to being ignored. Used to being shunned. And among them was one who was a head taller than the others. A giant of a man with a nasty white scar that ran from his forehead all the way across his cheek and down to his chin. As if someone had tried to split his head in half with an axe.

"So you have come to pay us another visit Odo!" Wendelin called out with a cold unfriendly smile as the giant rose to his feet holding a cup of beer, "and I see you have brought your boy with you this time. Brave of you. Considering the law on outcasts. What brings you out here to our humble camp? Have you come to offer us another barrel of beer. We are starting to run low."

"You know full well why I am here Wendelin," Odo replied as he came to a halt before the warriors in the midst of the forest camp. "You and I have business to discuss. You owe me, remember."

"I do?" Wendelin replied grinning.

"You do," Odo said grimly turning to look around at the small encampment. "I gave you blankets and tools so that you could survive the winter out here in the forest. I gave you that barrel of beer that you are drinking right now. And now in return I need you and your men to come and help me repair the roof of my barn. It burned down and I need to install a new roof. It will be two days work for five men like yourself. There will be no payment but I shall feed you and let you keep the tools and blankets that I gave you earlier."

"Your barn is of no concern to me," Wendelin said folding his arms across his massive chest. "Find someone else to do the work."

"A bit early to be drinking beer isn't it?" Odo shot back gazing back at Wendelin with an inscrutable look.

"It's good quality beer," Wendelin replied. "And I thank you for it Odo but I never said I would help you fix any barn. My men and I are warriors. We live to fight and raid. Come spring we shall be on our way west to the river to bag ourselves some fat Roman women."

"Maybe," Odo replied stubbornly standing his ground, "but before that you and your men shall help me fix the roof on my barn. A deal is a deal. When I first came to speak with you I said I would help you survive the winter and now it is I who has come asking for your help. You owe me."

"We made no deal, you and I," Wendelin sneered, dropping his cup of beer into the snow and taking a step towards Odo. "I thank you for the blankets and the tools and the beer but I made you no promises Odo. I do not need to do anything for you. Your people in the village treat us as if we were the scum of the earth," Wendelin snapped before angrily spitting onto the ground at Odo's feet.

"Well aren't you," Munatius said calmly gazing back at the giant. "Scum of the earth. You are outcasts. They say you murdered and raped a girl, Wendelin. That you refused to pay blood money to her family afterwards. That instead you fled from justice and came here to us. You should count yourself lucky that we have allowed you to stay out here in the forest and not thrown you all into slavers irons and sold you back to your own so that they could properly punish you."

As the forest camp went still Wendelin turned to Munatius in surprise.

"Well listen to you," the big man sneered. "Looks like you have finally managed to find your balls. Took you a while didn't it. You are what twenty-three, twenty-four? So tell me have you been raiding yet? Have you crossed the river and slaughtered Romans. Set their farms on fire and sent their soldiers fleeing in panic like I and my brothers here have?"

"No not yet," Munatius replied gazing back at the giant. "But I will one day."

"I thought so," Wendelin said with a chuckle, "you still have that softness about you. I can tell. You are just another young challenger who thinks he is now a man. Another young buck trying to make a name for himself. Someone who has not yet killed another man. Someone who has not bled with his brothers. I come across men like you all the time. Don't you ever speak to me like that again," Wendelin snarled his face abruptly darkening, "or I will cut you into pieces and feed you to my goat over there."

Staring back at Wendelin, Munatius remained silent before shifting his gaze to the four armed warriors standing arranged around their leader - the men watching him carefully.

"Odo has asked for your help," Munatius called out. "You are all honour bound to give it to him after the support he gave you earlier in the winter. No one else came out here to help you or speak with you. No one else came. But Odo did. And he helped you because he thinks you are not all bad men. So is it not fair now that he asks you for your help in return? Honest men would think so. You should do as Odo asks."

For a long moment no one spoke, the forest encampment pregnant with tension. Wendelin's harsh eyes fixed upon Munatius.

"He speaks sense Wendelin," one of the men with striking red hair said at last turning to his leader. "It is fair. Odo breaks the law by coming here to help us. He takes a risk for us. We should do as he asks. Two days labour is a small price to pay for what he has given us."

And as the red haired man spoke the other three men nodded silently in agreement but none made a move as they waited for their leader to make his decision. Looking annoyed Wendelin muttered something to himself. Then with a sneering dismissive gesture he once more spat onto the ground.

"Fine, if you insist," the giant growled as he stooped to pick up his mug and turned towards the barrel of beer. "You four will go and help Odo fix his barn but I am staying here and I am going to have a drink. I do not do women's work."

"Good," Odo said looking pleased as he turned towards the four warriors. "I will come back here tomorrow at dawn to fetch you and I will make sure to return you all before dark."

"You don't fear the wrath of the elders, of your village?" another of the warriors, the youngest among them, his hair tied up in a Suebian knot similar to Munatius's, called out. "If they see us with you they will not like it. They will throw stones at us like last time or something worse perhaps."

"Leave my people to me," Odo said turning towards the warrior with the Suebian knot. "Do not worry about them. I will speak up on your behalf."

"And so will I," Munatius said quickly turning to the warriors. "Those who have committed no crimes should have nothing to fear."

Staring at Odo and then at Munatius the four warriors remained silent as they glanced at each other before the man with the red hair shrugged.

As Odo and Munatius returned to the village through the forest, Odo was looking pensive.

"Tell me what you just learned back there?" Odo said at last as they approached the first of the longhouses.

For a moment Munatius did not reply, his eyes gazing at the ice bound lake.

"I thought you said that this was about leadership," Munatius said at last lowering his gaze. "But what I saw just now from Wendelin was not leadership. It was the opposite. Wendelin is no leader. He is just a big aggressive bully like Henrik and I do not know why his men follow such a piece of shit."

Crunching through the snow Odo turned his head away and started to laugh.

Chapter Twenty-Six - Vengeance

It was morning and Munatius was returning from the forest with a load of freshly chopped firewood slung in a net over his shoulder when he suddenly spotted Odo and Bertrada and a few other villagers standing outside the door to their home. And as he saw the grave, worried looks on their faces he knew immediately that something was wrong.

"What is going on?" Munatius called out as he came towards them.

But Bertrada was unable to answer, her face pale and drawn. While another woman standing beside her was staring at Munatius, fidgeting nervously with a necklace of beads.

"I am going to need your axe," Odo growled taking a step towards him, the older man refusing to look Munatius in the eye. "Give it to me and your knife too."

Refusing to comply, Munatius frowned as he turned to stare at the grave looking faces.

"What is going on?" he asked again in a calmer, quieter voice.

"It's Frieda," Bertrada gasped, "there seems to have been accident. She was with Henrik and it appears they had a quarrel and now she is dead. But it was an accident. Henrik swears that he did not mean to hurt her."

"Dead!" Munatius said as he let go of the net with the firewood, his face turning pale. The blocks of wood crashing into the snow. "Frieda is dead!"

"Henrik swears he did not mean to harm her," Odo said as he took another step towards Munatius and held out his hand for his axe. "It was an accident. Now give me your weapons boy. No one one wants any more trouble. The elders are going to pass judgement on Henrik for what he has done. He is in their custody right now. He will be punished according to our laws."

Turning to give Odo a strange disbelieving look Munatius remained silent, his breathing coming in fast gasps as if he were about to have a fit. Then from somewhere deep down fury and rage came welling up and with a terrifying bellow Munatius was off, stomping through the village towards the priest's house. One hand pulling free his knife, the other gripping his axe.

"Henrik! Henrik! Where are you! I am coming for you!" Munatius roared at the top of his voice as people emerged from their homes to stare at him.

Dimly aware of raised voices and the cries of alarm coming from behind him and the sound of running feet pursuing him, Munatius broke into a run. Refusing to be restrained. Pounding through the village he rushed towards the priest's house, shoving anyone out of the way who tried to stop him.

Standing outside the priest's door a gaggle of men were guarding Henrik whose hands had been tied behind his back with a piece of rope. But as Munatius came storming towards them the men turned to stare at him in shock. While Henrik yelped as he caught sight of the look on Munatius' face.

Bellowing in rage Munatius charged towards his rival and before anyone could stop him he had flung his axe straight at Henrik. The weapon hurtling through the air and embedding itself with a terrific thud into the wooden wall of the house right next to Henrik's head. Missing him by inches. Henrik screaming in response as he tried to hide behind one of his guards. But just as Munatius, clutching his knife, was about to throw himself onto his rival and stab him to death he was tackled to the ground from behind and moments later he found himself pinned face down in the snow as Odo and a few others got on top of him.

"Stay down son," Odo growled into his ear as Munatius felt his arms being pinned behind his back, his hands hurriedly tied together with rope. "You will get justice. Frieda will be avenged but not like this. Not like this son. You must let the elders decide upon the punishment. They must decide."

***

A light appeared to have gone out in his eyes as Munatius, looking pale, leaned against the wall of the longhouse. His hands were tightly bound behind his back and he was unarmed. His dull gaze was fixed upon the house across from him. It was afternoon and the snow covered village appeared to have settled down to some kind of normality. The people hurrying on by. The children subdued. Standing at the door to the house where the elders were holding Henrik were two armed men while a third guard had been posted at the end of the house to make sure no one was able to cut their way in through the side wall. And there were more guards inside. The men by the door now and then shooting Munatius worried glances as he silently stared back at them from across the way.

Odo had ordered him to remain calm Munatius thought and he was calm. The old man had tried to persuade him that Frieda would get justice. But there was only one sort of justice he was interested in. Odo had said that the elders would rule on what had happened and that he had to remain patient. But he was not patient. Odo had tried to convince him that it had been an accident, that there was a witness who claimed to corroborate Henrik's version of events. But he knew the truth to what had happened Munatius thought coldly. He just knew. Henrik had gone to see Frieda to try to persuade her to be his girl and when she had refused him, he had killed her in a fit of jealous rage. There was nothing accidental about her death. It was murder and now he could hear her outraged spirit calling for one thing, vengeance! Vengeance! Vengeance!

Spotting the door to the house opposite him opening Munatius tensed. Emerging from the building a slender boy of no more than sixteen had appeared. For a moment the boy hesitated in the doorway to look around. Then catching sight of Munatius watching him, the boy blushed, hurriedly averted his eyes and started out, heading into the village. Swiftly setting off after him Munatius's face darkened. Ahead of him the boy seemed to have sensed him for he abruptly increased his pace without turning to look around. Darting in between two long houses, anticipating where the boy was heading Munatius emerged right in front of the boy forcing him to a startled halt in the snow. The two of them were alone.

"I have a message for your brother," Munatius said coldly, his eyes fixed upon the boy. "I know he murdered Frieda. This was no accident. So you are going to take this message to Henrik. Tell that piece of worthless shit you call a brother that he and I are going to settle this in single combat. Tell him to meet me at first light tomorrow beside the old oak tree in the forest and that he is to come alone. The fight between us will be to the death. Tell him that if he refuses I will make sure everyone knows what a coward he is."

And with that Munatius pushed on past the boy and strode off.

***

It was dawn and across the forest the snow covered the ground and the branches of the trees. A bleak cold world of white and dark. The beautiful forest was still. The trees not moving. The first light, after the long night, was slowly warming the land. The rays of light piercing the forest like heavenly arrows. Alone. Sitting on the fallen tree trunk at the edge of the forest clearing Munatius was waiting. An axe resting across his lap while he was armed with a knife and a long Roman spatha sword he'd taken from Odo as the old man slept. Staring dully at the trees something seemed to have changed in him. Something appeared broken that could not be repaired. The light that had once shone brightly from his eyes had gone. Replaced by darkness. Swirling darkness and a burning insatiable rage.

At last, hearing the crack of a twig, Munatius spotted two figures emerging from the forest and heading towards him. And as he recognised Henrik and his younger brother, Munatius slowly rose to his feet and turned to confront them, holding his axe in his right hand. Coming to a halt in the midst of the clearing facing him Henrik had come armed with two axes and a knife. The big man's eyes filled with malice and hatred as he glared back at Munatius while his younger brother just looked worried and fearful.

"The elders have forbidden single combat," Henrik sneered. "We are breaking the law by doing this."

"I do not care," Munatius said dully gazing back at his opponent. "We are going to end this right now. Single combat. The fight will be to the death. And if you run now I will still find you and kill you."

Glancing away with a contemptuous look Henrik chuckled and it was clear that he too had come to fight.

"You are going to die slave," Henrik sneered. "First I am going to make you suffer. Then I am going to make you beg and then I am going to cut off your head and place it on a spike for all to see."

Saying nothing Munatius pulled his knife from his belt and went into a fighting crouch. Clutching his axe in one hand and his knife in the other. His dull eyes fixed upon his opponent. While Henrik quickly did the same. The bigger man holding an axe in each hand. The ominous, razor sharp blades gleaming dully in the growing light. The two young warriors slowly and warily circling, facing each other with their weapons raised, poised to attack. Then with a sudden sharp cry Henrik lunged. His axe sweeping in towards Munatius who sprang back, dodging the vicious blow. But Henrik was not yet done.

Lunging once more his axe swept in aiming a blow at Munatius' chest but again he missed and with a quick slicing blow of his own Munatius drove his opponent back. Both men failing to make contact. Gasping for breath they once again circled each other, glaring at each other. Weapons raised. The forest around them still and quiet. Henrik's brother looking on with a fearful look.

"I had her before she died you know," Henrik sneered. "I fucked your girl before I killed her. The bitch deserved nothing less. She dared to refuse me. She squealed and struggled until she could squeal no more. Like a pig that knows its about to be slaughtered. But you are not going to be able to tell anyone because you will be dead."

With a bellow Munatius charged at his opponent. His axe slicing through the air. Slashing at his opponent. Again and again. The fury of his attack forcing Henrik backwards. The blows kept on coming. Refusing to stop Munatius lunged at his opponent again and this time his blade tore across Henrik's arm causing blood to well up and Henrik to roar in pain. Swinging wildly at Munatius with both his axes Henrik tried to drive him back but his aim was poor and Munatius easily dodged the attack. Then as Henrik stumbled backwards grimacing, Munatius came at him again. Silent this time. His eyes were gleaming. His body impervious to pain and exhaustion. Some primeval force lending him strength.

Charging towards his opponent, Henrik prepared to receive Munatius's attack but at the very last moment Munatius ducked and went low, evading Henrik's clumsy slashing blows and before his opponent could recover, Munatius had buried his axe deep into Henrik's chest. The blow making Henrik grunt in surprise and drop one of his axes. The two struggling men tumbling backwards into the snow, wrestling, but Henrik's strength was rapidly failing. More and more of his blood staining the virgin snow and at last managing to raise his knife, Munatius thrust the sharp iron point deep into Henrik's throat cutting an artery and causing a stream of blood to fountain upwards. Henrik's hot blood splattering across his face and clothing.

"No!" Henrik's brother cried out weakly.

Lying on his back in the snow, gurgling up blood Henrik was nearly done. But Munatius was not. Grasping hold of his opponent's hair he yanked Henrik's head backwards before bringing his own face close to that of Henrik's. Their noses nearly touching. Munatius's cheeks and forehead stained in blood. His eyes wild. His face dark like a demon.

"You are not going to the eternal feast halls of the warrior gods Henrik," Munatius roared. "You are going to spend eternity in the fires of hell for what you did! This is for Frieda! This is for her!"

Then as Henrik's brother once again cried out in panic Munatius let go of Henrik's hair, raised his hand and with a vicious powerful blow from his axe he severed his opponent's head clean from his body. Grasping hold of Henrik's gory decapitated head Munatius stiffly got back to his feet as Henrik's young brother wailed in fright and terror.

For a moment Munatius did not move as he recovered his breath and stared at the head he was holding in his hand. His chest heaving. The long quarrel between him and Henrik finally settled. The rage in his eyes slowly dissipating. The darkness melting away as if he had been reborn. Suddenly Munatius became aware that he was no longer alone. Emerging from the trees and into the forest clearing, hastening towards him, were people. Lots of people. It seemed the whole village had come and leading them was the village priest. The old bald headed man looking outraged. And beside him was Odo.

"Seize him!" the priest shouted pointing at him as Munatius dropped Henrik's head into the snow.

***

The longhouse was packed with people. So many that most had to stand to get a view of the proceedings. It was evening and in the hearth the flames roared and leaped like dancing demons. The fire blasting out heat. While mice rustled about among the thatch roof over the people's heads. The smell of unwashed bodies and clothes filled the cramped space.

The mood inside the house was grim. The people were silent. Sitting on their three legged stools at the far end of the house near to the fire, the priest and the village elders were conferring with each other in low, quiet voices. Their faces stern and sober. Their long white and grey beards speaking of wisdom and experience. While laid out upon a table behind the elders was Henrik's body and head. Together with his weapons. Kneeling in front of the elders Munatius was clearly visible in the firelight, guarded by an armed man on either side of him. Their hands gripping his shoulders. Munatius' hands tied behind his back. His head respectfully bowed towards the earthen floor while standing to one side behind him Odo and Bertrada looked on. Odo looking ashen. Bertrada looking broken, fighting back tears.

"The facts speak for themselves," the priest called out at last as the elders ceased talking among themselves and turned their solemn eyes towards Munatius. "We all saw the defendant kill Henrik, son of Chlotar, with his own hands. In doing so he broke our laws. For it is forbidden for men to decide matters through single combat. So it is clear that you broke the law," the priest said turning to gaze at Munatius with a grave look. "You went against your own elders. You disobeyed us. We find you guilty."

"Elders," a man suddenly called out rising to his feet beside Odo. "I am Chlotar and that is my son who now lies dead behind you. Let me finish this murderer who took away my son. Allow me to fight him and when I kill him I shall have my justice for what he did."

"No Chlotar," the priest called out gravely shaking his head. "This matter will not be decided by single combat. But justice will be done. Our laws will punish the defendant and you shall get your satisfaction. The law for murder is death by strangulation."

And as the priest finished speaking Bertrada cried out in panic. Unable to stand it any more she fled from the hall.

"Elders," Odo now spoke up, his voice subdued, his expression grave. "You all know me. I respect whatever decision you come to. The boy here is not my son. He was my slave. I took him from the Roman lands as everyone knows. But over the years he has become like a son to me. I have trained him and watched him grow. He has a good heart. He has become one of us. He would not have broken our laws if he had not just so recently lost his woman. The pain of losing her made him temporarily go mad. The spirits who lust for vengeance lured him on. This should be taken into consideration. For I too have known the blood lust. I know what it can do to a man. And we should not forget too the fact that Henrik also broke our laws by agreeing to this single combat. I will abide by your decision elders," Odo continued, his face pale as he faced the judges, "but if his punishment is death then you shall have to kill me too. I ask you for clemency for my boy."

And as Odo fell silent, a murmur broke out among the people crammed into the house. While sat on their stools the elders gazed back at Odo with unhappy, silent looks. The tension inside the room rising.

"Silence," the priest at last called out. "The defendant will rise."

Stooping, the two guards quickly hauled Munatius to his feet and as they did Munatius raised his head, his expression calm and collected as he awaited to hear his fate.

For a moment the priest remained silent, his unhappy eyes resting upon Odo. Then his gaze shifted to Munatius and he sighed.

"Banishment!" the priest called out. "Ignatz is hereby banished. From this moment on none shall speak to the defendant ever again. His name no longer exists. He no longer exists. He shall be banished from our homes and our village forever and never be allowed to return on pain of death. He has until dawn to leave and if he has not left by then any man will be allowed to kill him. I have spoken. The verdict is clear. Justice has been done."

***

Standing beside the door to the longhouse, clad in his thick winter cloak, ready to leave, carrying his weapons, shield and a bag of personal belongings slung across his back, Munatius sighed as he turned to give the old house a final look. The fire was burning in the hearth and nearby his bed had not been slept in. He was leaving the home he had known for the last fourteen years for the final time. Never to see the old place again. Never to return. Standing by the door waiting for him Odo and Bertrada looked ashen. Bertrada's eyes damp. Odo looking shaken, his age suddenly showing. Turning to them Munatius said nothing as he gave them both a quick farewell hug.

"Where will you go?" Odo said refusing to let go of Munatius's shoulder.

"East I think," Munatius replied lowering his eyes as if in shame. "I will try and find a war-band to join. I am going to be all right. This is not the end. I will see you both again."

"Of-course you will," Betrada said hoarsely as she quickly wiped at her eyes. "You are my boy. You are strong and brave. You can do anything."

"Remember what I taught you," Odo said hurriedly. "May the gods favour you son. May you find your path."

Then with a final farewell smile Munatius turned for the door and moments later he had disappeared into the night.

Chapter Twenty-Seven - War-band

The five men were still asleep in their simple shelters, wrapped up in their blankets, the fire burning low, as Munatius appeared at the edge of the forest camp. It was dawn and the first light was creeping through the forest. The woods around him were still. The earth and tree branches covered in a thin layer of fresh snow. For a moment Munatius remained standing alone among the trees observing the five outcasts. Looking purposeful. Something about him had changed. As if he were no longer the same man he'd been just a couple of days ago. His grief had turned to determination and now he had the appearance of a man who was about to seize and grasp his destiny. He'd not had the heart to tell Odo and Bertrada what he had been planning in case they had tried to stop him. But it had to be done. The path ahead was clear to him now.

"Wendelin!" Munatius cried out in a loud voice as he lowered his pack containing his personal belongings to the ground. "Get up!"

Startled by his cry the five men woke and swiftly rose to their feet and hurriedly grabbing their weapons they turned to face Munatius. The warriors gazing at him with perplexed and uncertain looks.

"What do you want boy?" Wendelin shouted as fully clothed and looking annoyed the giant strode towards Munatius clutching an axe in one hand. "You come to offer us more beer."

"I want you fight you," Munatius called out. "Single combat. To the death. And when I kill you, your men will become mine. This war-band will become mine and I shall be its leader."

Coming to an abrupt startled halt Wendelin stared at Munatius in disbelief. Then he threw back his head and roared with laughter. His men grinning as they gazed at Munatius.

"Go home boy," Wendelin called out as he turned around and headed back towards his shelter. "I am not going to fight you."

But as Wendelin headed back to his shelter, his back turned, Munatius's throwing axe thudded into the tree right beside the giant's head. The impact bringing the giant to an immediate stop.

"Are you a coward," Munatius cried out. "Fight me! I don't think you have got the balls any more."

Slowly Wendelin turned around, his face suddenly dark with anger and for a long silent moment he stared at Munatius.

"You want to fight," the giant hissed at last.

"To the death," Munatius growled.

"So be it then," Wendelin snarled. "Shield," he roared and a moment later one of his men had tossed him a round shield which the giant smoothly caught with one hand in a practised movement.

Raising his own shield and pulling his long Roman sword from his belt Munatius went into a fighting crouch. His eyes fixed upon his opponent.

"Out of respect for Odo I am going to kill you quickly," Wendelin cried as he too took up a fighting position, armed with shield and his axe. "If it were not for him I would make you suffer as long as the day lasts. Prepare to die!"

As the men of the war-band backed away to give their leader the space Munatius and Wendelin watched each other warily.

Then Wendelin lunged but it was a faint and as Munatius fell back the giant laughed.

Once again the pair slowly circled, watching each other, their shields covering their bodies, their weapons seeking an opening in which to strike at their opponent. Launching his attack with a sudden savage roar Wendelin's axe came hammering down towards Munatius who caught the blow on his shield and moving with lightning speed he danced away. Enraged Wendelin came at him again, using his fearsome height and strength, but once again Munatius blocked the attack, moving fast on his feet.

"Come on fight me! Stop running away!" Wendelin bellowed.

But as Wendelin lunged again trying to decapitate him Munatius once again darted out of reach.

Grimacing Wendelin paused to wipe his nose with the back of his shield hand. His dark, furious eyes fixed upon his opponent. Then with another roar he charged at Munatius and as his axe went slicing through empty air, Munatius darted away but not before the sharp edge of his sword sliced across the giant's leg making Wendelin howl in pain. Enraged the giant turned and launched a series of blistering assaults, trying to batter his opponent into submission but to avail. Withstanding the furious assault, moving fast and remaining agile on his feet, Munatius suddenly made a lunge of his own, his sword slicing across the flesh of Wendelin's exposed arm and drawing forth blood. Crying out in pain and reaching out to clasp his wounded arm the giant retreated leaving a trail of blood droplets in his wake.

Dropping his shield into the snow Munatius calmly and silently reached up and pulled his throwing axe free from the tree trunk and now armed with only sword and axe he turned to face his opponent. Grimacing at him from across the forest camp, Wendelin was breathing heavily but still clutching his shield and axe. His eyes still filled with murderous intent. Then with a howl of rage the giant charged. Rushing towards Munatius through the snow, his axe raised and poised to strike. Waiting until the very last moment Munatius remained where he was before darting out of the way, dancing out of reach of his opponent's slashing weapon. But as Wendelin turned once more to face him, incautiously lowering his shield, Munatius's axe came whirling through the air and buried itself straight into the giant's forehead with a crack. The force of the blow bringing the giant to an abrupt halt before slowly he keeled over backwards into the snow and as he did the war-band gasped crying out in shock.

Coming up to Wendelin, Munatius paused as he looked down at the dying man. Blood pouring down his face. The axe firmly wedged into the bone. Then placing his boot on the giant's chest with a savage cry Munatius drove his sword point deep into Wendelin's throat, finishing him off. Staggering backwards, his breathing exploding in ragged gasps as if he had been holding his breath the whole time, Munatius cried out and raised his bloodied sword in the air in savage triumph. The forest camp silent. No one moving. No one speaking.

At last Munatius turned towards the four remaining men who were looking on in stunned disbelief.

"Wendelin is dead. I killed him in a fair fight," Munatius cried out. "You witnessed me killing him. I am your leader now. This war-band belongs to me and all of you will acknowledge me as your new captain. And if any of you has a problem with that then step forth now and we shall decide the matter right here."

But as the forest camp fell silent, no one spoke or made a move. The four warriors looking uncertain as they glanced at each other.

"Once you swore an oath to follow Wendelin into the fires of hell," Munatius cried out again. "Now I need you to swear the same oath of loyalty to me. For we are surely bound for hell but before that I am going to make you all rich, wealthy beyond your wildest dreams. Now swear your oath to me or be gone with you! I will not have cowards or disloyal men in my war-band."

Again the camp fire remained silent. The four warriors not moving. Then at last the man with the red hair took a deep breath.

"I am called Heller, blessed by the sun and I am the oldest," the man replied sombrely. "They call me lucky. We know who you are you, Ignatz, son of Odo," the man continued in the accent of the Franks. "We four have been with Wendelin from the beginning. We stood by him when the rest of our war-band abandoned him after he killed that girl. It was not right what he did to that girl but we had sworn an oath and none of us would break our word. For the gods favour those who are loyal. The gods favour those who have courage. Yes you killed Wendelin in a fair fight. It was done properly. So I will follow you. I swear now on Woden's head that I shall remain loyal to you captain. But please allow us to give Wendelin a proper funeral. So that we can formally end our oath to him and show his spirit how to find its way to the feast halls of the gods."

"I am no longer called Ignatz. That name is dead. I am called Munatius now and I was once a Roman," Munatius said sharply. "But now I am an outcast like you. I have been banished from my village for killing a man without the elders permission. A man who deserved to die. I no longer have a home to go to. This war-band is now my home and you are my brothers. I accept your oath Heller and I will give you permission to send Wendelin to his gods in the proper way."

Then Munatius turned to the other three men, remaining silent as he waited for them to speak.

"My name is Blaz, fast as the wolf," the youngest of the Frankish warrior's called out with a little youthful smile, his hair tied up in a Suebian knot as he turned towards Munatius. "I swear my oath to you, captain."

Then the third man with a badly disfigured face, the remains of a childhood disease, stepped forwards. His eyes studying Munatius carefully. "My name is Frederic and I am a Frank. They call me handsome for once I was," the man growled in a deep voice. "I swear my oath to you, captain. On Woden's head."

Nodding, Munatius's eyes lingered for a moment. Then he turned to the fourth and final man. A big warrior in his early thirties with bulging arm muscles. His face covered in the tattoo of a bear.

"They call me Penrod and I too am of Frankish blood," the man said lifting up his chin in a proud gesture. "Strong as the bear. I swear my oath to you captain, on all that is sacred in this world."

As the men fell silent, Munatius turned to look around the forest camp.

"Send him on his way to the gods," Munatius said pointing at Wendelin's corpse. "Then all of you, start packing your belongings. We are leaving. We have a long journey ahead of us."

"You said you would make us all rich," Heller called out as he folded his arms across his chest. "How? There are only five of us in this war-band. Not enough to go raiding across the river in Roman territory."

"We are not going to cross the river and raid in Roman territory," Munatius said turning to his warriors. "But I promise you that I am going to make you all rich. We are heading north-east towards the mouth of the Albis river. To the land of the Saxons. Come the spring a Roman ship transporting a fortune in gold coins will appear from the sea and try and sail upstream, all the way to Thor's Oak in the land of the Thuringians. I intend to seize that ship and the fifty pounds of gold that it is carrying. That is what we are going to do. So let's get going!"

Chapter Twenty-Eight - Competition

Spring 261 AD

Sitting on a fallen tree trunk beside the riverbank with a clear view of the wide Albis estuary, Munatius was repairing his cloak that had got torn. Working patiently with cloth, thread and needle. His Frankish throwing axe and Roman sword were strapped to his belt and his round shield was resting against a tree. His once clean shaven cheeks and chin were now marked by a short blond beard and on his head he was wearing a round black woollen cap.

It was afternoon and in the sky the warm spring sun gazed benevolently down on the land. The snow had gone. The frost exiled for another season. The last vestiges of winter had been banished and the forest along the river bank had turned increasingly green and lush. The woods and river filled with cautious new life that was increasing in boldness as it sensed the sun's growing support. Birds were chirping among the high branches. An otter's head quietly poking up out of the water. A family of ducks with young chicks hurriedly swimming away.

Pausing in his work Munatius turned to look round at the small forest camp where he and his war-band had been camped out for the last few weeks. Sitting beside the small burning fire Frederic was busy carefully sharpening his sword on a whetstone while Penrod was practising throwing his axe at a tree trunk. The men's belongings scattered about around their simple V shaped shelters. One of their blankets hanging up to dry on a tree branch. Animal bones lying discarded in a pile at the edge of the camp.

Hearing a sudden sound coming from the forest Munatius hurriedly rose to his feet. Moments later Heller and Blaz appeared, emerging from the woods and hurrying into the camp carrying some fresh food supplies slung across their backs. The men were looking excited.

"Well?" Munatius called out as Frederic and Penrod stopped what they were doing.

"We did as you asked, captain. We headed into Treva," Blaz called out excitedly with a cheeky youthful smile as he and Heller came up. "The market was busy today. The Saxon Thing starts tomorrow. The village is crammed with people from all over including King Hadugato. We saw him. The Saxon King is here and he has brought many of his warriors. There were ships in the harbour too. Several foreigners from the far north and also Roman traders. The Romans are finally here. They have come. We are sure of it."

"Shut up and let me talk boy," Heller growled as he cuffed his younger colleague over the head. "Captain," the older man continued taking over and turning to Munatius with a grave look. "You were right. There are Roman ships at anchor outside Treva. Some of them appear to be traders but there is one that does not appear to have come here to trade. A barge named the 'Frisian Glory'. It arrived today. I did not get a close look but I can tell a Roman even from a distance. I did not see any trade goods on-board her but the men who crew her are definitely Roman. This Frisian barge," Heller said fixing Munatius with a keen look, "it could be the ship we have been waiting for. The one carrying the gold."

"Good," Munatius said nodding in approval. "Good work, both of you."

"Captain," Penrod said turning to him with an eager look. "We will know that this is the right ship if after Treva they continue upstream. The others, the Roman trade ships, they will just be here for the Saxon Thing and the amber trade. If they are really here for just the trade then they will set sail for the sea and home. They would not venture further upstream."

"Yes," Munatius said nodding again. "But I still think I will take a closer look at this ship. Just to make sure we have the right one. Tomorrow I and Blaz will go into Treva and take a closer look. The rest of you will remain here in the camp and prepare to leave at short notice. If they start upriver, we follow. We watch them until we get a chance to attack them."

"There is however a complication," Heller said and as he spoke the others turned to look at him.

"A complication?" Munatius said.

"The Roman ship that just arrived in the harbour at Treva," Heller continued. "The Frisian Glory. The locals say the Romans are accompanied by a high priestess. One of the old ones. Ganna, seeress of Nerthus is on-board."

"With the Romans!" Penrod called out, looking surprised.

"Ganna!" Munatius exclaimed, frowning. "What the hell is she doing mixing with Romans? She hates Rome."

"I don't know why or what she is doing in their company," Heller shrugged. "But if Ganna is there to protect them it will complicate matters. You know the power and influence these women wield."

"Ganna was King Hadugato's seer," Frederic said darkly as he examined the edge of his sword. "But then she fucked things up for him and as punishment he banished her to Hallig Island. Looks like the Romans have brought her back. I wonder if these Romans know what they are doing."

"I can't imagine the Saxon King will be pleased by that," Penrod said with a chuckle. "Bringing her back will just embarrass the Saxon King and challenge his authority. Banishment is no laughing matter, right captain?"

Ignoring Penrod, Munatius turned his eyes towards the flames of the small camp fire and for a moment he looked thoughtful. Then he shrugged.

"It doesn't matter if Ganna has become involved with these Romans," he said. "We continue as before. And if the seeress gets in my way I will kill her myself. She may be a high priestess but she is also still just a woman who can bleed like the rest of us."

"Killing a high priestess of Nerthus is a crime among all the tribes, captain," Heller said hastily, looking worried. "The punishment for which is death by fire. We would be hunted down like animals."

"When I was eight years old," Munatius said slowly turning towards the red haired warrior with a cold uncaring look, "when I was still a Roman, I helped murder my step father. I lured him into an ambush while my elder brothers stabbed the bastard to death. And afterwards I kept my mouth shut. No one but us three knew what we had done. I am outcast Heller. I am banished from ever returning home. Do you think I fear what else they can do to me? Screw Ganna. Screw the Romans. That gold which they carry belongs to us."

For a long moment no one spoke.

"Shit captain," Blaz exclaimed at last with a little impressed chuckle, "that is seriously bad ass. You killed your old man."

"He deserved to die," Munatius said looking away. "He abused us three. He meant nothing to me."

"I counted at least eleven people on-board that Roman ship," Heller continued turning to Munatius. "Including a woman. Some of the men on-board looked like trained warriors who know how to handle a weapon. They are not ordinary sea folk. They looked like proper soldiers. There are just five of us captain," Heller said biting his lip with a frown. "How do you intend to take on these Romans when they have eleven and a priestess and we have just five. The odds are not in our favour. The odds are pretty shitty to me."

"We will find a way," Munatius said turning to Heller. "But that ship and the gold is not going to reach its destination."

Munatius was about to say something else when abruptly he froze. At the edge of the forest a band of silent men had suddenly appeared. The eight strangers were armed with swords, axes, spears and shields. Five trained warriors and three nervous looking youths. One of the men was clutching a battle horn shaped like a boar's head with black streamers. And as they slowly emerged from the forest Munatius's warband hurriedly reached for their own weapons. The men hastily arming themselves and turning to face the newcomers. Quickly heaving his shield from the ground Munatius pulled his long Roman sword from his belt, as his eyes swept across the strangers faces.

"So I was right," a tall man clad in a bears hide and holding a spear and a round shield whined speaking in a Saxon accent as he picked out Munatius. "So there is a nest of Frankish snakes hiding along the river bank after all. Fancy that. You boys are a long way from your own territory."

"Our business is our own, Saxon," Munatius growled guardedly as the Saxons started to spread out in a line threatening to outflank him. "We are not here to cause any trouble for you and your people."

"Maybe," the tall Saxon said smiling coldly, "but we are certainly here to cause you trouble. This is our land and you are not welcome here Frank. What are you doing here? Spying?"

"Like I said," Munatius retorted as his four companions inched closer to each other, their shields raised and their weapons drawn, "our business is our own. So why don't you just fuck off to where you came from and leave us be."

But the tall Saxon showed no signs of backing away. A cold confident smile plastered across his face. For a moment the man paused to look around the forest camp, taking in the shelters and the war-band's belongings. Then he turned his eyes back to Munatius.

"You know what I think," the man said. "I don't think you are here to spy on King Hadugato. I think you are here to steal the gold on-board that Roman ship which is currently anchored in the harbour at Treva. I think you are here for the gold. The problem is," the man continued with a smile, "so are we."

Staring back at the tall Saxon, Munatius tightened his grip on his sword. For a long moment nothing happened and no one spoke.

"We could share it," Munatius called out at last. "We could share the plunder. Half and half. There is enough for all."

"Yeah I don't think so," the Saxon retorted. "This is our land. That Roman ship and its cargo belong to us, not you."

Once again the forest camp fell silent. Taking a deep breath Munatius steadied himself. Then without warning the Saxons charged.

"War-band! Shield wall!" Munatius roared.

Acting on instinct and training Heller, Blaz, Frederic and Penrod hurriedly bunched together to form a shield wall and it was not a second too late. Catching a Saxon's spear on his shield Munatius fended off the blow. His opponent snarling in rage. But the enemy outnumbered them and from the corner of his eye Munatius saw one of the untrained youths storming towards him from his exposed flank. The boy armed with a shield and a sword. Breaking away from his companions Munatius leaped towards the youth, caught his clumsy slashing blow on his shield and before the boy could react he had driven his sword deep into his unprotected stomach causing the youth to gasp and spit up blood. Pulling his bloodied sword free Munatius kicked the dying boy to the ground. But there was no time to finish him off. With an enraged howl he was instantly set upon by another Saxon. The man battering at him with a spiked club that threatened to splinter Munatius's shield into pieces. The attacker howling like a demon.

His attention drawn completely to preventing the Saxon from hammering him into the ground there was no time for Munatius to see what had become of the rest of his war-band. They were fighting their own personal battles. Their raised voices and sharp cries ringing out. The clash of weapons against shields reverberating across the forest camp. Then with a terrifying crack the Saxon's devastatingly powerful club shattered Munatius's shield into two pieces and he yelped in shock as the painful tremors from the blow shot up his arm.

Falling back towards the water's edge Munatius hurriedly dropped his broken shield onto the ground and pulled his axe from his belt as his opponent came lunging and swinging at him again. The Saxon howling, his eyes bloodshot. As if he were out of his mind. Darting out of the way of another swinging blow Munatius tried to stab his opponent but the Saxon too was fast and evaded his attempt. Grimacing Munatius retreated, his back now just feet from the water's edge. His breathing coming in gasps. He was in danger of getting trapped. Feinting one way he tried to escape the other way but the Saxon had read his move and blocked it, his club swinging and missing Munatius by inches. Snarling in fury Munatius lunged at his opponent with his sword trying to drive the steel into the man's flesh, but the attack too missed, striking empty air instead.

Then just as the Saxon was about to strike again and drive Munatius into the river, Penrod suddenly loomed up behind the man and his axe thudded into the Saxon's neck, nearly severing his head from his body.

"You owe me captain!" the strong man yelled as their eyes met briefly.

Surging back into the fight Munatius said nothing as he swiftly came to Blaz's aid who was battling a Saxon armed with a huge two handed axe. Swiftly cutting the Saxon down from behind, Munatius staggered backwards as Blaz cried out in a mixture of rage and terror and leaped onto his opponent, stamping his boot repeatedly onto the dying man's face.

Turning to look around at the forest camp Munatius saw that the fight was over. Five of the Saxons lay dead on the ground including their tall leader with Heller's sword still sticking out of his chest. While one of the other Saxons had been wounded and was limping back into the forest as fast he could go, clutching his side, accompanied by two of the remaining youths. Watching them go Munatius took a deep angry breath but made no attempt to go after the survivors. Then hurriedly he turned towards his own men but they seemed to have all survived with nothing more than a few scratches, bruises and minor cuts. Heller looking grim and tired as he gasped for breath. Blaz red in the face, his youthful eyes wild. Frederic silent and seething with fury. Penrod, calm and collected, as if the fight had just been another day's work for him.

Steadying his breathing Munatius looked on as Heller quietly retrieved his sword and Blaz gave a corpse a final contemptuous kick. Then spotting something lying on the ground in between the corpses Munatius moved towards it, stooped and picked up the abandoned boar head shaped war trumpet. Holding it up in the air he turned to examine the instrument.

"Well will you look at this!" Heller suddenly exclaimed as he stood over one of the corpses, looking down and pointing at the dead men with his sword. "Come and have a look at this."

And as the others inquisitively crowded around him and turned to look down at the corpse, Heller shook his head with a sudden amused smile. "I did not believe it possible but there was actually someone who was even uglier than Frederic here. Look at the poor bastard's face."

And as he finished speaking Heller began to laugh. His booming laughter drifting away into the forest. His laughter proving infectious for moments later the others too had joined in until the whole war-band was laughing together.

Chapter Twenty-Nine - The Watchers in the Forest

It was morning and hurrying across the small island towards Treva, leading his war-band; the five of them carrying all their belongings and weapons slung across their backs; Munatius could see that something was going on inside the Saxon settlement. Some sort of public disturbance. For the noise of raised voices and shouting could be heard coming from the direction of the harbour. As if some violent confrontation was taking place. Gathering together in large swarms, children were shrieking excitedly. Dogs were barking wildly. Armed men rushing past. No one paying Munatius and his war-band any attention.

Frowning as he jogged across the field towards the first of the longhouses, Munatius glanced at the sacrificial pit from which a large fire was leaping up into the air, blinking as he thought he recognised the blackened and shrivelled remains of a human body lying among the embers.

"What is going on?" Munatius called out as an elderly man came hobbling past going as fast as he could with the aid of a wooden walking staff.

"The Romans," the old man shouted back, "they have taken Ganna hostage. They are threatening to kill her. They are heading back to the harbour. They have a ship but King Hadugato is not going to let them escape."

"We are going to burn the Romans alive when we catch them!" another angry man cried out as he overheard the conversation.

Swearing to himself Munatius turned to stare in the direction of the harbour which was hidden from view by the houses. The Saxon war trumpet he had taken from the men they had killed yesterday stowed away among his gear that was resting across his shoulders. Then he was off again, increasing his pace. His warriors following in silence. Entering Treva, Munatius's pace slowed as he started to push his way through the excited and angry crowds that thronged the spaces in between the houses.

Reaching the muddy harbour front, with its solitary wooden jetty poking out into the river, Munatius came to a halt as he caught sight of the ships lying at anchor. Moving out into the wide estuary, heading down-stream in the direction of the sea, one of the Roman ships was trying to escape. Her square sail unfurled and bulging in the breeze. And from his position Munatius could see figures rushing frantically across her deck, but he was too far away to make out any individual faces. The vessel was being pursued by a single large sea going Saxon ship and an armada of small one man dugouts. The Saxon warriors shouting to each other from across the still waters as they sought to catch up.

"That's our ship, captain," Heller hissed looking alarmed as he came to stand by Munatius's shoulder, the two of them staring across the harbour at the solitary Roman vessel. "That is the Frisian Glory. What the fuck just happened? Why are they fleeing?"

"You heard the old man just now," Munatius said as he hurriedly turned to look across the crowded harbour front towards the spot where King Hadugato was sitting on his horse watching events, surrounded by his personal bodyguard. "Seems the Romans have had a falling out with Ganna. Fuck knows why. But if those Saxons on-board that ship over there catch up with them then we are going to lose our gold. That's certain."

Standing at his side Heller swore out loud but there was nothing any of them could do about the situation. Feeling suddenly helpless Munatius took a deep unhappy breath as he turned his attention back to the fleeing Roman ship and folded his arms across his chest. His eyes fixed on the two big ships slowly drifting out into the broad estuary.

"They are going to board the Roman ship, captain, look," Blaz called out suddenly pointing excitedly with his axe.

Out on the placid waters the large Saxon ship had indeed managed to draw level with the fleeing Roman barge and as Munatius watched, a dozen armed men suddenly leaped onto the Roman boat. Their savage sounding war cries carrying across the water. The Saxons swiftly closing in on the crew. Driving most of the Romans back to the stern of the boat. But as he watched the hand to hand combat Munatius began to frown as one by one the Saxon warriors started to get cut down, their bodies slumping onto the deck. The crowds gathered around him abruptly falling silent as they too saw that the unexpected was happening. The Romans were winning the fight. At last Munatius shook his head in surprise as the Romans started to advance across the deck driving the surviving Saxons back onto their own ship. The crowd gathered around him groaning in dismay as defeat loomed. The two big vessels parting company and starting to drift apart. The Romans were going to escape after all.

"Well fuck me," Frederic growled, his disfigured face looking startled. "I sure did not see that coming. They won. Those Romans know how to fight. Look. They are getting away."

"Good," Heller replied lowering his voice with a sudden look of satisfaction as he turned to gaze at the crowds around him.

"Look, there is Ganna! The Romans still have her," Penrod called out pointing at an unmistakeable figure clad in a white cloak who had suddenly appeared - dragged out onto the Roman deck. "They have the priestess."

And as he spoke the crowds gathered along the shore went silent with sudden foreboding. Then they groaned in dismay as without warning one of the Romans suddenly caught hold of the priestess and sent her unceremoniously tumbling overboard and into the river where she landed with a spectacular splash. The priestess vanishing under water before resurfacing and as she did Munatius was unable to contain a snorting laugh that instantly drew him hostile looks from the crowd.

"Shit," Penrod muttered as around him the crowd began to grow angry, hurling insults at the retreating Roman ship.

"What now captain?" Blaz said quietly turning to him.

For a moment Munatius did not reply. His eyes fixed upon the Roman ship that was drifting away down the river. Then Munatius shifted his gaze to the armada of dugouts who were converging on the spot where Ganna was thrashing about in the water.

"That's our ship, lads," Munatius said at last lowering his voice and turning towards his warriors with a determined look. "No ordinary trader would fight like that. They are protecting something valuable. We are going to follow them. That is what we are going to do. Come. Let's go."

***

Pushing on through the thick and dark forest that came right up to the edge of the river bank Munatius led the way. The war-band spread out in single file. The warriors carefully and silently picking a path through the undergrowth, past moss covered rocks and ancient trees. The trackless green wilderness around them bursting with cheerful new life. Insects buzzing over their heads. The noise of a woodpecker hammering away from somewhere out of sight. It was a sunny morning and several days had passed since they had set out from Treva, following the course of the Albis towards the south-east. Leading the way, weighed down by his gear and weapons, Munatius looked grave, his round black cap pushed back across his head as he glanced in the direction of the river, where the Roman ship was just about visible through the thick foliage. The solitary Roman barge was sticking rigidly to the middle of the two hundred yard wide river. The barge's oars dipping silently into the water in rhythmic harmony as they steadily propelled the craft upstream. The Romans were visible as they moved about on the deck. Oblivious to the presence of the watchers in the forest who had been tracking them for days. The dense forest helping hide them from view.

"Captain, question," Blaz said quietly as he quickly closed the gap, coming up behind Munatius, the young man laden down with his gear. "You speak the Roman language. You were a Roman once. How come then you are willing to attack and kill your own people?"

"The Romans are not my people any more," Munatius said softly as he came to a halt and once again turned to observe the solitary Roman ship out on the river. "I belong to the Franks. I am a son of the northern light just like you. I fear Woden. I sing of Thor and his hammer. I wish all women looked like Freya. I am a free man and will go and do as I please."

"Talking of women, captain," Blaz said quietly with a little cheeky and cocky smile as the others came ambling up. The five of them pausing to take a break among the trees. "I never told you the story of Frederic and his woman. Well once long ago Frederic did have a woman and a very fine woman she was. So fine that we started to wonder why she was with him for he is not the..," Blaz said before pausing as he caught the silent warning look in Frederic's eye, "well he is as he is. So we made inquiries and guess what," Blaz said with a triumphant look. "Turns out that she was blind and could not see how fucking butt ugly he was!"

Grinning in silence at the old joke Blaz, Heller and Penrod remained standing while Munatius kept his eyes on the Roman ship that was just about visible through the forest cover.

"So Frederic," Munatius said at last in a quiet voice, without looking around, "what happened to your woman?"

"She died," Frederic said curtly, killing the conversation.

Sticking as close to the water's edge as he dared Munatius started out again through the forest, leading the way. His boots scraping softly across the forest floor. The others coming on silently behind him.

It was some time later when Munatius came to an abrupt, startled halt. His face turned towards the Albis. For out on the river one of the Romans, too distant to make out any specific features had suddenly pointed an arm straight towards him as if the man had spotted him moving through the forest. For a moment Munatius did not move. Frozen in place. Then silently he raised his fist in the air in warning and went into a crouch as the war-band immediately did the same. And for a long moment no one moved or made a sound.

"What is it?" Heller whispered as he quickly worked his way up to the spot where Munatius was crouching in the undergrowth peering at the Roman ship through the thick foliage. "You think they have spotted us?"

"I don't know," Munatius growled sounding uncertain. "But one of the Romans was pointing straight at us just now. Or maybe he was pointing at something else," Munatius muttered. "Look. They don't seem alarmed. Maybe I am just being too cautious but then so are they. Have you noticed how they always anchor in the middle of the river for the night or along that sand bank that was sitting in the middle of the stream the other day. They are worried about being attacked. They are not taking any chances."

Gazing at the Roman ship on the river Heller remained silent for a moment. Then he slowly exhaled.

"Well I wouldn't either. Not when I am carrying such a valuable cargo. So what is the plan captain," the older man said quietly. "The odds are still the same. They have eleven and we have five. How are we going to take that gold?"

"We will continue to follow them," Munatius said quietly, his eyes fixed upon the Roman boat. "We are not far from the confluence of the Marsh river. If they are heading for the Thuringian Thing at Thor's Oak as expected then I suspect that they will leave their boat behind at the confluence of the two rivers and continue their journey on foot from there. And once they are in the forest we shall have an opportunity to ambush them."

"Good," Heller growled with a sudden hungry look. "For its about time we got some fucking payback for all our work."

***

The afternoon was wearing on when Penrod came hurrying up behind Munatius, as the war-band carefully picked their way through the forest following the river and keeping pace with the Roman ship out on the water. Quickly grasping hold of his shoulder he brought Munatius to a halt.

"What is it?" Munatius said quietly, turning around and noticing the sudden troubled look on the strong man's face.

"I don't know for sure," Penrod said as he turned to look back down the forest trail they'd just come through, as the others came to a wary halt nearby. "But I can't shake this feeling that we are being followed. I think someone is pursuing us, captain. They are not far behind."

Gazing at Penrod for a moment Munatius eyed him with a serious and concerned look. Then hurriedly he shifted his gaze towards the forest but among the trees he could see nothing untoward. No sign of people. Nothing but the dark, trackless forest. Shifting his attention back to the river and the Roman ship rowing upstream Munatius took a deep breath.

"Who? Who would be pursuing us?" he said quietly. "Did any of you talk to anyone while we were in Treva?"

"No captain," the others replied quietly, their faces sombre and serious.

"Someone is coming after us captain," Penrod said once again turning to look back down the trail. "The bear knows when it is being stalked. I just know they are there. What do you want to do?"

Biting his lip Munatius hesitated, conscious that the war-band was watching him.

"All right," he said at last quickly turning to look around and spotting a massive fallen tree that had pulled up its roots and big chunks of the earth, creating a natural sheltered hollow in the ground. "We will get off the trail and hide for a while and see if you are right Penrod. Better to be safe than to be caught unprepared. Over there," Munatius said gesturing towards the fallen giant. "We will hide over there, behind that tree."

"And the Roman ship, captain?"

"We will catch up with them later," Munatius said as he started out towards the fallen tree.

Crouching in the hollow, hidden by the massive tree trunk and the tangle of roots and clumps of earth Munatius peered into the forest in the direction in which they had just come. His hand clutching his throwing axe. His round shield resting against the side of his body. While beside him the war-band were squashed into the same confined space. The warriors gripping their weapons, prepared for all round defence. Their eyes searching the forest.

For a while nothing happened. The forest remaining undisturbed. Nothing moving among the trees and undergrowth. Munatius was about to lean back and replace his axe in his belt when Heller suddenly reached out and gripped his shoulder in silent warning. Then Munatius saw them too. Running silently through the forest a man had appeared. Leaping nimbly over the bushes and around the trees. Bare-chested and carrying an axe, a round Saxon shield slung across his back. The agile warrior was swiftly followed by five more men, all armed. All utterly silent, running without boots or shoes. Flitting through the forest like ghosts. And as a seventh man appeared and came running through the forest, Munatius's eyes widened in shock for clinging to the warrior, piggy back style. was an old woman. Ganna! The high priestess having swapped her white cloak for a black one. But it was her. There was no mistake.

Running through the forest and leaping over the obstacles the seven men and the priestess moved on by, oblivious to the watching eyes. Holding his breath Munatius stared at them, not daring to move. Then as swiftly as the men had appeared they had disappeared back into the forest, leaving no trace of their passing. The men heading upstream in the same direction as the Roman ship. For a long moment Munatius stared at the forest into which the men had vanished before coolly exhaling.

"Looks like we have some new competition for that gold, lads," Munatius whispered. "I don't think the priestess is after us. No. She is following that Roman ship. Looks like Ganna wants to get her hands on that gold too. They should have let the fucking bitch drown in the river."

"Well at least they did not have any dogs with them," Frederic growled. "I hate dogs."

Chapter Thirty - Who has the Gold

Lying stretched out on his stomach in the waterlogged marsh that lined the banks of the tributary river Munatius peered across the reed infested water at the anchored Roman ship from his concealed position less than a hundred paces away. His forehead and corn blond hair were covered in mud and in his hand he was gripping his Frankish throwing axe. The marshy ground and reed-beds that lined the river bank were still and quiet as if the animals who normally lived there were holding their breath. Unsure of what to make of these intruders into their world. Lying stretched out in the marshy ground beside him the war-band were tense and silent like a pack of hungry wolves observing their prey. The men carefully watching the Roman crew as they went about their business oblivious to the fact that they were being watched. It was afternoon and drizzling. The soft rain soaking their cloaks and gently patting their heads.

Across from him Munatius could see that some of the Romans had already gone ashore while the rest were still moving about on-board their barge. Observing them Munatius slowly exhaled. His keen eyes darting between the shore party and the men still on the ship - too far away to get a good close look at the faces of the Romans. Two of the Romans appeared to have been sent ahead in advance to guard the landing site Munatius thought. They looked like soldiers. Seasoned warriors from the way they were holding their weapons. The Romans observing the edge of the forest were looking for signs of trouble but they were not bothering to shift their attention towards the marshy river bank where he and his men lay hidden. Oblivious to the danger they were in.

Turning his head slightly Munatius swore softly as he was alerted by a Roman cry. Up on the deck of the ship the Romans had started to carefully lower a large chest overboard and into a waiting dugout, floating on the water below. The Romans calling out to each other in sharp, urgent voices as the chest slowly and steadily descended into the dugout where a man was sitting waiting and guiding it into the small, simple boat.

"That must be our gold, captain," Heller whispered, lying next to Munatius. His hungry eyes fixed upon the Roman chest. "See how much care they are taking getting that loaded. They don't want to drop it into the river. The gold must be inside that chest."

Saying nothing Munatius peered at the dugout as he watched the chest successfully reach its destination. Then his eyes came to rest upon the man sitting in the dugout and suddenly he frowned. The Roman had his back turned to him and he was too far away to see his face but as Munatius stared at him a strange sense of recognition had suddenly taken hold of him. As if he knew the man sitting in the boat. As if the Roman had brought back memories from long ago. Memories he had long suppressed. But how could this possibly be so?

Blinking rapidly Munatius tried to drive the thought from his mind as he watched the three Romans carry the chest up onto higher ground. The men coming to a halt as they waited for the others to join them. Peering at the waiting trio of men Munatius frowned again, unable to shake the strange feeling that had overcome him. "No," he murmured to himself looking confused, his voice making Heller turn and glance at him.

"Captain?" Heller whispered.

"It's nothing," Munatius murmured quietly, shrugging off the strange sensation. "Just some stupid thought. We will let them go ashore and follow them once they set out into the forest. Then tonight when they are asleep we will attack and take the gold. You are right. The gold must be inside that chest they were carrying. It looked heavy. They needed two men to carry it."

"The heavier the better," Heller said with a greedy grin.

Peering at the Romans from his hiding place, lying stretched out in the marsh, Munatius watched in silence as the Romans were finally joined by the rest of their party, leaving just two of their crew behind on-board the anchored Roman ship. An older man and a young woman. One of the Romans raising his hand in farewell. The gesture immediately reciprocated from those left behind on the barge. The Romans were preparing to set out into the forest with the chest and all their gear just as he had expected and anticipated Munatius thought. Grunting in satisfaction Munatius was about to turn to Heller when to his astonishment loud, urgent shouts suddenly rang out. Moments later Munatius's eyes widened in shock as two of the Romans were sprinting towards the water's edge and their transport anchored just beyond in the river. The two men swiftly pursued by some of the other Romans. The men yelling at each other.

"Fuck, what is going on?" Munatius heard Heller whisper in confusion.

Looking on Munatius frowned as he saw the Romans tackle one of the fleeing men to the ground and seize him. But the other one had managed to reach the river and as he plunged into the water Munatius grunted. His shocked grunt followed swiftly by another as he saw the two crew members on-board the Roman ship raise their weapons and hit one of the Romans with an arrow. The man sitting down abruptly on the ground in shock with the arrow protruding from his stomach.

"They are attacking each other!" Heller hissed. "What the fuck? What are they doing that for?"

But Munatius did not have the answer. Staring at the wild scene he took a deep breath. Things appeared not to be turning out like he had expected after all. Quickly his eyes darted from one party to the other. Taking in the Romans onshore and those left on-board the ship. The river forming an impassable barrier between the two rival groups. For a moment nothing further happened. The two groups appeared to be in a stand-off. Shouting at each other, their weapons trained on each other, but he was too far away to hear their words properly. Then one of the Romans on-board the ship appeared to throw something onto the land and in exchange the shore party released their captive. The young Roman hurriedly entering the water and clambering back onto the ship.

"Exchange, captain," Heller hissed. "That was an exchange. The men onshore got something in exchange for releasing that man."

Saying nothing Munatius stared at the Romans with a perplexed expression as the men on-board the ship hurriedly raised their anchor and the Roman barge started to drift away downstream on the current leaving the shore party behind, stranded on the land.

"Fuck," Munatius swore at last.

"Who has got the gold?" Penrod whispered. "Is it still on-board the ship or did they just bring it onto the shore? How are we going to know which group to follow now, captain?"

"The gold has to be in that chest that they brought ashore," Heller murmured in an irritable sounding voice. "It has to be. The men onshore have the gold. Look. The others are heading off downstream. That way lies the sea. They are going home. They are done. They do not have the gold. We should follow those seven men over there when they set off into the forest. They have the gold."

"Captain?" Frederic said quietly glancing over at him.

Looking troubled Munatius was peering at the seven Romans left stranded beside the river. The men clustering around there wounded comrade. One of them kneeling on the ground beside something that was hidden by the the long grass. Then as he heard sudden peels of laughter he shifted his gaze towards the Roman ship that was drifting away and out of view. And as he stared at the Romans on-board and heard their loud heartfelt and infectious laughter ringing out, Munatius was unable to suppress a little smile of his own.

"They are laughing!" Heller hissed in dismay. "Can you believe that! Those Romans are laughing. What do they have to laugh about?"

Turning his attention back to the seven remaining Romans Munatius carefully reached up to rub his blond beard. The Roman who had been kneeling on the ground had risen back to his feet and appeared to be having a fit of rage. Violently waving his arms around in the air. His face turned towards the departing ship. His shrill voice raised in anger. His men standing around him looking a little lost and aimless.

At last as the Roman ship vanished downstream the seven Romans turned and supporting their wounded comrade they picked up their gear and started out into the forest heading westwards in the same direction as the sun. The men quickly vanishing from view among the trees.

Staring at the spot where they had vanished Munatius's eyes narrowed.

"Captain," Heller said his voice sounding urgent, "you have to make a decision. Which group of Romans are we going to follow? We cannot let them get away with our gold."

"Stay here," Munatius said quietly. "I will be back."

Then carefully he started to crawl forwards through the muddy and waterlogged ground. Slithering through the marsh on his stomach like a crocodile. Quietly entering the cold reed infested water of the tributary, Munatius started to swim the short distance to the other side. Emerging on the far shore he crouched in the mud and pulled his axe from his belt. Water dripping from his soaked clothes as he turned to observe the forest into which the seven Romans had disappeared but there was no sign of anyone. No sign that they had returned. Boldly rising to his feet he started out towards the spot where the Romans had come ashore before at last he came to an abrupt halt. Gazing down at the iron Roman chest that had been left behind and abandoned in the long grass Munatius eyes widened as he saw the spilt white sand that filled the chest. Hurriedly squatting down beside the strong box he quickly rummaged around in the sand with his hand but there were no gold coins hidden inside.

Abruptly Munatius rose back to his feet and his head whipped round to stare downstream in the direction in which the Roman ship had vanished and as he stared at the river he began to laugh.

Chapter Thirty-One - My Wolves

Half submerged in the water, holding onto the floating tree trunk, his head just about visible, Munatius quietly swam towards the anchored Roman ship. Kicking his way silently and powerfully across the river towards the small marshy island. Fighting the current. His shield strapped across his back. His weapons hanging from his belt. The war-band were doing the same. Their heads just visible above the water as they used the piece of flotsam to draw nearer to their quarry. Their hungry eyes fixed upon the deck of the ship that was nestling alongside the river island, half concealed by the marshes and green trees.

It was morning and the river and forest were quiet and peaceful. No one was about. Peering at the stationary Roman ship as it loomed up in front of him Munatius could see no one up on deck. The Romans had posted no sentries. Nor could could he hear anyone or smell a cooking fire. As if the boat had been abandoned. And as the unsettling thought entered his mind, that he was too late and the Romans had already left with the gold, Munatius bit his lip. Suppressing his frustration. Reaching the side of the hull he carefully let go of the tree trunk and as quietly as he could he caught hold of the ship's anchor chain and tightly wrapping his hands and feet around the sturdy iron chain he began to climb. His war-band silently moving around the edge of the ship to attack it from the side of the island. The men pulling their weapons from their back and belts.

"I know you are there," a gruff voice suddenly called out from somewhere on-board the ship, speaking in a Frisian accent. "There are just two of us but I will sure take one of you with me," the voice growled. "And my daughter will take another. So who wants to go first?"

Cursing Munatius quickened his efforts and moments later he was clambering over the side of the hull and onto the deck of the Roman ship. Pulling his sword from his belt. The other hand hurriedly reaching for his round shield. Standing watching him from the stern of the barge was an old man with fierce yellow blond hair. The man gazing back at him with a grave, sombre expression. Holding a spear and a round Saxon shield. While at his side a young woman who looked no older than sixteen was clutching an axe. The girl sporting long blond braided hair. Her youthful face covered in freckles. The two of them warily backing away as Munatius came towards them.

Pausing as the rest of his war-band came hurriedly scrambling over the side of the hull Munatius studied the two ship's crew in silence. His eyes hard as flint. Then quickly he checked the cabin but it was empty.

"The hold is clear," Penrod called out as he knelt and hurriedly checked the open cargo hold. "Looks like he's speaking the truth, captain. There are just two of them."

"Can't see anyone on the island, captain," Blaz reported.

"Where are the others?" Munatius said addressing the old man who was pointing his spear at him. "There were four of you on-board the ship when we last saw you. Where are the other two? Where is the gold?"

For a long moment the Frisian did not reply. Studying Munatius warily. His daughter gazing back at Munatius with a flushed, defiant look. The war-band watching them closely. The men poised to launch their attack and kill the crew as soon as Munatius gave the order.

"Why should I tell you anything, Frank," the old man said. "When you are just going to kill us anyway."

"I am not going to kill you," Munatius replied. "Nor will we touch your daughter if you tell us where the gold is. We know you have it. We know you have been carrying it on-board this ship. Now I will not ask again. Where are the other two? Where is my fucking gold?"

"If you value your daughter, old man," Heller called out in a harsh voice, "you will tell us the truth."

Keeping his wary eyes on Munatius the Frisian did not immediately reply. Then muttering something to his daughter the old man slowly and carefully stooped and lowered his spear and shield onto the deck and his daughter followed suit with her axe. Leaving the pair of them unarmed. Their hands raised in the air.

"I will trust in Frankish honour and tell you what I know," the Frisian called out slowly showing the war-band the palms of his hands. "My daughter and I are just ship's crew. This boat belongs to me. We are just doing a job, captain. The Romans have left. We abandoned seven of them yesterday and I do not know what has become of them. But they were bad men and not our friends. They did not have the gold. The other two left before dawn this morning. You have missed them by many hours. You are too late. They took the gold with them."

"All of it?" Heller cried out.

"Yes, they took it all," the Frisian replied nodding.

Studying the Frisian Munatius remained silent.

"Search the boat," Munatius said at last turning to Blaz and Frederic. "The two Romans who took the gold," Munatius said quickly turning back to the Frisian. "Where are they heading and don't lie to me, old man. For I shall know if you are lying and I will kill you myself and take your daughter."

"They are heading for Thor's Oak and the Thuringian tribal assembly, captain," the tall Frisian replied calmly. "The tribal council starts in a few days. On the night of the full moon. The Romans have business to conduct with the Thuringians.

That's all I know. They are good men, those two Romans. Take the gold if you must but spare their lives. They are our friends. I beg you. As fellow followers of Woden and Thor and fair Freya."

"Friends with Romans," Penrod sneered. "I don't think so Frisian."

"You said they left before dawn," Munatius said, turning to look southwards at the vast forest that stretched to the horizon with a sudden thoughtful look. "Two men carrying fifty pounds of gold. They may have a head start on us but they won't be able to go very fast carrying such a load." Then Munatius turned his eyes back to the Frisian. "Why is Ganna pursuing you? We saw her in the forest following you when you were on the river. What does the high priestess want from you? Does she know about the gold?"

"Ganna!" the Frisian exclaimed and from his reaction it was clear the news had come as a surprise to him. "How the hell would I know what a priestess of Nerthus would want from us? I am just a simple repairman."

Studying the Frisian, Munatius's face darkened. "You are not just a simple repairman," Munatius said shaking his head. "The Romans chose you for this mission. You are friends with these men. You said so yourself. Now tell me the truth. Why is Ganna after you? And do not lie to me again old man. You know what will happen."

"I mean no offence to you, captain," the Frisian replied quickly. "We had some trouble with Ganna before. Back when we were at Treva in the estuary but it sorted itself out. My Roman friend threw Ganna overboard. Tumbled her straight into the harbour and I am only sorry that she did not drown. But I swear I did not know that she was coming after us."

"Nothing, captain," Blaz called out as he poked his head out of the hold. "We searched everywhere. The gold is not here."

Turning back to the Frisian and his daughter Munatius eyed them with a displeased look. "Now you speak the truth, Frisian," he said lowering his sword. "Now we are getting somewhere."

Coming up to the unarmed girl who backed away from him until she was pressed up against the ship's hull, Blaz eyed her for a moment. No one speaking a word. Then his hand caught her by the chin forcing the girl to look up at him. Turning to inspect the woman as if she were some prized possession, Blaz's silently examined her from top to bottom before grunting, letting go of her chin and taking a step back. His eyes gleaming. A little cold smile playing across his lips. The girl gazing back at him in disgust.

"Two men, captain," Heller said turning to Munatius with a hungry look. "Two Romans all alone in the forest with a fortune of gold. Looks like our task has just become a lot easier. Frederic is our best tracker. If we leave now we should be able to overtake them before dark."

Nodding in approval, Munatius however kept his gaze upon the Frisian, his expression suddenly changed.

"We are going to leave you now, Frisian," Munatius called out to the old man with a cold smile. "You spoke the truth so you shall live. I promised that I would not harm you or your daughter and I am a man who keeps his promise. But when you get back to whatever shit-hole you call home you will tell everyone that it was I Munatius and my wolves - the men from my war-band who showed you such mercy. You will tell all you meet that in free Germany there is now a new war-band whose fame and exploits are going to be greater than all others. You will tell them that we are going to set the world on fire and that whoever dares stand against us will lose their head. That too is a promise. Soon Frisian, every tribe in every land is going to know our name. Everyone is going to learn to fear me and my wolves!"

Chapter Thirty-Two - Pursuit

In single file with Frederic leading the way the war-band hurried through the forest in single file, swiftly and silently picking their way past the noble and ancient trees. Like a pack of bounding wolves on the scent of their prey. The men carrying their gear across their backs and their weapons in their hands. Their boots softly scraping across the forest floor. Their eyes and ears straining to detect human presence within the vast, silent forest. It was getting late and in the heavens dark storm clouds were gathering. Looking up as he suddenly heard the distant roll and clap of thunder Munatius frowned. The two Romans they were pursuing appeared to have been moving faster than he had expected. For they had still not caught up with their quarry. But they could not be far away now.

Hurrying on through the dense, wild forest it was not long before Munatius felt the first drops of rain and soon the drizzle had turned into a downpour as the dark skies were lit up by flashes of lightning and the rolling claps of thunder. The storm growing in strength and intensity as it drew nearer. Abruptly ahead of him in the pouring rain Frederic came to a halt. His disfigured face looking suddenly troubled as he turned to look around at the forest.

"What is it?" Munatius said as he slowed his pace and came up to Frederic.

"Sorry captain," Frederic growled. "I have lost the trail. It's this rain. The storm. I can't see the trail any more. I can't track the Romans."

Swearing to himself Munatius hurriedly looked around but among the trees there was no sign of their quarry.

"What's going on, captain?" Heller called out as he and the others came up. Their heads and faces plastered by the streaming rain.

"We've lost the trail," Munatius replied looking unhappy. "Damn! All right. There is no point in continuing to look for them in this weather. It will be dark soon. We will just have to find a place where we can shelter and sit out this storm. We will continue again at dawn."

"Shit," Heller muttered.

Moving on through the forest at a slower pace, their clothes and belongings soaked by the incessant rain it was some time later when Munatius came to a halt. His nose working. Sniffing at the air. Then through the trees he suddenly spotted the lonely hut. The little house sitting all alone in the midst of a small forest clearing. Its steep roof nearly reaching all the way to the ground while from a hole in the thatch roof a column of smoke was escaping upwards. The scent of wood-smoke dissipating across the forest.

For a moment Munatius stared at the hut as the rain plastered his bearded face and over his head the heavens thundered and the lightning flashed. As if the gods were having a brawl. He could see no one about but the rising smoke indicated that there was at least someone inside the hut.

At last half turning to his war-band who had come to a halt behind him in the pouring rain he silently pointed at the hut and then cautiously started out towards it, gripping his sword. But just as Munatius was about to leave the forest and enter the clearing and approach the hut, Heller caught him by the shoulder forcing him to a halt. The red haired man suddenly pointing at an oak that stood at the very edge of the clearing. His breathing coming in rapid excited bursts.

"Captain," Heller said hastily. "Look. See. The tree. There are runes of power carved into the trunk. We can't approach. It is forbidden."

And as he noticed what he had missed Munatius softly swore to himself. Heller was right. Carved into the oak were a series of runes. The ancient language unmistakable. For a moment Munatius did not move as he stared at the runes. Knowing their meaning. Then he quickly shifted his attention to the hut. Whoever lived inside was warning people to stay away. Whoever lived there wished to be left alone. The runes were the language of someone sacred. Perhaps a god. Thor in disguise. Woden, Freyr or Loki the trickster. Entering the clearing and the hut was forbidden. The ground sacred and out of bounds. Swearing softly again Munatius bared his teeth. Then signalling to his war-band to follow him he turned around and started back into the forest.

***

Coming to a sudden halt along the forest path as he heard the distant noise Munatius quickly raised his fist in the air bringing his war-band to a stop among the trees. Frowning he turned his head, straining to listen. It was afternoon and throughout the vast and dense forest all appeared peaceful. The storm had blown itself out and the rain had refreshed everything. Behind him along the path the war-band too appeared to be listening. Their heads cocked to one side. Their faces looking tense. No one speaking. Then Munatius heard the sound again. The distant barking of dogs.

"Dogs," Frederic growled, his disfigured face looking unhappy. "Did I tell you that I hate dogs. One bit me when I was still a boy. I nearly died."

"Who, captain?" Heller called out softly, fixing his questioning gaze upon Munatius.

For a moment Munatius did not reply, straining to listen. The distant sound of barking coming again. Drifting through the trees. Then he turned towards his deputy, his expression suddenly grim. "Listen!" he whispered. "The dogs they sound excited. They are chasing something. Someone. They have the scent. Ganna!" Munatius whispered again. "It's the priestess. It has to be. She has found the two Romans. She is hunting them. They cannot be far away."

Staring back at him with a serious look Heller said nothing. Then silently he nodded.

Turning to stare into the dense dark forest Munatius paused before abruptly veering from his path and plunging off into the wilderness. Picking up the pace he started to run. His war-band following. The five warriors silently flitting through the forest, leaping over boulders and around trees. Like a pack of wolves on the hunt. Heading towards the distant sound of barking dogs. Their steel bladed weapons gleaming evilly in the sunlight.

Up ahead among the trees the sound of barking dogs had grown louder as Munatius at last slowed his pace. His keen eyes peering into the trackless forest. Then he heard men's excited shouts and as he reached a storm felled tree he came to a halt and went into a crouch. His war-band quickly following suit. The men's breathing coming in a quick controlled gasps. Their eyes and ears straining to decode what was happening up ahead. Peering through the trees Munatius caught sight of movement. Two men were rushing through the forest, one of them carrying a heavy looking back pack. The two fugitives were being pursued. For as the pair disappeared from view Munatius spotted a dog bounding after them through the trees followed by running men. Staring at the men Munatius took a deep breath. Then through the trees he spotted Ganna. The priestess was being carried along on the back of one of her men.

"It's Ganna," he said quickly leaning back into cover. "She is chasing two Romans on foot. They have the gold."

"I counted nine men and three dogs, captain," Penrod said softly. "And the priestess, that makes ten."

"I am not giving up on that gold," Munatius whispered as he caught Heller watching him. "No fucking way. That gold belongs to us. We are not giving up now. Not now we are so close."

Turning his head as he heard sudden yelling coming from the forest Munatius frowned. But among the trees he could see no one. Dumping most of his gear onto the forest floor Munatius carefully rose to his feet and gripping only his shield and sword with the boar headed Saxon war trumpet resting across his shoulders, he started to cautiously advance through the forest towards the sound of the raised voices. Reaching a large tree he crouched again in the undergrowth. Ahead the woods thinned out into a forest clearing and beyond he could make out an ancient burial mound. The earth and grass covered tumulus surrounded by armed men and barking dogs. Spotting Ganna standing close to the entrance of the passage grave Munatius grunted. The priestess appeared to be talking to someone inside the tumulus.

"The Romans," Heller whispered as he crouched beside Munatius, his eyes fixed upon the forest clearing and the tumulus. "They must be inside the grave. Not a bad defensive position."

"They are trapped," Munatius said quietly. "Ganna will simply wait them out. Then when they surrender she will kill them and take the gold."

"So are we doing this, captain? Its ten plus three dogs against five."

Shifting his gaze to the spot where two of Ganna's men were standing guard watching the forest Munatius's expression hardened.

"Take Blaz and kill those two men," Munatius said quietly indicating the two look-outs. "Do it quickly. Ranged weapons. I will let the priestess know that we are here. Then we go in and kill them all. This is it," he said reaching out to tightly grip Heller's shoulder. "We are either going to be the greatest and most famous war-band that has ever been or we are going to be nothing. Woden looks upon us now. To see if we are worthy. We are about to be judged."

Giving Munatius a silent grim look Heller paused. Then softly calling out to Blaz the two of them were off, flitting through the forest towards the unsuspecting look-outs. Watching them go Munatius reached up and pulled the boar headed Saxon war horn from his back.

Out in the forest Heller and Blaz swiftly and silently closed in on their targets. Like wolves stalking their prey. Creeping closer they edges forwards. Slinking through the thick undergrowth. Then as the forest went still the warriors spears came flying out of the forest. The weapons striking Ganna's unsuspecting men, bringing them crashing to the ground. Instantly the forest clearing was beset by consternation. Alarmed voices crying out. Reaching for his horn, Munatius placed the instrument to his lips and moment later the forest had come alive with a great deep humming noise. The horn ringing out summoning his men into battle.

Emerging from the forest in a tight V shaped formation with Munatius at the very tip of the V the war-band started to advance into the clearing. Their round shields covering their bodies. Holding their weapons in their hands. And as the war-band came on the five warriors started to sing their battle song. Their voices steady and deep, rising in unison. Beating like a drum. Their grim eyes fixed upon their opponents.

Startled and caught off-guard by the attack and the sudden appearance of the war-band, Ganna's men rushed towards them. While their dogs barked wildly, straining at their leashes. Spotting a warrior, naked from the waist up, charging towards him clutching an axe and shield Munatius, caught the man's slicing blow on his shield boss before thrusting his sword straight through the man's chest. Dropping him to the ground. His boot stamping down on the dying man's face with a sickening crunching sound. Then three more attackers came storming up towards the war-band. The men screaming as they wildly hacked and jabbed at their opponents. Trying to find an opening in the tight shield wall.

Ducking as a warrior swung an axe at his head Munatius swiftly slammed the edge of his sword into the man's exposed lower leg, sawing the razor sharp edge of his sword along the warrior's calf and causing his opponent to howl in pain. Losing his balance and concentration the man stumbled and the next moment Penrod's axe struck his head, taking off half his face, blood and gore flying through the air. Rising to his feet Munatius snarled as a dog came charging towards him. The beast leaping up towards his throat, displaying a row of sharp, drooling teeth. Catching the animal full on his shield the two of them crashed backwards onto the ground, struggling with each other as they rolled through the grass. The beast growling as it sought to tighten its grip. Breaking free Munatius caught hold of the dog's head and sinking his teeth into the animal's ear he tore a chunk out of it. Causing the dog to whimper, release its grip and race off.

Struggling back to his feet Munatius saw that four of their opponents were lying dead around him and Frederic was gasping in pain, his hand placed over a nasty gash he'd taken to his side. Blood staining his tunic.

But there was no time to go to his aid. Suddenly Munatius was aware of a high pitched shrieking voice and a moment later he saw Ganna rushing towards him. The priestess's face contorted in rage. Dark as if a shadow had taken possession of her. Her hand clutching a knife, ready to strike. Acting on instinct Munatius dropped his sword and pulled his axe from his belt and sent the weapon hurtling through the air. The axe neatly slamming into Ganna's head, the force of the blow knocking her clean off her feet and onto her back. Swiftly retrieving his sword Munatius leaped forwards as the forest clearing went silent as if in shock. The remaining three men hesitating. Lying on the ground Ganna was still alive, just. Her eyes staring up at the sky. The axe sticking out of her head.

"No!" Heller yelled suddenly, his eyes bulging with sudden fear. "No Munatius! It is forbidden! It is not allowed!"

Ignoring his deputy Munatius looked down at the priestess. Then swiftly he wrenched free his axe and slamming it into the woman's neck with a series of blows he decapitated her. The act bringing forth startled cries of horror from everyone in the forest clearing. Raising Ganna's bloody head in the air Munatius turned to face her remaining men who recoiled from him in shock and horror. As if they were witnessing something terrible. Something indecent. Something unholy. For a moment the men stared at him. Then crying out to each other they turned and fled, vanishing quickly into the forest.

"What have you done, captain?" Penrod yelled, his face blushing, his eyes bulging. "You killed Ganna! But it is forbidden to kill a priestess of the earth goddess. Now all the tribes will hunt us down wherever we go. You have turned us into outlaws. We are dead men!"

"When I first came to you," Munatius cried out, his eyes blazing as he thrust a discarded spear into the ground and stuck the priestess's head on top of it. "I told you that I would lead you into the very fires of hell. Well I was not lying. The priestess had a choice. Ganna could have fled but she did not. So now she is dead. And if the gods wish to punish me for that then so be it. And if they do then I will know that the gods are a bunch of fucking cowards!"

"You killed Ganna!" Blaz blurted out as he stared at Munatius in shock. "Penrod is right captain. When this becomes widely known every tribe will hunt us down for this sacrilege. We are dead men."

"They will have to catch us first, lads," Munatius growled as he turned to survey the dead bodies lying across the forest clearing. Then at last he turned his attention towards the dark and narrow entrance to the tumulus.

Approaching the narrow entrance with his war-band gathering around him Munatius cautiously peered into the darkness beyond. But from within the passage tomb he could see or hear nothing.

"Romans," Munatius said taking a deep breath as he switched to Latin. "I know you are in there. I know there are just two of you. I do not wish to hurt you. Give us the gold and we will let you go on your way. You have my word and I am a man who keeps his promise."

For a long moment there was no reply. But as he peered into the darkness Munatius thought he suddenly saw movement.

"Fuck off," a sullen voice growled back in Latin.

"Ah this is no time for games," Munatius called out in a patient voice. "Ganna is dead and so are most of her men. You are lucky we arrived just in time. We saved you Roman. Come on. Your position is hopeless. We just want the gold. You and your companion will live. Is that not a fair trade?"

Once again there was no immediate reply from within the grave. Then suddenly a face appeared from the darkness and then a shortish sized man squeezed out of the narrow passage and as he caught sight of the Roman, Munatius froze. His face growing pale in shock. The Roman suddenly looking equally shocked. The man staggering backwards against the rock as if he had just seen a ghost.

"No!" Munatius whispered shaking his head in confusion. "No! It can't be. Veda! Brother!" he exclaimed blinking rapidly. "Is it really you?"

Staring back at him the Roman remained silent but it was clear that he too was struggling to comprehend what had just happened. Looking uncertain the Roman cleared his throat. His eyes fixed upon Munatius. His cheeks flushed. "Once there were three brothers," the man called out in Latin, his voice hoarse. "What was the eldest brother called?"

"Corbulo! He was called Corbulo and the middle brother was called Veda and I am the youngest brother," Munatius exclaimed and as he did the Roman laughed, sounding incredulous.

"Holy shit!" Veda cried out. "Munatius! Munatius! I thought you were dead. But look here you are! I can't fucking believe it!"

Then with a delighted incredulous cry the two brothers were advancing towards each other and a moment later they embraced. Breaking apart laughing for joy Munatius turned to inspect Veda. The two sporting pleased and incredulous grins. "Fuck," Veda cried out. "I still can't believe it is you. Look at you little brother. All grown up. Fuck you have grown tall. When I last saw you, you were just a little squirt. And now look at you. You are a fucking beast, brother! A beast!"

"Fifteen years!" Munatius called out. "It has been fifteen years since the day we were parted. This is a good day. This is a great day! Do you remember when we were attacked on the road?"

"I do," Veda replied nodding, beaming. "I got away. You did not. We all thought you were dead. That the Franks killed you."

"They didn't," Munatius said grinning. "They took me as a slave instead. Took me back across the river to their village. I am a son of the northern light."

"Right," Veda replied looking a little confused.

"Corbulo, does he still live?" Munatius said hurriedly observing his brother with a sudden cautious look.

"Yes," Veda said nodding. "I think so. He is a high ranking officer in the army now. They sent him to the east. I have not seen him for fifteen years either but he writes to aunt Helena. We get a letter from him once a year. In his last letter he said he was doing well so there you go. As is our sister Cata. Do you remember her? She and Helena still live at the old estate on Vectis. The old farm. Fuck, it is good to see you brother!"

Munatius was about to agree when behind Veda another figure suddenly emerged from the passage tomb. The young man dragging a heavy back pack with him. The youth blinking in the light before turning to give the war-band a wary look. His hand holding an axe.

"The gold," Munatius said taking a deep breath. "I am afraid we are going to have to take it from you, Veda."

"Right," Veda said lowering his eyes with a sudden painful expression. For a moment Veda remained silent. Then he looked up.

"I can't give you the gold," Veda said with a resigned look. "I have a job to do and I need that gold. We are heading for the Thuringian Thing at Thor's Oak. There is a treaty of alliance between the Thuringians and Rome and I am going to renew the treaty. The gold is the subsidy that Rome has agreed to pay. I can't give it to you brother. I am sorry."

"What's he saying?" Heller growled as he took a step towards Veda, his face set in a menacing manner.

Looking away it was Munatius's turn to look pained. "These are my men, my war-band," Munatius said sticking to Latin. "We have been tracking you and your colleagues for weeks now. I promised them the gold and if you do not now hand it over they will kill you and take the gold anyway."

"Yeah I suppose they will," Veda said giving Heller a resigned look. "But I have a job to do and I am going to renew that treaty of alliance," he added turning back to his brother with a sudden determined look. "I am going to do my duty to Rome. And no one, not even you and your men are going to stop me. Is that not what our family has always done? Serving Rome. But hear me out brother," Veda continued quickly as Munatius was about to interrupt him. "I am not a soldier like you or Corbulo. I work for a bank," Veda continued with a little amused smile. "Yes a fucking bank out of Londinium. Can you believe it. That is why I am out here in the midst of this forest with a fortune in gold coins. The money technically belongs to the bank and I have been tasked with seeing that it gets safely delivered to its destination. I made a promise, brother. It's my job. But I have no desire to die either. So maybe you and your men will settle for a deal," Veda said fixing Munatius with a serious look. "To make things proper and legal with the bank I will pay your men four pounds of gold each but in return you will agree to work for me as my bodyguards. You and your men will escort me to the Thor's Oak. You will remain with me until the alliance with the Thuringians has been renewed after which your contract will come to an end and your men will be paid."

"Four pounds of gold per man," Munatius said eyeing Veda with a careful look. "And we work for you until this business with the Thuringians is done?"

"Yeah," Veda said nodding. "A few days work at most for four pounds of gold. It's not a bad wage if you ask me. It is the best that I can offer you. If not you are going to have to kill me."

Staring at his brother Munatius hesitated. Then he turned to Heller. "This Roman is my brother," he called out in German. "He and his companion are one of us. But my brother is also a stingy Roman bastard. He is tight like a Frisian. He offers you each four pounds of gold but we must work for him as his bodyguards until we get paid. A few days work at most. So," Munatius said with a shrug as he gazed at his war-band, "four pounds of gold per man. What do you say? Will that do or should I kill him now?"

Watching Munatius and Veda the four warriors remained silent. Frederic grimacing in pain. Penrod looking pensive. Blaz looking curious. Then at last they glanced towards Heller as if delegating their decision to him and in response Heller simply nodded in agreement.

"We will take the four pounds of gold," Heller called out.

Chapter Thirty-Three - Thor's Oak

Standing all alone in the midst of the forest clearing the massive and ancient oak rose out of the ground. Thor's Oak. Its branches reaching towards the skies like outstretched fingers. Its thick gnarled roots visible above the ground. The tree impossibly old. Offerings sitting at the base of its venerable trunk. Ribbons adorning its branches and fluttering in the gentle breeze. Little bells tinkling in the wind. A black raven sitting on one of the high branches. Four armed men guarding its trunk. The warriors facing north, west, east and south.

It was morning as Munatius, Veda, Caledonus and the warband emerged from the forest and entered the vast Thuringian encampment that had sprung up around the old oak tree. The rugged, hard-faced warriors carrying their belongings, shields and weapons slung across their backs. Caledonus weighed down by his heavy pack containing the gold.

The temporary camp around the oak was bursting with activity and growing as more people kept arriving. The newcomers streaming in from the forest, individually or in family groups. The people moving past the tents and simple shelters that had already been erected everywhere among the clearing and into the forest beyond. Thousands of men, women and children were already there moving about. The people going about their business. Cooking over camp fires. Talking with friends. Selling to the newcomers. Negotiating trade and marriage alliances. Sleeping. Eating. Laughing. Others practising single combat. While rowdy competitions were spilling over onto their neighbours spots. The attendees of the Thuringian Thing gathering to hear what their elders and leaders had to say. To decide and to vote on the important decisions that had to be made this year and to use the opportunity to meet up with old friends and family members. The mood one of bustling and growing excitement. The forest alive with human shouts and cries. Swarms of rushing children. Laughing and singing women. The barking of dogs and the mooing of cattle. The camp filled with the scent of wood smoke.

Pushing on towards Thor's Oak, ignoring the curious and startled glances that were cast in his direction Munatius led the way with Veda and Caledonus following closely behind. The war-band bringing up the rear. The warriors gazing about them with silent, grim faces. Frederic grimacing in pain. His body moving stiffly. His wound bandaged up and slowly starting to heal. The men's hands resting idly upon the hilts of their weapons.

His clothing, weapons and appearance were unmistakeably Frankish Munatius thought and the tribesmen had noticed. And as he came on by more and more Thuringians stopping what they were doing to stare at him and his war-band before hurriedly shifting their attention to Veda and Caledonus. Taking in their foreign appearance and clothing. Some of the men rising to their feet. Their faces looking unfriendly. Swarms of dirty, bare footed, blond haired children clad in furs observing the newcomers in silence. But no one made an effort to block his path or challenge him.

Coming to a halt near to Thor's Oak Munatius paused as he turned to look at the old venerable oak. Then he shifted his gaze to the camp around him before at last turning to Veda.

"All right we are here. I got you safely to your destination," Munatius said quietly in Latin. "We are now in the camp of the sworn enemies of the Franks. Just the place to be for a Frankish war-band."

"They don't like your men being here," Veda said cautiously turning to look around at the mass of people. "I understand. The Thuringians are the sworn enemies of the Franks. But you are with me and you brother are a Roman. I will make sure that you and your men will have diplomatic immunity."

"No. I am a son of the northern light," Munatius said quietly as he turned to look around at the camp, searching for any sign of the Thuringian elders. "I am a Frank. I am not a Roman any more. I left that life behind me years ago."

"Right," Veda said turning to give his brother a confused look.

"You need to do your shit Veda and soon," Munatius continued. "It's best if we do not hang around for too long in the open like this. The Thuringians are sober right now but come nightfall this place will be heaving with drunks just spoiling for a fight. And what better opponent than a band of Franks. Do your shit Veda. Get it done. We will wait for you here. Just call out if you need help and we will come."

"All right. I will," Veda said turning to look around as approaching from the direction of a large tent he suddenly noticed a group of Thuringian elders. The men were carrying venerable wooden staffs and sporting long white and grey beards. Their ancient faces looking grave and stern. The collective wisdom of the tribe advancing towards him. Standing their ground as the elders came up to them, Munatius and Veda remained silent, observing the men. The Thuringians in turn taking in the newcomers, examining them closely. Some of the men sniffing the air. Others reaching out to run their fingers over their clothing.

"Honoured elders," Veda called out suddenly with an amused smile and in a voice that nearly made Munatius laugh out loud. "My name is Veda and I have been tasked by emperor Postumus to renew the treaty of alliance that exists between you and Rome. I bring you honest and sincere greetings from my emperor. These men with me," Veda said gesturing at the war-band, "are my companions. My bodyguards and all shall fall under the protection conferred on them by the law of nations which I know your tribe takes most seriously."

With Veda falling silent no one spoke. The silence lengthening. The Thuringian elders studying Veda cautiously.

Some frowning. A few of the men staring at Munatius with displeasure.

"You represent Rome," one of the elders called out at last speaking in his distinctive Thuringian accent. "We were expecting to meet the legate Laelian. We know him. We do not know you. Where is he? Where is Laelian? Why has he not come this year?"

"He is not here," Veda replied curtly. "But I am and you shall deal with me regards the renewal of our treaty. I am fully authorised to represent Rome and the new government of emperor Postumus. I have brought you the subsidy of gold that Rome has promised to pay you. Like what was agreed before. You will find that it is all there, elders."

And as Veda finished speaking he gestured for Caledonus to open his pack. The freedman silently complying. The mass of Roman gold coins suddenly gleaming in the sunlight. Taking a quick step towards Caledonus to get a better look at the gold the Thuringian elders muttered among themselves as they crowded around. Then at last one of them turned to Veda. His eyebrows knotted together. Looking perplexed.

"This is unusual," the elder exclaimed. "A Roman envoy arriving in our camp with a bodyguard of Frankish warriors, to conclude a treaty with us against our common enemies the Franks. I do not believe it has ever happened before."

"Shit happens," Veda said beaming brightly. "But don't worry. These Franks who accompany me, they work for me. They are loyal to me and me alone. They have no interest in the grand affairs of nations. These are extraordinary times that we are living in, elders. Shall we move inside to conclude the renewal of our alliance? I have travelled a long way to be here and was expecting some hospitality as is the custom of the tribes."

"Well we will need to count the coins. To make sure it is all there as agreed," the elder growled.

"Absolutely," Veda said smiling, "and I am going to need to get a receipt from you for the safe delivery of the gold. I insist. This treaty must be done properly would you not agree."

As the elder gestured for Veda to follow him back towards the large tent from whence he and the others had come, Veda quickly glanced at Munatius and as he did Munatius dipped his head in a little silent acknowledgement. The war-band starting to follow Veda towards the tent.

Looking on as Veda and Caledonus disappeared into the Thuringian tent together with the gold and the group of elders, Munatius sighed before taking up position directly outside the tent entrance. As if to guard his brother. The war-band idly hanging about. The men coolly turning to look around at the encampment as they settled down to wait.

It was some time later when still standing outside the tent entrance, Heller suddenly nudged Munatius, gesturing with his head at a group of five men who were coming towards the tent.

"Fuck and I thought we were the only Franks in this camp," Heller muttered. "I do believe they look like some of our own elders. What are they doing here in the heart of the enemy camp?"

Staring at the group of five Frankish elders Munatius frowned. Then he groaned as he remembered.

Approaching the tent entrance the delegation of Frankish elders looked formidable. Their faces stern and hard. Their long beards speaking of wisdom and years of experience. Their status and rank in society assured. Their confidence palpable. But as the five men prepared to head for the entrance into the Thuringian tent where Veda was conducting his negotiation, Munatius stepped out in front of them barring the way.

"Honoured elders," Munatius said calmly. "I have no quarrel with you but I cannot allow you to enter this tent and speak with the Thuringians."

"What?" one of the Frankish elders growled. "Why not?"

"They are busy right now," Munatius said straightening up, "renewing their alliance with Rome. You are too late to change their minds. You should return home. Your journey has been in vain."

"What?" another of the Frankish elders cried out, looking furious. "Who the hell do you think you are? Stand aside at once! We have travelled a long way to speak to the Thuringian council. We are here to conclude an agreement with them. A very important agreement."

But as the elders tried to push their way past Munatius, he and the war-band swiftly moved to block their path again, preventing the elders from reaching the tent entrance. The little silent scuffle, a dance of bodies trying to get past each other and being physically blocked continuing for a few more embarrassing moments.

"How dare you!" an elder snarled at last conceding defeat as he turned to confront Munatius. "You! You would betray your own people in favour of the Romans. Shame on you!"

"Listen," Munatius growled starting to lose his patience, his hand falling to his axe that hung from his belt. "I am not here to shed blood but I will if you don't get the fuck out of here right now. We are not letting you into that tent. You are too late. So I am going to count to five and if you have not turned around by then and started to walk away the killing will begin. Do not come back! One…"

Glaring at him the elder swore out loud but there was nothing he could do. For a moment he stared at the tent entrance just beyond reach. Then with a deep breath he gestured to his companions, turned around and started off back the way he had just come.

"Well that was fun," Heller muttered as he came to stand beside Munatius and the two of them watched the Franks retreating. "We seem to be making new enemies at an alarming rate. How did you know they were here to make an agreement with these Thuringians?"

"Because I was supposed to be accompanying them," Munatius replied. "It's a long story but the short of it is that they wanted me to spy on the Romans. Because I can speak the language of the Romans."

"I see captain. But was it really wise to make an enemy of those elders," Heller said quietly, frowning. "I mean they are right. The Romans are not our friends either. Why favour them over our own?"

"My brother," Munatius growled gesturing at the tent behind him with his thumb. "He is not finished in there and he has not paid us yet so until he does we still work for him and we do as he says. We do what he would want us to do. He would not want those elders interfering in his negotiations. So until he pays us we do as he asks. I am a man who keeps his promise."

It was an hour later when Munatius spotted the three women walking towards him. Rising to his feet from where he had been sitting on the ground in the shade of the tent he frowned as he saw that one of the women appeared to be blind. Her sightless eyes a milky white colour while escorting her the two other women had their hoods drawn over their heads. All three of them were clad in long white woollen cloaks that were fastened at the waist by leather belts. Little bells attached to their clothing tinkling as they moved.

"It's a con," Blaz called out sounding bored as he studied the approaching women from where he was sitting on the ground in front of the tent entrance. "They are either going to offer to tell you your fate or they are going to say that we are cursed and that they can lift the curse for you. Either way it is going to cost you money. You have been warned boys."

Standing his ground, his arms folded across his chest Munatius waited as the three women came up to him. His frown deepening as he tried to understand what they wanted from him.

For a moment no one spoke. The strange confrontation drawing a few curious glances from the passers-by. Then the blind woman sighed and taking a step towards him suddenly with the speed of a striking snake her hand leaped out and her long razor sharp nails scratched across Munatius's cheek drawing blood and causing him to cry out in shock.

"What the fuck!" Munatius cried out as he quickly reached up to touch the scratch marks and his bleeding cheek and the war-band hurriedly rose to their feet behind him. But the blind woman appeared not to care. Bringing the tips of her fingers close to her nose she inhaled sharply gasping as she did. Before licking and tasting Munatius's blood and skin which had accumulated under her nails. For a moment nothing happened. Then the woman's white sightless eyes turned to look directly at Munatius and as they did Munatius felt a sudden chill run down his spine. This woman was no ordinary con-artist he thought. She was a witch.

"The three old sisters who sit beneath the tree at the centre of the universe," the woman said starting to speak quickly in an even voice that neither rose or fell, "pause to pluck at their threads. Unsure of what fate to spin for the man. The blood of she who he has killed will come seeking vengeance upon him. He will never be safe and at peace. His crime is too great even for the greatest of kings to bear. All shall hunt him. Death looms. Death will be woven into his fate. Sooner than he would like. His friends will abandon him and flee in fear. None shall sit at the tables of the gods. They shall know only eternal darkness and shame. Still the three maidens pause their weaving. Hesitate to decide upon his fate. For there is a way back for the man. A way back from the terrible sin that he has committed. In the shadow of Thor's Oak arrives the price he and his men must pay. Two strangers he will obey. Service as Thor's hammer will be demanded. Champion of man he must be if he wishes to remain free. The man must decide."

"What the fuck are you talking about witch?" Munatius cried out glaring angrily at the blind woman.

But in reply the blind woman just laughed. Her harsh cackling laugh ringing out as she and her two companions turned around and started to walk away.

"She's a witch," Heller said his cheeks flushed as he quickly came to stand by Munatius's shoulder and the two of them guardedly watched the women move away. "They have the power of prophesy."

"And sharp nails too," Munatius growled once again reaching up to touch the scratch wound across his cheek. "She marked me."

"We are all marked men, captain," Heller said quickly and sombrely lowering his eyes. "When it becomes widely known that we killed Ganna everyone will hunt us down. Every tribe. We are dead men walking."

"Maybe," Munatius said looking grim. "But the witch spoke of a way back. A way back for us. Like Thor we must become the champion of man. Whatever that may mean."

"Thor is a god with a massive hammer," Heller said glancing towards the old venerable oak tree with a dissatisfied look. "We are no gods or giants. What can we do?"

Munatius was about to say something else when two men suddenly approached him. An older man and a younger one. The pair looking subdued.

"Captain," the older man said addressing Munatius in a respectful manner. "We see your war-band. We see your warriors. We see strength. We see idleness. We come from the east where the river rises in the Giant mountains. Our village is under attack from bandits and we seek your help. We wish to hire you and your men to defend us from these raiders."

"Can you pay?" Heller snapped.

"We can feed you and your men," the older man said looking grave. "But we are poor and have no gold or silver. My name is Wilfred and this is my son Hennig. Will you come?"

***

It was starting to grow dark when Veda and Caledonus finally emerged from the Thuringian tent. The two men looking like they had been through an ordeal. Veda blowing air from his mouth. Caledonus blinking, carrying his substantially lighter looking pack across his shoulder.

"Well?" Munatius said quickly as the two of them started to walk towards Thor's Oak.

"It is done," Veda replied looking relieved. "The treaty of alliance with Rome has been renewed for another year. I have handed over the subsidy. All fifty pounds of gold and I even got my receipt," Veda added with a grin. "So," Veda continued quickly. "We are done here. My mission is complete and so is the employment of you and your men."

Gesturing at Caledonus Veda looked on in silence as in the shadow of Thor's Oak the freedman reached into his pack and moving over to the four warriors he handed each member of the war-band a large bag of gold coins.

"Four pounds of gold per man, just as agreed," Veda said. "Not bad for just a few days work."

"You kept your promise Roman," Heller growled grimly as he held up his bag of coin and nodded at Veda. "It saved your life."

Ignoring Heller Veda sighed and turned to look up at Thor's Oak. Then he shifted his gaze to his brother.

"Come back home with me," Veda said studying Munatius with a sudden serious look. "Come back to the estate on Vectis. Come back to Britain. It has been so long since you last saw Cata and Helena. They will be so happy to see you again, brother. It's our home. You belong there. You could have a good life there with us. Will you come?"

Epilogue

The West Breaks Away is historical fiction. The second book in a series of books that will follow the exploits of three brothers, Corbulo, Veda and Munatius, direct descendants of the characters in my Veteran of Rome and Soldier of the Republic series.

Some of the characters in this book were real life characters. Ulpius Cornelius Laelianus (Laelian) is one such historically attested person. The Thuringians (modern Thuringia in Germany) were indeed enemies of the Franks for centuries but whether and how the Romans actually paid them subsidies is hinted at but largely unknown. Emperor Postumus apparently did come to Britain in the winter of 260/1 after which the province went over to him without any fighting as did Spain. Postumus may have been a Batavian but nothing is entirely certain. Treva was the oldest name for Hamburg and appears to have existed. It exists on early Roman maps. The Albis is the Elbe river. The Marsh river is the Saale. Hallig Island is my name for modern Heligoland Island. The description of the "Frisian Glory" and the idea for its owner Abbe and his daughter Jorina were taken from a Dutch archaeological discovery in 1997 of a nearly intact Roman barge found in Utrecht province, The Netherlands. De Meern 1. The art work for the book cover was done by my wife.

Until the next book my friends!

The Romans, Celts and Germans

Veda's Family

Tadia, mother of Corbulo (deceased)

Vennus, biological father (fate unknown)

Gamo, step father (murdered)

Hostes, uncle, Gamo's brother

Helena, aunt, Tadia sister

Corbulo, eldest brother

Munatius, youngest brother

Cata, sister

Holda, Hostes wife

Jutta, daughter of Hostes and Holda

Badurad, son of Hostes and Holda

Caledonus, family slave and now freedman

Other characters

Sulpicia, Tadia's female friend

Adron, estate manager at Veda's farm

Linus, Badurad childhood friend

Odo, Munatius's former master, a Frankish warrior

Bertrada, Odo's wife

Senovara, young junior banker in London

Buccaddus, partner at B&M Brothers banking house

Dubnus, rival banker at First Imperial bank

Laelian, Roman diplomat

Mobius, prefect of the Rhine vexillation (Deceased)

Crastus, a centurion with the 1st cohort of the Thirtieth Legion

Harald, centurion of the 2nd company of the 1st cohort of Salian Franks

Atlas, A Roman speculatore attached to the first cohort

Macrianus, Emperor Valerian's chief treasurer

Balista, Valerian's praetorian prefect

Uranius Antoninus, lord of Emesa (deceased)

Claudia, Antoninus' wife and sister of the future Emperor Probus

King Odaenathus, king of the city state of Palmyra

Queen Zenobia, second wife to king Odaenathus

Asher, Sasanian born Jewish lord (deceased)

Fadel, Bedouin slave and Asher's man servant

Arif, leader of the Arab mercenaries (Deceased)

Hypatia, Christian woman

Probus, future Roman Emperor

Wulfaz, Ripuarian Frankish leader, Balista's bodyguard

Kartir, Zoroastrian priest

Macrianus Junior, Macrianus son and co emperor

Quietus, Macrianus's son and co emperor

Heller, member of Munatius's war-band

Blaz, member of Munatius's war-band

Frederic, member of Munatius's war-band

Penrod, member of Munatius's war-band

Abbe, captain and owner of the Frisian Glory

Jorina, Abbe's daughter

Ganna, high priestess of Nerthus (deceased)

King Hadugato, Saxon King

Roman Glossary

Acta, News reports

Achaean League, the city states of Corinth, Argos, Sicyon and Megalopolis in the Peloponnese

Adyton, small holy room at the back of a temple which was never open to the public.

Aemilii, Roman aristocratic family/clan

Aesculapius, the God of healing

Aesculapius temple, on Tiber island, Rome, dedicated to the God of healing and medicine

Aetolian League, city states of Elis, Messene and Sparta

Agora, the central marketplace

Alpheus, god of rivers

Amposta, modern Castell D'Amposta, Spain

Aoos river, now known as Aoos or Vjose river, northern Greece and Albania

Aphrodite, Goddess of love

Apollo, God of healing and music

Apollonia, Greek speaking city on the Illyrian coast, now known as Pojani, Albania

Appian Way, road connecting Rome to Capua

Apulia, region in south eastern Italy

Aquae Appia, the oldest of Rome's aqueducts

Achaean league, Greek city state defensive alliance

Arethusa, Syracusan nymph, water spirit

Arevaci, Celti-Iberian tribe

Argiletum, the street in Rome of the booksellers

Ariminum, modern Rimini, Italy

Arno river, still called the Arno and it flows through the city of Florence

Arpi, ancient town in south eastern Italy

Artemis, Greek Goddess of the hunt, the Roman goddess Diana

Arx, the most northerly of the two summits of the Capitoline hill.

Asses, simple Roman coinage

Atanagrus, capital city of the Ilergetes, in the region of modern Lleida, Spain

Atellani, Iberian tribe

Athena, patron goddess of Athens

Atrium, the open-living-space at the heart of a fine Roman house

Aufidus, now known as the Ofanto river, Italy

Aufidena, now known as Alfedena, Italy

Augur, fortune teller, religious priest

Bacchus, god of wine, liberation and a good time, otherwise known as the Greek Dionysus

Baebulo silver mine, mine location near Linares, Spain

Baetis river, now called the Guadalquivir

Balearic slingers, slingers from the Balearic Islands

Belerion, ancient name for Cornwall

Belli, Celti-Iberian tribe

Beneventum, Latin colony, now known as Benevento, Italy

Boii, Gallic tribe living in the Po valley, Italy

Bononia, now known as Bologna, Italy

Brundisium, a Greek speaking city in the far south of Italy, now known as Brindisi

Brutians, ancient peoples living in southern Italy

Calabria, region in southern Italy

Calatini, ancient Italian tribe

Campanians, people from the Italian region of Campania

Candida, the official clothing of a candidate up for election

Canusium, modern Canosa di Puglia, Italy

Capitoline Hill, one of the hills in ancient Rome

Capua, Campanian city close to Naples

Carales, capital of Roman Sardinia, now known as Cagliari

Caer Bran, West Cornish iron age settlement

Carn Brea, West Cornish iron age settlement

Carnyx, boar headed Celtic war trumpets

Castra, fort

Casilinum, stood on the spot where now stands modern Capua, Italy

Castulo, near modern Linares, Southern Spain

Celtici, Celti-Iberian tribe in southern Portugal

Cenomani, a Gallic tribe in northern Italy, who were friends and allies of Rome.

Chakka, a small handheld mill stone to grind grain into flour

Chun Castle, West Cornish iron age hill top fort

Cis-Alpine Gaul, Roman name for the Gallic lands in northern Italy between Alps and Apennines

Cispadana Gaul's, Gauls living south of the Po river

Cissa, small ancient town just north of modern Tarragona, Spain

Clastidium. now known as Casteggio, Italy

Clepsydra, a Greek time keeping machine, a water clock

Cloaca maxima, the old sewage system in central Rome

Cloacina, the goddess of cleaning

Colline Gate, Rome's most northerly gate

Comitium, the circular public space right outside the Curia Hostilia in Rome

Consul, highest elected Roman war leader and magistrate

Corcyra, Greek speaking city on the Illyrian coast, now known as Corfu, Greece

Cornicen, trumpeter

Cornus, town on the west coast of Sardinia, now known as Caglieri

Cryptologist, code breaker

Cremona, Cremona, Italy

Croton, now known as Crotone in southern Italy.

Cumae, now known as Cuma, close to Naples

Curia Hostilia, the Senate house in Rome

Decimomannu, now part of the city of Cagliari, Sardinia, Italy

Decurion, Roman cavalry officer

Demeter, goddess of the harvest

Diana, Goddess of hunting otherwise known as Artemis

Dilectus, the conscription process by which Roman military tribunes would choose new recruits for the legions during the Republican period.

Dimale, Greek speaking city on the Illyrian coast, now near modern Krotine, Albania

Discordia, Goddess of strife and discord

Drepana, modern Trapani, Sicily

Druid, Celtic holy man

Dugouts, canoes

Emporiae, modern Empuries, Catalonia, Spain

Epidamnum, Greek speaking city on the Illyrian coast, now known as Durres, Albania

Equestrian, Roman social class, just below the senatorial class

Equites, Roman cavalrymen

Etruria, Tuscany, Italy

Etruscans, tribe of Tuscany

Factionalism, old-fashioned party politics and personal rivalries.

Faesulae, town of Fiesole, Italy

Falacrinum, Roman village near town of Rieti

Falcata sword, curved Iberian sword

Fasces, the bundle of rods symbolising the power of the office of the consul.

Firedogs, a bracket support on which logs are laid for burning

Focale, Neck scarf

Fortuna, Goddess of Fortune/Luck

Forum, central market square

Forum Boarium, the ancient cattle market of Rome.

Forum Romanum, the ancient Roman forum

Gades, Cadiz, Spain

Garum, fermented fish sauce

Gaesatae, Feared professional Gallic mercenaries, from north of the Alps

Gaul, France

Geronium, ancient town in Molise, Italy

Gladius Hispaniensis, double-edged, pointed sword

Grumentum, now known as Grumento Nova, Southern Italy

Gwenap, settlement in West Cornwall

Hades, the underworld

Hamae, ancient sacred grove, only three miles from Cumae

Hasta, Roman spear

Hastatii, Roman infantrymen, formed the first line of a Roman army

Herdonia, modern Ordona, southern Italy

Hibera, modern Tortosa, Catalonia, Spain

Hippocrates of Kos, father of medicine

Hirpini, ancient Italian tribe

House of Aemilia, Roman patrician aristocratic family

Ictis, modern St Michael's Mount or Plymouth - location still uncertain

Ilergetes, Spanish tribe living around modern Lleida, north-east Spain

Llercavones, Iberian tribe

Illyria, modern coast of Croatia, Montenegro and Albania including the old cities of Apollonia, Oricum, Dimale, Epidamnus, Pharos and Lissos

Impluvium, basin set in the floor to catch rainwater

Insubres, Gallic tribe living around Milan

Insulae, apartment blocks in Rome

Juno, Wife of Jupiter and Queen of the Gods

Juno Moneta, temple housing the state Mint

Jupiter, Rome's patron god

Klepsydra, a Greek water clock

Lacetani, Iberian tribe in northeast Spain

Lares, the guardian spirits who protected the household.

Latinitas, citizen without the right to vote in the public assembly

Latium, region of Lazio around Rome

Lebbade, Punic cap

Leontini, Lentini, Sicily

Liburna, small, light and fast ships with a single rowing-bench and twenty-five oars on each side.

Lictors, attendants to a Roman consul

Ligurians, tribe living around Genua, Italy

Lilybaeum, modern Marsala in Sicily

Llorca, located near modern Cartagena, Spain

Locri, now known as Locri in southern Italy.

Lucania, region in southern Italy now called Basilicata

Lucanians, ancient peoples living in southern Italy

Luceria, Latin colony, now known as Lucera, southern Italy

Ludi Consualia, the festival of the harvest.

Lusitanii, Celti-Iberian tribe living around Lisbon, Portugal

Maniple, Roman army unit of up to 120 men

Mars, God of war

Massalia, Marseille, France

Massaliot, people of Massalia

Messana, modern Messina, Italy

Messene, town in southern peloponnese, Greece

Mount Eryx, mountain in western Sicily

Narnia, modern Narni, central Italy

Naupactus, now known as Nafpaktos, Greece or Lepanto

Neapolis, Naples, Italy

Nemesis, the winged goddess, the collector of dues.

New Carthage, now known as Cartagena, Spain

Nola, still called Nola, Italy

Okilis, now known as Medinaceli, Spain

Optio, second in command of a maniple unit

Oricum, ancient city in Albania

Ortygia – the site of the original colony at Syracuse, Sicily

Ostia, ancient port of Rome

Paenula cloak, Poncho

Parthini, city on the Illyrian coast, now known as Dimale, Albania

Patrician, Roman aristocratic class

Pella, historical capital of Macedonia

Peloponnese, southern Greek mainland

Persephone, wife of Hades, co-ruler of the underworld

Pharos, city on the Illyrian coast, now known as Stari Grad, Croatia

Phocaea, Greek speaking area on the west Anatolian coast

Phrygian helmet, ancient helmet

Picenum, region of Italy

Pila, Roman spear

Pisae, Roman town now known as Pisa

Placentia, now known as Piacenza, Italy

Plebeians, commoners

Plebeian tribune, Magistrate tasked with championing and looking after the political interests of the common people

Pontifex Maximus, the Roman High Priest

Poseidon, Greek God of the sea

Praetor, Consul's military subordinate

Prefecture, the administrative building housing the colony's authorities and public records

Principes, second line of Roman infantrymen

Principia, Roman camp HQ

Pro-praetor, Roman magistrate, commander and official

Pugio, army knife

Punic, Carthaginian

Quinquereme, heavy warship propelled by sail and five banks of oars

Reate, Rieti, central Italy

Revetments, banks to hold river water back

Rhegium, modern Reggio, Calabria, Italy

Rion, straights of Rion, Greece, western entrance to the Gulf of Corinth

Robigus, Roman god of agricultural disease

Rostra, a wooden elevated platform from where Rome's magistrates would traditionally address the people

Sabine country, region north east of Rome

Saguntum, Sagunto, near Valencia, Spain

Salapia, now known as Salapia, Italy

Salaria, old Salt road

Samnites, Italian peoples living in south central Italy

Sandaracha, a gold coloured mineral from which arsenic dust was derived

Saturn, God of plenty and wealth

Saturnalia, festival of Saturn in december, comparable to Christmas

Scorpions, bolt-throwers mounted on tripods

Scutum, shield.

Sentinum, now known as Sassoferrato, Italy

Sicyon, now known as Sicyona, Greece

Signifier, officer who keeps a unit's banner

Sora, modern Sora, Lazio, Italy

Spolia opima, Rome's highest military decoration,

Spoletium, modern Spoleto, Italy

SPQR, Senate and People of Rome

Strategos, Greek commander in chief

Stylus or styli, Roman pens

Sibylline books, the books of destiny

Stoa, a Greek style covered walkway with stone columns supporting a high tiled roof

Stylus, iron-tipped pen

Subura, slums in the heart of Rome

Syracuse, still known as Syracuse, Sicily

Tabula Valeria, painting in Rome depicting the Roman victory against Hiero of Syracuse and Carthage in the first Punic war

Tarentum, modern Taranto, Italy

Tarquinia, now known as Tarquinia, Tuscany, Italy

Tarraco, modern Tarragona, Spain

Taurini, Gallic tribe living near modern Turin

Taurasia, Turin, Italy

Terra Mater – the mother earth goddess, called Gaia in Greek

Tesserarius, the watch commander

Tharros, town in Sardinia

Thrace, modern Bulgaria

Ticinus river, modern Ticino

Tifata, mountain above Capua, Italy

Toga candida, specially whitened toga worn by candidates during elections

Torc, Celtic neck ring, denoting high social status

Tramontana wind, local wind that blows in the Apennines

Trebia river, modern Trebbia

Trencrom, hill fort in West Cornwall

Triarii, Third class of Roman infantrymen. The most senior and experienced class of heavy infantry

Triplex acies, Roman battle formation comprising three battle lines

Triremes, ancient warship

Tullianum, Rome's central prison

Tumultus Gallicus, A state of emergency referring to a Gallic invasion

Turma, Squadron of around thirty cavalrymen

Umbria, Italian region of Umbria

Ushant, island off the west Brittany coast

Utica, Carthaginian colony on the coast of Tunisia

Velites, Roman light infantry - skirmishers and javelin throwers

Venusia, Latin colony, now known as Venosa, Southern Italy

Vestal virgin, female priestess dedicated to the goddess Vesta

Via Aurelia, Roman road from Rome to Pisa, Italy

Via Flaminia, Flaminian way, ancient Roman road

Via Salaria, the old salt road, in Rome

Victoria, goddess of victory

Villa Publica, building where the censors had their base and where the public records were held. Stood on the fields of Mars.

Volturnus river, now known as the Volturno river, Italy

Vulcan, god of fire and carpenters

Zeus, Greek king of the Gods, Roman Jupiter

Printed in Great Britain
by Amazon